Getting a Job
Abroad

Getting a Job Abroad

The international jobseekers' directory

ROGER JONES

Seventh edition

howtobooks

By the same author
Getting a Job in America
Retire Abroad

British Library Cataloguing in Publication Data
A catalogue record for this book is available from the British Library.

© Copyright 2003 Roger Alan Jones

Roger Alan Jones has asserted his moral right under the Copyright, Design and
Patents Act, 1988, to be identified as the author of this work.

First published by How To Books Ltd, 3 Newtec Place,
Magdalen Road, Oxford, OX4 1RE, United Kingdom.
Tel: (01865) 793806.   Fax: (01865) 248780.
info@howtobooks.co.uk
www.howtobooks.co.uk

First edition 1989
Second edition 1991
Reprinted 1992
Third edition 1994
Fourth edition 1996
Fifth edition 1999
Reprinted 1999
Sixth edition 2001
Seventh edition 2003

Note: The material contained in this book is set out in good faith for general guidance
and no liability can be accepted for loss or expense incurred as a result of relying in
particular circumstances on statements made in the book. The laws and regulations are
complex and liable to change, and readers should check the current position with the
relevant authorities before making personal arrangements.

Produced for How To Books by Deer Park Productions
Cover design by Baseline Arts Ltd, Oxford
Typeset by Anneset, Weston-super-Mare, North Somerset
Printed and bound by Cromwell Press, Trowbridge, Wiltshire

Contents

List of illustrations   9

Preface to the seventh edition   11

Part One: Introduction   **13**

1   Working abroad: Is it an option for you?   **13**
Changing work patterns   13
Reasons for working abroad   14
Coping with a strange environment   16
Do you fit the part?   17
Other considerations   22
How to use this book   23

Part Two: Finding a Job   **25**

2   The search for a job   **25**
Getting fixed up before you leave   25
Answering an advertisement   26
The speculative approach (in the UK)   28
Making visits 'on spec'   34
Pros and cons of different approaches   35

3   The recruitment process   **37**
Impressing the selectors   37
Getting through the process   37
Replying to an advertisement   41
Sending a speculative letter   41
Writing a letter of application   44
Preparing a curriculum vitae   44
Completing an application form   47
Sending your documents   51
Preparing for tests and interviews   53
Aftermath   57

4   Coming to a decision   **58**
Knowing your employer   58

Understanding the salary package 59
The job itself 61
Family matters 62
Adapting to your new environment 68
Sources of information 71
Contract checklist 76

Part Three: Preparation and Acclimatisation 80

5 Preparing to leave 80
Banking 80
Your car 81
Clothing 82
Arranging education for the children 83
Financial planning 83
Protecting your health 85
Your home 87
Insurance 88
Language learning 88
Sending luggage and personal effects 90
National Insurance 91
Passport 91
Pension 92
Shopping 93
Travel planning 94
Visas and work permits: Are they necessary? 95
Final checklist 96

6 Settling in 97
Facing culture shock 97
Creating a friendly personal environment 98
Keeping in touch 104
Attending to the paperwork and other details 105
When things don't work out 105

Part Four: Surveying the Opportunities 109

7 Working holidays and work experience 109
Considering short-term work 109
Vacation jobs 110
Seasonal work 114
Gap Year employment 115
A year out as an undergraduate 117
Exchange schemes 117

8 Contract work 120
Short-term contracts 121
Longer contracts 123
Looking beyond the end of the contract 129

9	**Permanent jobs and self-employment**	**132**
	A home base with visits abroad	132
	Secondment abroad	133
	A home base with postings abroad	134
	Permanent relocation	136
	The ultimate option: working for yourself	138

Part Five: The Regions of the World   **141**

10	**Europe**	**141**
	The European Union	141
	The rest of Europe	145
	Further information	148

11	**The Arab World**	**149**
	The opportunities	149
	The influence of Islam	150
	Political attitudes	151
	Israel and the Palestine problem	152
	Dealing with Middle Easterners	153
	Finding jobs	153
	Further information	154

12	**Asia**	**155**
	Central Asia	155
	The Indian Subcontinent	156
	South East Asia	157
	The Far East	158
	Understanding differences	159
	Further information	160

13	**Africa**	**162**
	West Africa	163
	Central and East Africa	163
	Southern Africa	164
	South Africa	164
	The continent and its people	165
	Further information	166

14	**North America**	**168**
	Canada	168
	United States of America	171
	Further information	174

15	**Latin America and the Caribbean**	**175**
	Central and South America	175
	The Caribbean	177
	The Falklands	177
	Finding jobs	178

Further information   178

16   Australasia and the Pacific   180
      Australia   180
      New Zealand   183
      The Pacific   185
      Further information   185

Part Six: Reference   187

17   Job opportunities by profession   187

18   Recruitment directory   217

19   Country directory   268

20   Useful addresses in the UK   311

21   European applications   317

22   Further reading   328

      Index   332

List of Illustrations

1. Specimen request for job details   42

2. Model speculative letter of application   43

3. Specimen accompanying letter for CV   45

4. Specimen CV for a younger applicant   48

5. Specimen CV for a mature applicant   49

6. Specimen accompanying letter   52

7. A follow-up letter after an interview   55

8. A reply to a rejection letter   56

9. The decision-making process for a married person   78

10. The decision-making process for a single person   79

11. Application letter in French   317

12. Application letter in German   318

13. Application letter in Spanish   319

14. A sample CV in French   320

15. A sample CV in German   321

16. A sample CV in Spanish   322

17. A sample European Commission application form   323

Preface

to the Seventh Edition

This combined handbook and directory is intended for anyone planning to work abroad, whether for the first or the umpteenth time. It discusses the implications of such a step, surveys the wide range of opportunities on offer and offers advice on how to land the job you want.

Whether you are a school-leaver in search of adventure or a retired executive in search of new challenges - or somewhere in between - you should find most of the answers to your questions on working abroad in the following pages.

Chapter 7, for instance, is of particular relevance to students (including Gap Year students) and others looking for either holiday employment or work experience. Chapter 8 looks at contract opportunities for qualified and experienced professionals. Chapter 9 focuses on long term careers abroad and business opportunities in a foreign location.

The book also deals with the job search at some length with a key section devoted to the best ways of presenting yourself effectively to prospective employers. Other chapters deal with such matters as finance and contracts, which will be of considerable relevance to people planning to spend substantial part of their careers abroad.

However, finding a job is only part of the story. Taking up a posting in a foreign land can be fraught with unforeseen problems which can lead to frustration and misunderstandings.

Obviously you will want your experience to be worthwhile and successful. So to get you off to a good start I include tips on preparing for your assignment and coping with life in a strange land. Personnel officers and others who have to prepare staff for overseas assignments should find this information useful too. So should any members of your family who plan to accompany you.

As usual the advice is backed up with a comprehensive reference section providing thousands of contacts both at home and abroad. But before delving into this I recommend that you start by reading the introductory chapter which weighs up the pros and cons of living and working abroad, and recommends how to use the material in this book to the best advantage.

As with previous editions, I have undertaken a thorough revision of the book in order to reflect current conditions, including the growing importance of the Internet. Unfortunately, on the fast-moving international employment scene, information can go out of date very quickly, and it is not always possible to predict future trends. This means that inevitably some details will be incorrect or out-of-date – for which I offer sincere apologies. If you spot an error or have any suggestions, do please let me know c/o How To Books or e-mail arle@ukonline.co.uk and I shall make amends in future editions.

Finally, I must thank the many people who have supplied me with advice and information over the years. And to those of you who are encouraged to take the plunge, may I wish you a very happy and successful time working abroad.

Roger Jones

PART ONE: INTRODUCTION

1

Working Abroad:
Is It an Option for You?

CHANGING WORK PATTERNS

As the third millennium unfolds, our work patterns are changing. No longer do we expect to stay in the same job or with the same organisation all through our lives. Another change is that more of us are no longer constrained by national boundaries. We are beginning to think globally.

At one time very few people ventured abroad unless they had to – to fight wars on foreign soil or to escape poverty and injustice at home, for instance. Today we think nothing of jetting to the furthest corners of the planet for a holiday, and more of us are opting to live abroad these days out of choice rather than necessity.

Nowadays, just as people from every country under the sun come to find jobs in Britain, similarly UK nationals can be found working in every corner of the globe. We are becoming less insular, and more cosmopolitan. A new opinion poll reveals that, given the chance, 54 per cent of the population of the UK would like to live and work abroad. And around a quarter of a million are reckoned to leave every year for this reason for either short-term or long-term assignments.

While some of these are Walter Mittys who feel the grass is always greener over the hill, most have genuine motives for wanting to move. They include:

- a lack of opportunities at home

- a desire to travel or live abroad

- the chance to extend their professional experience

- a better salary

- promotion

- the wish for a more vibrant lifestyle

- family reasons (e.g. marriage to a national of another country)

- a sense of vocation (e.g. to help the Third World or spread the Gospel).

Others have to. It is a requirement of the job.

A quarter of a million may seem an enormous number, but it must be remembered that relatively few of these will be taking up permanent appointments abroad. Many of the posts in foreign countries tend to be on contract terms – so a similar number of expatriates will be returning at the same time.

This contrasts with the situation in the past when a posting to another country usually represented a lifelong commitment. You joined the Colonial Service, the Indian Army or a firm with extensive overseas involvement, and stayed overseas – apart from intermittent leave – until retirement. Nowadays it is virtually impossible for people to spend the whole of their careers in one location, Moreover, the need is for people with particular skills – IT specialists, engineers and teachers – rather than generalists who learn the job as they go along.

Another difference is that the age range of people taking up posts abroad has widened. The jobs market is more fluid than it used to be, and people are more prepared to change direction these days, either by choice or from necessity.

REASONS FOR WORKING ABROAD

What kind of people want to work abroad?

- At one end of the scale there are young people who are keen to see the world before they settle down to a fixed career. They may decide to take a year or two off between school and college or between college and the world of work, and want a job – or a succession of jobs – that will help them support themselves in this venture.

- Further up the scale there are people who decide from the outset on a career that will enable them to spend much of their life in foreign countries, in the Diplomatic Service or in a multinational company, for instance. A fair proportion of these will already have had experience of living abroad and know more or less what to expect.

- There are also professionals who are not interested in long-term careers abroad, but see a spell overseas as an important part of their career development. As organisations adopt flatter structures, employees are moving laterally rather than upwards in a bid to broaden their experience and learn new skills. If it is a way to improve their finances as well, so much the better.

- Older people are less likely to regard working abroad as a means to an end. They will already have progressed in their careers, but may feel the urge to try something different – even if only for a short spell. Age no longer seems to be a barrier to overseas employment, provided that a person is adaptable and resilient.

- A final category consists of people who have never thought of working abroad but find themselves sent off to a foreign posting. This is very much a sign of the times. Companies – particularly large ones – are no longer confined within national boundaries, and are keen to create an international cadre of key staff.

Dream and reality

People in Britain who have never worked abroad are often envious of those who have. They are persuaded by glossy holiday brochures into believing that every foreign location is highly desirable. They think of the sunshine and the sights but not of the mosquitoes or the business hassles.

But working in a foreign country is very different from a brief holiday visit where your sole aim is enjoyment. On vacation you are so entranced by the novelty of a particular place that you do not stop to consider that the heat, the traffic jams or the quaintness of the locals could begin to get you down after a while.

An overseas posting is not a holiday from your normal humdrum life. Indeed, anyone who is merely looking for escape from the challenges and traumas of life at home would do well to forget the idea of a posting abroad altogether. A job in Java is no haven for escapists, but requires realists who are able to meet challenges on all sides, not just one.

Even moving to another job in your own country can be something of an upheaval. You have to learn new methods and become acquainted with a new set of people. But moving from Guildford to Guinea involves a good deal more readjustment than a relocation to Grimsby. You will need to come to terms with a different living environment:

- different food

- different customs

- a different language

- a different climate

- different value systems.

'Variety,' notes Cowper, 'is the very spice of life that gives it all its flavour.' A successful expatriate is someone who is able to appreciate life's infinite variety – the good and the bad. This involves accepting unfamiliar vistas, values and traditions, and also giving something in return. You cannot stand aloof from what is happening around you. Instead, you will need to modify your behaviour and attitudes to blend in with your new surroundings.

COPING WITH A STRANGE ENVIRONMENT

Environment is a factor that should not be overlooked. Your skill and that of your nearest and dearest in adapting to it could be just as crucial to your success as your ability to do the job.

This is particularly true if your family is with you. So long as they are content, you will have a stable home base where you can retire and relax after the traumas of the day. If they find the place a drag, their feelings will in turn begin to sap your morale.

In some jobs you are protected to some extent from your environment, particularly if you live within an expatriate community. A British military base in Germany or Belize bears many similarities to its counterparts in Britain. If you are posted to a major capital, the chances are you will find a substantial community of fellow expats there who can help you acclimatise.

On the other hand, you might find yourself out on a limb both at work and away from the workplace. You could be the only non-local employee in a particular organisation, and opportunities to socialise with your fellow countrymen and women might prove few and far between. In such cases your qualities of resourcefulness and adaptability will be tested to the full.

How would you cope in such a situation? This is the kind of question that you need to ask yourself before you make any binding commitment. Don't assume that conditions in Tuvalu are the same as they are in Tunbridge Wells. If you do, you could be in for an enormous shock when you get there. The stories you hear of people arriving at their post and taking the next flight home because they can't cope are, unhappily, very often true.

Such disasters benefit no one. And so one of the aims of this book is to persuade people to look before they leap. There are plenty of work opportunities in foreign countries for the right person. Finding them is in many respects the easy part of the business; convincing an employer that you can make a success of the job and your period abroad is harder; coming to terms with your new environment can be hardest of all.

What makes working abroad so different?

The days have gone when you could go out to some distant clime and recreate your own little England around you and expect the local populace to adjust to your whims and fancies. Nowadays, the adjustment needs to come from *your* side. Here are a few of the major differences you will need to contend with:

- **Minority status**. For the first time in your life, perhaps, you will find yourself in a minority. Even if you do not manifest different racial features from the bulk of the populace your behaviour, attitudes and accent may make you stand out.

- **Climate**. At home you are used to a climate which avoids extremes. Other climates can be much harsher. Would you be able to cope with temperatures in excess of 90°F or below -25°F, flash floods or hurricanes?

- **Communication**. There is always plenty of scope for misunderstanding, particularly if you have an imperfect grasp of the language of the locals, whether it is the spoken language or body language.

- **Working practices**. Working hours and vacation entitlements may be different, and the whole company culture may seem strange. Your responsibilities could turn out to be more all-embracing than you expect.

- **Social customs**. What is acceptable in one culture (e.g. consumption of alcohol, backslapping or kissing in public) may not be so in another. You will need to learn the traditions of the country in order to avoid causing offence.

- **Different values**. You might find yourself in a country where the values are different from your own. For instance, loyalty to one's company may take second place to family loyalties, and nepotism could play an important role in the selection process.

DO YOU FIT THE PART?

You may be quite certain you would like to work abroad. The question is: will any employer be prepared to send you abroad on an assignment or offer you an overseas contract? This section is designed to help *you* decide.

First, forget the idea that the only qualities needed for an overseas posting are youth and a willingness to learn. While this may be sufficient for a holiday job or work experience, today's employers are more discriminating. They want candidates with relevant qualifications and experience, some of it gained abroad. Your nationality is not an advantage these days. American or British companies, for instance, no longer feel obliged to put their own nationals in charge of their foreign operations if there are local staff who can do the work just as competently – and possibly more cheaply. Where vacancies occur for expatriates they are often to cover a temporary skills' shortage.

To put it in a nutshell, recruiters are looking for **competence** and **value for money**. If they can find someone who can do the job as well as you for half or a quarter of the salary, they will do so. The main reason, for example, that the demand for British craftsmen in the Middle East has declined is that 'local' labour costs less to employ.

However, the law of the jungle can also work to your advantage in the international labour market. In recent years, for instance, British managers have been more popular with multinational employers than people from other countries – partly because British salaries are often lower compared with those in North America and on the European Continent.

For any job abroad – apart from work experience schemes for young people and casual work – employers require:

- good qualifications
- professional experience
- the right personal qualities
- language and communication skills.

The right qualifications

The days when a school leaving certificate was sufficient to find you a job in an overseas location are now past. It may be fine for a Gap Year assignment abroad, but most countries have plenty of people educated to this standard now, and so they no longer require the services of a semi-skilled expat.

This applies not only to the well-paid jobs. Voluntary service organisations that would take people straight from school 30 years ago are now much more demanding. A **degree** or **equivalent qualification** is generally the minimum requirement for this kind of work these days.

In my survey of agencies recruiting for abroad, the importance of a degree-level qualification was frequently stressed. While some recruited for vacancies at the supervisory level – for which a City & Guilds qualification was sufficient – generally speaking, this particular qualification was regarded as the absolute minimum.

Foreign employers tend to place more importance on degrees and certificates than on experience, and often recruit the person with the best qualifications – even if there are others who can acquit themselves more ably.

There is usually a particular reason for this – namely, government restrictions on expatriate labour. In order to be able to employ an expatriate, firms may well have to prove to their Ministry of Labour that they cannot recruit a sufficiently qualified local national. This applies as much to Australia and Canada as it does to the Third World countries.

So if you are keen to work abroad, have a look at your qualifications first of all. Are they really likely to impress? If not, see if you can improve them by attendance at night courses, doing correspondence courses or taking a year or so off for full-time study.

The right experience

Experience is important. A glance at the recruitment literature of several large multinationals will confirm that they are unwilling to send any of their permanent staff abroad until they have spent a few years gaining experience at home.

The importance of experience also applies to contract work. Employers are not interested in raw recruits. They want people who:

- have proved themselves in their chosen vocation
- are familiar with the world of work and its responsibilities
- are able to discharge their duties without the need for supervision.

Experience of working abroad is regarded as a plus.

Most recruitment firms will tell you that three years' work experience is generally regarded as an absolute minimum, and many more years are demanded for senior posts.

Similarly, voluntary service organisations require people who are not only qualified, but have plenty of practical experience under their belt. That is obviously why the average age of today's volunteers is around 30. Some may be over 50.

The right personal qualities

Sending a person abroad is an expensive business, but nothing is more expensive than an assignment that has to be aborted, because an individual has problems in settling down to a posting in an unfamiliar environment.

It is not just leaving the job early that can be a problem. Some employees manage to stick it out till the end, yet operate at a much lower level of efficiency because they or their families have not adjusted to the environment properly. And once more their company or organisation is losing out. Non-technical considerations are just as essential to the success of an overseas posting as any amount of professional skill.

Organisations that have had their fingers burned in this way now take greater care in choosing personnel. The wise ones no longer choose expatriate employees on the strength of their technical expertise alone, but realise that professional competence and suitability for an overseas assignment are by no means the same thing.

Handling cultural differences

The crux of the matter is whether you can perform as effectively in a foreign environment as you can on your home ground. It is all very well to arrive in a country with the best of intentions and a clear idea of what needs to be done, but things may start to go wrong when it comes to implementing your plans.

In his book *Riding the Waves of Culture,* Fons Trompenaars cites the case of an American multinational company that decides to introduce a performance-related pay scheme for its salespeople all round the world: the more a person sells the greater his bonus. But while managers from Northern European branches of the firm like the scheme, the Italians object strongly.

For Italians, working for a company is akin to being a member of a family. If a salesperson receives a bonus and his colleagues do not, he feels guilty about it and next time round tries not to earn a bonus – thus defeating the purpose of the bonus scheme. In any case in Italy it is unthinkable that a good salesman should earn more than his boss; over there pay is normally related to the position a person holds, not to how he performs.

It is only too easy to blame the foreigner if things do not work out as expected. Western businessmen who have to deal with the Japanese often get frustrated at the time it takes for them to secure an order or for their Japanese clients to reach a decision.

It just so happens that Japanese procedures differ from those of the West. The Japanese like to become thoroughly acquainted with a firm before they do business with it and decisions are made collectively – not just by one person. In their eyes they are not just signing an agreement but entering into what they hope will be a long-term relationship.

You also need to be able to function effectively on a personal level, and this may mean a modification to your customary behaviour patterns. In Turkey it is quite customary to kiss your colleagues, both male and female; but this should not be attempted in Hong Kong. In Africa raising your voice can engender respect; in China you should lower your voice: shouting causes 'loss of face'.

I have come across expatriates who are paranoid about the way the people of the host country go about their affairs, but the fault normally lies at their door. When you arrive to work in a foreign country – even one which you regard as similar to your own – you have to learn a new set of rules, and you will find learning easier if you understand the reasons behind a particular form of behaviour.

To seek to impose your way of doing things upon people may not lead to the desired results, as the American firm discovered with its payment by results policy. 'Rather than there being ''one best way of organising'' there are several ways, some very much more culturally appropriate than others,' comments Dr Trompenaars.

Assessing your own suitability

'The most underrated, though the most effective, method of selection is self-selection. Really thorough briefing will give unsuitable candidates a chance to see their unsuitability for themselves, thus saving all concerned much pain and grief.' Clare Hogg.

Ask yourself the following questions and invite other members of your family to do the same.

- Do you have very firm convictions/prejudices?
- Is your health indifferent?
- Do people sometimes find you brusque and tactless?
- Do you distrust 'foreigners'?
- Do you tend to be very set in your ways?
- Are you easily upset – by delays, the inadequacies of others, and so on?
- Do you have difficulty in seeing the funny side of situations?
- Are you intolerant of methods that conflict with your own?
- Are you reluctant to abandon home comforts?
- Are you ever moody?

If you find you have answered 'yes' to the majority of these questions, you need to resign yourself to the fact that you are probably not cut out for a foreign lifestyle. You will feel much happier staying in your own country and the rest of the world will heave a sigh of relief if you do!

To be a success in a foreign location, this is the sort of person you need to be:

- open-minded – prepared to accept alternative points of view

- adaptable – able to fit in to your new surroundings

- balanced – possessing a stable outlook on life

- resourceful – able to respond appropriately to new situations

- healthy – able to cope physically and mentally with stress and strain

- diplomatic – careful not to offend cultural sensibilities

- patient – a particular virtue in many Third World countries

- tolerant – of others' methods, religions, lifestyles, and so on

- communicative – able to put your ideas across clearly and effectively

- empathetic – able to understand and respect foreign cultures.

Of course, how important these qualities are will depend very much on your prospective environment. You could form part of an extensive expatriate community and have little contact with local people, as might be the case in the armed services, a large metropolis or a construction camp. But in more out-of-the-way locations you could be very much on your own, and your qualities could be tested to the utmost.

To help you decide whether working abroad is right for you, you might enlist the help of Christians Abroad World Service Enquiry who offer careers advice on an individual basis for people planning to work abroad. ECA International publishes a self-assessment guide, *Planning to Work Abroad*. For addresses see Chapter 20.

OTHER CONSIDERATIONS

Age

Mature people, who find that British employers prefer young recruits, may find that this is less of a problem with posts abroad. Foreign employers do not discriminate so much against older candidates. Indeed, in some countries age is regarded as synonymous with wisdom, and the older you are the more the employer likes it.

Indeed, the only potential problem is your physical health. But provided you are fit, mentally alert and adaptable, there should be few obstacles to your securing and taking up an overseas posting.

Your spouse

It is becoming common for accompanying wives and husbands to be invited to participate in an interview, particularly in the case of senior appointments, and this is a practice to be welcomed.

Spouses may have to play a much more significant role in their partner's careers than they do at home. There may be visitors to be entertained, company spouses to be looked after, and possibly even responsibility for some of their partners' duties to be shared. Indeed, the personality of the spouse could be crucial for the success of the overseas assignment.

The working woman

While the status of women has improved enormously as far as employment is concerned in Western Europe, North America and Australasia in recent decades, this is not really true in most of the rest of the world. Male-dominated societies still see the woman's place as being in the home, and have difficulty in accepting women on equal terms in the workplace.

For this reason many organisations operating in these areas prefer to recruit male candidates rather than female ones; so while there are certainly opportunities abroad for women, they are by no means as numerous as postings for men.

HOW TO USE THIS BOOK

This is not a book that needs to be read from beginning to end like a good thriller. You will need to delve into different parts of it according to your needs. Here are a few suggestions.

I am keen to work abroad, but I'm not sure where. Any ideas?
You need to start off reading the chapters of Part 5 which survey the conditions and the prospects in different parts of the world. For more information on individual countries see the Further Reading section (Chapter 22) or make contact with one or two addresses in the Country Directory (Chapter 19).

I have skills that I want to use abroad. Where do I start?
Start with Chapter 17, Job opportunities by profession. At the end of each job section you will find a list of organisations which recruit for this kind of job. For more information on these agencies and employers look them up in the Recruitment Directory.

I want to work abroad, but I am not sure if I want to do so permanently. What options are there open to me?
Read the Chapters 7, 8 and 9 which consider all types of assignments ranging from holiday jobs to permanent positions.

I have received an overseas job offer. Should I take it?
Read Chapter 4 with great care and take note of the suggestions.

I have a job lined up, but I want to find out more about what is involved.
Read Chapters 5 and 6 and the relevant chapter in Part Five: The Regions of the World. Consult the Further Reading section for books which would be of use and the Country Directory for other sources of information. Some of the contacts in Useful Addresses in the UK are worth following up.

I have never applied for a job abroad before. How do I set about it?
Start by reading Chapters 2 and 3. Then identify suitable employers in the appropriate section of Chapter 17: Job opportunities by profession.

I have plenty of experience of working abroad and know the ropes. What is there in this book for me?
The Reference section pre-eminently. In Chapter 18: Recruitment Directory you will find out who is currently recruiting whom, and in Chapter 19: Country Directory you will pick up more useful contacts.

PART TWO: FINDING A JOB

2

The Search for a Job

GETTING FIXED UP BEFORE YOU LEAVE

First of all, forget the idea of becoming a Dick Whittington who books a flight to a distant land in the belief that he will find a job soon after landing – such a plan is likely to land you in deep water with the immigration officials! Even if it doesn't, it can prove an expensive lesson if your plans don't work out – as they probably won't.

If at all possible, get yourself fixed up with a position before you board the plane or ferry. There are several good reasons for doing this:

- There is a well-developed international job recruitment market, especially in the UK, offering a wide range of opportunities that are open to everyone.

- If you are recruited in the UK you will probably be provided with your airfare to your job and other perks.

- The organisation that recruits you will be used to dealing with applicants like you, which means there should be little, if any, misunderstanding.

- With luck you will be offered a briefing on the job and the country, which will enable you to get off to a good start. If not, there are plenty of other sources of information and advice to prepare you for life in the country or region in question.

- Most governments nowadays impose restrictions on foreign nationals who wish to work in their countries, so you will need to obtain an appropriate visa before you arrive there. (EU countries are an exception to this rule provided you are an EU citizen.)

This last consideration is the most crucial of all. In many cases you need to have your paperwork in order before you leave this country, otherwise you might find you are regarded as an illegal immigrant.

As for the process of finding a job, there are basically two approaches, no matter when you are looking:

- You see one advertised and apply for it.

- You use a speculative approach.

Both methods can work when it comes to getting a job abroad, but you must know where to begin.

ANSWERING AN ADVERTISEMENT

This is the most common way of getting a job, either here or abroad. But first you have to find the vacancy.

Looking through the overseas job advertisements is a good starting point, since you get some idea of the range and locations of jobs on offer. Here are some suggestions as to where you might look:

- **UK daily and Sunday newspapers.** Some of these have specialist appointments sections on certain days of the week, e.g. banking and accountancy; public appointments; educational appointments. Generally speaking, in others Thursday is the best day for job advertisements.

- **Specialist journals.** These are particularly numerous, and periodicals that appear weekly tend to be more likely to carry extensive job advertising than monthlies and quarterlies. Examples are:

  Accountancy   *Construction News*
  British Medical Journal   *The Economist*
  Caterer and Hotelkeeper   *Nursing Times*
  Computer Weekly   *Times Educational Supplement*

- **Vacancy bulletins** which are normally only obtainable on subscription. Here are some UK ones:

  Opportunities Abroad (World Service Enquiry). This deals mainly with vacancies in voluntary, missionary and aid organisations. Ten issues a year.
  Nexus (Expat Network) monthly.
  Vacancy supplement to *Home and Away* (Expats International).
  Overseas Jobs Express (Island Publishing), fortnightly.
  The Health Exchange (International Health Exchange). Medical jobs in the Third World mainly with non-governmental organisations.

- **Foreign newspapers**. Although you can always take out a subscription to foreign journals this can be expensive; one alternative is to visit the reading rooms of some larger embassies and high commissions which often have them. Some large public reference libraries have a selection of these newspapers too – e.g. the City Business Library in London. One final possibility is to ask any friends or relations abroad to send you any promising job ads in their local papers.

- **Other publications**, which might include house journals or job annuals such as *Graduate Opportunities*. *World Service Enquiry*, a free guide from Christians Abroad, lists a number of organisations in the voluntary sector which accept unqualified people.

- **The Internet**. The Internet is becoming a popular medium for recruitment – which is good news for people in far-off places who do not have access to the various publications mentioned above on a regular basis and so miss out on the best opportunities. Most of the recruitment contacts in this book now have their own websites and e-mail addresses, and these are included, if known. Otherwise, if you are adept at 'surfing the net' you could try a number of sites. Here are a few to start you off:

www.overseasjobsexpress.co.uk (any country)
www.monster.com
www.eures-jobs.com

Many foreign newspapers and journals, like their counterparts in the UK, have their own websites which often feature a recruitment advertising section. You can find these websites in media directories, such as *Willings International Press Guide.*

For instance, if you are seeking work in the US you might try the website of the *Los Angeles Times* (www.latimes.com) or that of the *Washington Post* (www.washingtonpost.com). For jobs in Canada you could try accessing the website of *The Globe and Mail,* which is www.theglobeandmail.com

---

Health warning: There have been instances in the past of rogue businesses advertising non-existent jobs abroad and asking would-be applicants to send money for air fares. Such advertisements should be treated with scepticism. If the job is genuine you should normally expect an interview and the fare paid to your posting by the employer. Normally, it is illegal for agencies in the UK to charge candidates fees.

THE SPECULATIVE APPROACH (IN THE UK)

If you wait around for the right vacancy to crop up in the advertisement columns, you could be waiting in vain. Not all vacancies abroad are advertised, simply because employers already know of people they can call on to take up the post. After all, why should they spend money on expensive advertising when they already have a bevy of suitable candidates?

Rather than merely responding to events, it often pays to take the initiative and let prospective employers know that you are ready and willing to work in a foreign location. You are, in fact, advertising yourself, though in a way which may seem less obvious.

Some people imagine that the speculative approach means sending off a round robin indiscriminately to all and sundry. This method has been known to work, but more often than not the results are disappointing.

The key to success is **targeting**. You need to identify the companies and organisations that may well have a need for people like you and the agencies that specialise in recruitment for your particular area of work. You also need to make use of your network of personal contacts. Let's look at these ideas in greater detail.

Finding opportunities within your own organisation

If you are in the employ of an organisation, what better place to start your quest?

- Many larger firms have subsidiaries and associate companies in foreign locations, and personnel transfers between countries are increasingly common. A survey of 100 leading companies by Cendant International Assignment Services showed that 59% expected expatriate employment to grow during the next five years.

- Smaller outfits could offer opportunities in foreign parts as a representative or on secondment to a client. According to the Cendant survey 71% of smaller companies surveyed predicted an increase in expatriate employment.

- In the public sector there will also be opportunities – most notably in the Foreign and Commonwealth Office, the Department of Trade and Industry, the Department for International Development, the armed forces, GCHQ – but also in other branches of the Civil Service.

The fact that your staff noticeboard contains no foreign vacancies does not mean that they do not exist. Mention to your superiors that you are keen to work abroad and ask for suggestions. Organisations sometimes have problems in finding suitable candidates for overseas assignments, and the fact that you are interested in working abroad could count in your favour.

Do not expect quick results. To attain your goal you might need to transfer to a different department within your organisation – export sales, for instance. You might also need to undergo a course of preparation, such as language training. But in the long run it could be well worth the effort. According to a survey by ECA International 88% of firms regarded a spell abroad as useful and helpful to career prospects.

Using personal contacts

Do you know anyone who works abroad or has done so in the past? If so, you could ask him how he set about getting the job and if he knows of other vacancies in his particular organisation.

Don't be afraid of mentioning your overseas aspirations to others who may not be such obvious leads, such as your companions down at the Red Lion, colleagues at your aerobics class or even your Uncle Donald; they may have connections with organisations abroad, or be able to suggest useful contacts.

Other contacts you might consider approaching are business colleagues (past and present), tutors (past and present), pen friends, former classmates, former employers, Internet newsgroups and so on.

Using official contacts

Your professional association or trade union may have suggestions or even be able to arrange a placement. The Royal College of Nursing, for instance, operates a scheme to enable nurses to gain experience abroad, and the National Federation of Young Farmers Clubs also operates an exchange scheme for its members.

Foreign embassies and high commissions in the UK are *not* usually equipped to advise on job opportunities in their respective countries, and the same is true of most British diplomatic missions abroad. However, they may well have reference material you can consult and several have reading rooms where you can peruse the newspapers for job advertisements.

Chambers of Commerce are likely to be more helpful, whether they are foreign chambers in Britain or British chambers in other countries. **British Council** offices abroad can be a useful source of information, too, particularly for anyone looking for a job in education. (Useful addresses like these are included in the Country Directory at the end of this book.) Many towns and cities have close links with places abroad, and may be able to suggest or arrange employment opportunities via the local twinning committee.

Approaching employers direct

This is becoming more and more common as an approach, but your chances of success will be greater if you set about your task systematically.

1. Keep an eye on overseas news items in the trade and professional press. If you read that a company has been awarded a contract in Madagascar, that the government has decided to set up development assistance to Vanuatu, or that a leading consultancy plans to extend its activities to Mongolia and you have the requisite qualifications, skills and experience, it may pay you to approach these organisations immediately – before they get round to advertising for additional staff.

2. If possible, find out before applying whether the international company relies mainly on local expertise abroad, or whether you will have to spend some years working in the UK before being sent overseas. If either of these is the case, you may have a long wait for an overseas posting.

3. On the other hand, there are organisations with significant overseas interests where a high proportion of their permanent staff will be expected to work in foreign countries as a matter of course, such as Unilever, BAT Industries, the Standard Chartered Bank, the British Council and Oxfam. If in doubt, look at their recruitment literature or under their entries in directories such as *Graduate Employment and Training*.

4. Once you have chosen a company, send off your CV along with a covering letter explaining why you are keen to work for that particular outfit and what skills you have to offer.

5. Don't be disappointed if you hear nothing. Some organisations are inundated with speculative applications and are just not equipped to handle them. If you send a stamped, addressed envelope with your application, however, they might at least acknowledge your letter.

Some people submit speculative applications to foreign employers or subsidiaries of multinational firms. Names and addresses can be found from national trade directories, telephone directories and Expat Network's *Contact Directory*, *SE Asia Contact Directory*, *Far East Contact Directory* and *Middle East Contact Directory*.

If you have specific companies in mind, but do not know their addresses or contact numbers, a useful source of information is the *International Fax Directory* (Jaeger & Waldman) which can be found in most business reference libraries.

Using agencies/recruitment consultancies

An increasing number of jobs are handled by intermediaries on behalf of both foreign and British-based employers. They have various names – **employment agencies**, **recruitment consultants** and **executive search consultants** being the most usual descriptions. Normally the first category handles general appointments while the latter two are involved in the recruitment of top or middle management through advertisement, candidate register or by a process known by the alarming title of 'headhunting'. However, a considerable number of employment agencies handle executive recruitment as well, sometimes through a subsidiary. Many, although by no means all, of these agencies specialise in particular employment sectors – nursing, computer staff, accountancy staff, and so on – so find out who specialises in what before you make an approach. Otherwise you might unwittingly approach a catering agency when your area of expertise is heavy engineering!

Looking at the classified advertisements in specialist journals is a good way to discover which agencies are active in your field. In the Recruitment Directory (Chapter 18) you will find a select list of agencies that were involved in overseas recruitment when this book was being compiled. Not all of them are equipped to deal with speculative applications and may only reply if they have a suitable vacancy at the time you approach them.

There are certain advantages in using agencies, provided they are reputable organisations with plenty of experience of recruiting for jobs abroad:

● They generally recruit for a number of employers rather than just one.

● They can sometimes indicate the type and level of jobs open to you.

● They may be able to give you an idea of trends in the overseas jobs market.

● They can often give you a frank assessment of both job and employer.

● Many operate a candidate register – which you should try to join.

● They should know precisely how to present your credentials to a foreign company.

● No fee is charged to candidates by agencies in the UK. (There are exceptions, e.g. au pair agencies, Gap Year organisations.)

Although recruitment agencies are often helpful to applicants, remember that their clients – the people who pay for their services – are the employers rather than you the applicant, so don't expect them to move heaven and earth to place you in a job. Ringing them up every day demanding to know how your application is progressing will probably be a waste of time. On the other hand, you could get a phone call right out of the blue to see if you are still interested in a position.

Many of the large recruitment organisations have branches overseas, though they are often run as separate organisations. Walker and Walker include details of employment agencies abroad in some of their *Emigration Packs*. *The Executive Grapevine* and its *International Directory of Executive Recruitment Consultants* are worth perusing for higher level recruitment.

Private recruitment agencies and the law

You should have no qualms about using a recruitment agency operating in the UK. Although UK employment agencies no longer have to be licensed by the Department for Work and Pensions they are still regulated by the Employment Agencies Act 1973, and the Department has responsibility for ensuring that they comply with the law.

The Act includes the following provisions which are of relevance to anyone taking up an overseas posting:

- An agency must not charge you a fee for finding you work except in certain cases, mainly in the modelling and entertainment industries.

- An agency employing you to do temporary work should pay you whether or not it is paid by its client.

- An agency which finds you work abroad must give full written details of the job, employer, travel arrangements and accommodation.

- An agency must not supply a worker to a hirer abroad who has no business premises in the UK unless satisfactory written testimony has been obtained which states that the work will not be detrimental to the worker's interests.

- An agency must not send a worker to a hirer abroad unless thay have made arrangements to pay the worker's return fare themselves when the job ends or if the job does not commence, or else have obtained a written undertaking from the hirer to do so. If a hirer defaults on such an undertaking the employment business must pay the return fare.

Please note, however, that these regulations do not apply to agencies outside the UK, although other countries may well have their own laws governing the conduct of such agencies.

Job Centre facilities

Many countries have their own state employment agencies which recruit for jobs at all levels. In Europe they have formed a network known as EURES, which means you can find out about vacancies in other countries through your own national jobs agency.

In the UK the Overseas Placing Unit of the Department for Work and Pensions handles international job vacancies, including jobs in other European countries. It also has a network of advisers who can offer guidance on applying for jobs in the European Economic Area.

There is no need to contact the OPU's Sheffield office direct to find a job abroad. You should be able to conduct a search of its overseas jobs database from your local Job Centre. The OPU can also circulate your details to foreign employers. You simply have to fill in a form obtainable from the Job Centre.

Finally if you have access to Teletext you will find some overseas vacancies advertised on Job Finder (Page 368). Alternatively you can log on to the OPU website.

Placing a 'Situation Wanted' advertisement

This is a similar approach to a speculative letter except that you are using the advertisement columns of a newspaper or journal which circulates internationally to publicise your availability for employment. If you are keen to work in a particular country, you could try placing an advertisement in a suitable publication in the country in question.

You can find details of many foreign newspapers - including their websites and e-mail addresses – in *Willings Press Guide* or *Benn's International Media Directory*. Most capital cities and international centres have at least one English language newspaper, eg *International Herald Tribune* in Paris. Some of these have offices or representatives in Britain who can deal with your queries. You could also try circulating your details on the Internet.

There is no statistical evidence on how successful this approach is. Clearly, if you have skills which are much in demand, e.g. advanced IT skills, you are likely to fare better than someone who doesn't. You might increase your chances by being accessible – e.g. by having your own website giving full details of your skills and qualifications or by indicating if you will be visiting the area in the near future. You should also look out for suitable websites – particularly ones dedicated to your particular profession – which offer opportunities to advertise your skills and availability.

Sample classified ad

Journalist, 27, with five years' experience on business and financial publications seeks position with newspaper in East Asia. Excellent credentials. Visiting Hong Kong, Japan and Korea in June. E-mail: jswift@johnbull.com.

Miscellaneous

If you are a client of an outplacement or careers counselling agency, it may operate a system whereby your details are circulated to prospective employers. The expatriate service organisations, Expats International and Expat Network, run a similar service for their members.

MAKING VISITS 'ON SPEC'

Much of this chapter has been devoted to finding a job abroad before you leave Britain. Why not go abroad and conduct your job search on the ground?

This may seem the obvious way to go about things, but in practice there are snags. One major problem is that many governments impose restrictions on foreign nationals who want to work in their countries, so as not to put at risk the employment opportunities of their own nationals.

While it is possible to visit many countries as a tourist or in order to transact business, in the majority of places you will not be allowed to take up paid employment without the correct visa. If you do find a job, you may well have to leave the country, apply for a work visa (or similar document) and wait for your application to be approved. In the case of the United States this process can take up to a year, by which time the job you found may have gone.

There are exceptions. Within the European Union there is free movement of labour between most member countries which means that a UK or Irish passport holder may enter these countries both to look for a job and to take up employment without restriction. But in other parts of Europe and the rest of the world – including Commonwealth countries – you have to go through the proper formalities if you want to work.

On the other hand, if you happen to be visiting a country for other reasons – on a business trip or on holiday, for example – there is no harm in enquiring whether there are work opportunities available. An offer might come right out of the blue, as happened to a friend of mine who went for a holiday on a Pacific island and was asked if he would like to take up the post of Deputy Attorney!

There are certainly advantages in visiting a country before you decide to apply for a job there:

● You will be able to see what conditions are like there at first hand rather than relying on second or third hand information.

● You will be able to meet prospective employers and decide whether you are likely to get on well with them.

● You will have an opportunity to assess whether you would be able to adapt to the way of life of the country.

● You may be able to start making domestic arrangements such as finding accommodation for yourself or schooling for your children.

To find a job in the country itself, look through the advertisement columns, surf the Internet, approach recruitment agencies, write off speculative letters – just as you would do in the UK. However, do not expect the same kind of terms you would be entitled to if you applied for a job from the UK, such as travel and luggage allowances. You are likely to be offered a contract on local terms, i.e. on the same conditions as a local person. As this might mean no housing allowance and liability to local income tax, the implications of the contract would need to be looked into carefully.

PROS AND CONS OF DIFFERENT APPROACHES

Method	Pros and Cons	
Through advertisements	*pro*	The commonest method. You know a vacancy exists.
	con	You may be up against stiff competition.
Job with current employer	*pro*	You do not need to transfer to another employer.
	con	Relatively few employers offer jobs abroad.
Use of personal contacts	*pro*	You may be able to circumvent recruitment procedures.
	con	They will tend to offer suggestions, not firm leads.

Use of official contacts	*pro*	They may be able to offer information or foreign contacts.
	con	They are unlikely to offer a recruitment service.
Speculative approach to individual employers	*pro*	A well-targeted approach can sometimes open doors.
	con	Success usually depends more on luck than judgement.
Speculative approach to recruitment agencies	*pro*	Agencies usually have a wider range of vacancies on offer.
	con	Not all operate candidate registers or recruit for abroad.
Using Job Centres	*pro*	A service that circulates jobs' and candidates' details.
	con	Somewhat bureaucratic with no certainty of a match.
Situation wanted advert	*pro*	Your details will be read by a wide selection of people.
	con	It may not be seen or acted on by recruiters.
Foreign visits on spec	*pro*	You can find out about the country and job prospects.
	con	It is a costly exercise if you don't land a job.
Surfing the Internet	*pro*	You can access thousands of vacancies at the touch of a button.
	con	Some of the sites may not offer genuine jobs.

3

The Recruitment Process

IMPRESSING THE SELECTORS

Hopefully, by now you will have unearthed an interesting vacancy or identified an organisation that could use your skills. The next step is to convince the recruiters that you are the man or woman for the job.

It sounds simple, but it isn't – particularly in these days of increased competition. It's not really enough to rely on your native wit to win the day. You have to impress the selectors right from the word go. This means:

- a well-written letter of application on unlined A4 notepaper

- a clear and well thought out curriculum vitae/personal history/resumé

- a neatly filled-in application form supplying all the required information

- a recent photograph (or photographs) of yourself and photocopies of your qualifications (although this is not usually needed for jobs in Britain, it seems almost standard for overseas recruitment).

If you can produce all your documentation on a word processor (or have it produced for you), **do so** – even if it seems a chore (especially if, like mine, your handwriting is not your strong point!). Word processors will produce a more impressive document even than a manual typewriter, since you can remove all the mistakes and improve the layout before printing it out.

GETTING THROUGH THE PROCESS

If your application is good enough, you will hopefully be invited for an interview. Sometimes you may just have to take some tests (in recruitment competitions for the European Commission, for instance). The interview could be just an exploratory interview with a recruitment consultant – the first of a succession of interviews – or it could be the real thing.

Eventually, on the basis of your documentation, your performance at the interview, and your references, the organisation will decide whether or not to offer you the post.

This sounds simple enough, yet recruitment for positions abroad can be a lengthy process lasting months rather than weeks. This can prove irritating for anyone not well-endowed with patience, so in order to understand what you are letting yourself in for, let us consider a hypothetical case.

Case study: Richard recruits a training manager

1. Richard Wagner, manager of the Sierra Madre copper mine, decides he needs a training manager. He asks Giuseppe Verdi, personnel manager at the HQ of the El Dorado Mining Group, to recruit someone.

2. Verdi decides he will recruit from abroad so he contacts the London based recruitment consultancy Gilbert & Sullivan. Edward Elgar, a consultant at Gilbert & Sullivan, says he will be quite happy to help, and asks Verdi to send a detailed job description together with terms and conditions of service.

3. Verdi does so and Elgar looks through his register of candidates to see if he can find a suitable person. As he can't, he drafts an advertisement and places it with *Mining Monthly, Training Officers' Gazette* and *The Sunday Times*.

4. The advertisement appears in the latter two journals, Elgar receives 60 enquiries and sends off job details to each of the enquirers. He cannot begin selection yet as he is still waiting for the advert to appear in *Mining Monthly*. Eventually the next issue of *Mining Monthly* is published and the Sierra Madre advertisement attracts another 100 enquiries. Elgar sends off more job details.

5. Elgar sits down and sifts through the final applications – some 130 in all – and decides to interview a dozen or so of the candidates. He sends off invitations to the twelve most promising and informs the others that he does not propose to take their applications any further.

6. In the end he interviews ten candidates – two fail to turn up for interview – and decides to recommend four of them to Verdi. He sends off their papers to Verdi for him to make the final choice.

7. Verdi announces that the company's managing director Hector Berlioz is coming to Europe the following month for an international mining conference and would like to drop in to interview the four

shortlisted candidates. Elgar arranges for the four to meet him, contacts their referees, and informs the other six on the shortlist that they are not included on the final shortlist.

8. Berlioz interviews the four and provisionally accepts one John Constable provided his medical proves satisfactory and the El Dorado government grants him a work permit. Elgar arranges for Constable to have a medical, while Berlioz instructs Verdi to send Constable's details to the Ministry of Labour. (Verdi warns Elgar that the government vetting process may take time since none of the civil servants in the El Dorado Ministry of Labour speaks English.)

9. Eventually the permission is granted, Constable is pronounced fit, and he is given a contract to sign. However . . .

10. There are certain clauses in the contract which are extremely hazy, so Constable asks for some clarification before he signs. Elgar contacts Verdi; Verdi has a word with Wagner; and Constable receives a reply which satisfies him. He signs.

11. Constable now has to go to the El Dorado Embassy in London, present his passport, the work permit, his contract of employment, birth certificate, marriage certificate and six passport size photos in order to gain an entry visa. He completes a detailed visa application form and is asked to return to collect the documents in seven days.

12. Once Constable's documentation is in order he boards the plane for El Dorado.

When I say that recruitment for an overseas posting can seem an endless rigmarole, I really mean it. In fact, the hypothetical case I have described has been fairly straightforward. What would have happened if some hitch had occurred in the process?

Dealing direct with foreign employers
In a sense Constable is fortunate in being able to use a British intermediary who is familiar with recruitment practices in both Britain and El Dorado. Elgar is therefore able to explain Constable's qualifications and experience to his client Verdi and advise on the appropriate conditions of service for a person of his calibre. Thus there should be little scope for misunderstanding.

Misunderstandings *can* occur, however, if you are dealing direct with a foreign employer.

- **Language difficulties**. Try to be as precise as possible in expressing yourself and be prepared to explain unfamiliar terminology. The problem can be both of language and of culture. Mention that you were the President of the Oxford Union, for instance, and it might be assumed you are a leading trade unionist. Reference to your treasurership of the Duckington-in-the-Mud Bowling Club is more likely to confuse than enlighten.

- **Unfamiliarity with British qualifications**. While some employers will understand what a BSc stands for, they might be bewildered by such acronyms such as MIEE, MIMM or MICE.

- **Differences in recruitment practice**. A continental employer will be more interested in your certificates than in your achievements outside the world of work, and, like many American employers, may ask for transcripts of your grades or open testimonials.

Who should you send the letter to? If you put Director of Overseas Recruitment on the letter, this will ensure that it arrives in the right in-tray. Or better still, telephone the organisation, ask who you should send your application to and put this name on your letter. Don't forget to add the job title as well.

If you are dealing with an employer or agent whose mother-tongue is not English you need to express yourself carefully and precisely:

- Write in his or her language if you can.

- If you can't, keep your language clear and reasonably simple.

- Keep your letter polite and fairly formal.

- Have your CV translated, if possible.

- Avoid unfamiliar acronyms, if possible. Qualifications should be written out in full. You may need to explain how much study they entailed.

Chapter 21 includes examples of applications and CVs in foreign languages.

Some professionals avoid recruitment consultancies, regarding them as an extra and unnecessary link in the recruitment chain. In fact, good recruitment consultants can often speed up the process if they understand exactly what the overseas client wants and have experience of finding the type of person who would best fit into the organisation. Let's look more closely at the recruitment process.

REPLYING TO AN ADVERTISEMENT

When you see a job advertised, read the instructions carefully.

- Do you have to telephone, fax, send an e-mail or write for an application form?
- Do the recruiters just want you to send along a CV or will they send you a form to fill in?
- Whom or which department should you contact?

It is important to get it right. If the employer mentions an application form, there is no point in preparing an elaborate application of your own. At the early stage a short note asking for a form and further details is all that is needed (see Figure 1).

If, on the other hand, they want a CV, send a good and relevant one . . . accompanied by an effective letter of application.

If applying for a job advertised on the Internet you may find that you are expected to key in your details on-line.

SENDING A SPECULATIVE LETTER

The important thing about a speculative letter is that it has to arouse interest. A letter opening with the words 'My name is Aloysius Merryweather and I am looking for a job' is likely to be consigned to the waste-paper basket before you can say 'Jack Robinson'; so you need something that is short and snappy and draws attention to your strengths as far as this particular vacancy is concerned (see Figure 2). Emphasise any of the following if they apply to you:

- a successful track record abroad
- an ability to work with people of other nationalities
- technical skills
- achievements – particularly in a foreign environment
- adaptability and resilience
- specialised knowledge of the area in question
- language ability.

Should you send a CV as well? There are two schools of thought. One is

Tel: 01111 222222
E-mail: plum@apple.com

Blackberry Cottage
Sloe
Brambleshire BR1 2YZ

5 April 200X

Jack Mulberry
Consultant
Damson International
Strawberry Hill
London SW30 1AB

Dear Mr Mulberry

I am writing in response to your advertisement in this week's *Horticultural Express* for a Horticultural Adviser to the Guava Soft Fruit Project in Papua New Guinea.

The post sounds an exciting one to which I could undoubtedly make a substantial contribution. I would therefore be grateful if you could send me further details on the position, together with an application form, if required.

Yours sincerely

Josiah Plumb

Fig. 1. Specimen request for job details.

Tel: 01678 987543   13 Tanner Court
E-mail: Ivor@britnet.com   Crown Hamlet
                                         Stirling ST5 8MT

                                         31 September 200X

Managing Director
Mark Dinar Bank (Overseas Division)
50 Dollar Square
London EC1 9ZZ

Dear Sir

The recent report in *The Financial Times* about your ambitious expansion plans prompts me to enquire whether you have any vacancies in your international operations.

I am very keen to become involved in overseas banking as I believe it offers intellectual stimulation as well as the opportunity to work with people from other countries. I have lived abroad for extended periods – in Zambia, Guatemala and Austria – and developed close relationships with people of other nationalities.

I am proficient in three foreign languages and have recently been awarded a degree in economics by the University of Liverpool. As for practical experience, during my time in Austria I helped organise an international seminar entitled 'Banking 2000', and was consulted on a number of occasions by a leading bank in Innsbruck.

If you feel it would be useful, I would be very happy to drop by for an exploratory chat – with no obligation, of course.

Yours faithfully

Ivor Catchpenny

Fig. 2. Model speculative letter of application.

that at this stage you are only trying to interest the prospective employer and therefore don't want to give too much away. The other is that to present a detailed CV will save time in the long run. The decision is yours.

If you are dealing with someone in a non-English speaking country you may make an impression if you can send a letter in the language of that particular country, but make sure it's accurate. However, if you are after a job in Abu Dhabi or China and cannot write Arabic or Chinese, don't panic! Just pen some good, clear English prose.

Increasingly people are now communicating by e-mail or fax. These methods have the advantage of being much speedier processes which let you know whether or not your communication has reached its destination.

WRITING A LETTER OF APPLICATION

If you are applying for a particular job, don't assume that a completed application form or CV should stand alone or be accompanied by only a cursory note. The accompanying letter is the first contact the selector has with you, so it needs to look good (see Figure 3).

A letter can answer a lot of questions about you:

Can you spell?
Are you prepared to make an effort?
Can you communicate well?
Do you know how to write a business letter?
Are you keen on the job?
Do you understand what the job entails?

Most important of all it gives you an opportunity to make a statement about yourself to the selector before he starts wading through your CV or your application form. It should:

● explain why you want the job

● give three or four factors which mark you out as the ideal candidate

● finish on a positive note.

PREPARING A CURRICULUM VITAE

Like the letter of application, a CV has to look impressive, but don't try to impress the recipient with a document of inordinate length. Recruiters are

Tel: 01234 87654

Shelley Cottage
Coleridge Walk
Tennyson Wells TE4 2TZ
United Kingdom

31 December 200X

Mr Bruce Foster
Personnel Manager
Maugham IT Series
O'Casey Close
Sydney, NSW
Australia

Dear Mr Foster

I am most interested in your vacancy for a Senior Programmer advertised in this week's edition of *Computer Weekly*, and wish to be considered for this key post.

Although very happy with my present employers, I believe the time has come for me to try something new. Australia's IT sector seems to offer plenty of challenges these days, and I am sure I would feel at home in a progressive firm such as yours.

I have many years' experience in computers, as you will see from the enclosed CV, and have worked on IBM, ICL and Nixdorf machines. Apart from successfully completing assignments for both British and foreign firms, I have also been involved with public sector installations in a number of different countries.

In this particular field you need someone who is well-balanced, can communicate effectively with people who may not be computer-literate, and work to the most exacting standards. I believe I am such a person.

May I look forward to meeting you to discuss the contribution I feel I can make to the continued success of your organisation?

Yours sincerely

W A Wordsworth

Fig. 3. Specimen accompanying letter for CV.

not usually interested in people's memoirs! Instead, keep it concise and to the point (ideally, just one side of A4 paper; two sides at the most). Have it word processed if you can't do that yourself. Preparation of a CV can be a lengthy process, but if you get it right first time it is well worth the time and effort. There are basically two types:

- **The chronological CV**. This is the most familiar type which details your experience in chronological order. Examples are given in this book.

- **The functional CV**. This type of CV is sometimes used by candidates with many years of experience behind them. Instead of using a chronological approach for the work experience it focuses on particular areas of expertise.

While the latter can be a powerful tool, some recruiters may find it confusing. I therefore suggest that, when applying for jobs abroad, you use the chronological method and highlight your expertise in the letter of application. Your CV should contain:

- **Personal details**. Your name, address, telephone numbers (work and home), date of birth, nationality. Place of birth, marital status, religion are optional.

- **Education**. Educational institutions attended with dates and examinations passed. If you left school decades ago there is no need to go into details about your GCE results. Include any courses you have attended in recent years and any diplomas/certificates you are currently studying for.

- **Summary of work experience**. An optional section in which you outline your main areas of expertise.

- **Employment record**. List the jobs you have held, the organisations you have worked for with addresses and dates. Give a concise description of your responsibilities in each post, particularly in the case of those you have held during the past five or ten years. If you have had a long and distinguished career, be brief about the jobs you held twenty years ago. On the other hand, if you are right at the beginning of your career include details of holiday jobs and traineeships.

- **Interests and activities**. Foreign employers are unlikely to pay much heed to this section. British recruiters will, because they like evidence that the applicant has a well-rounded personality. List the sports you play, the clubs and societies you belong to, particularly those in which you hold office.

● **Other information**. Possession of a valid driving licence or passport, language abilities, membership of professional associations, awards you have received, time spent abroad – these are just a few of the items you might mention.

Don't assume that the length of your CV should be commensurate with your age. The CV of a young applicant could well take up as much space as that of an older person. The differences lie in the approach.

Younger applicants at the beginning of their careers will need to *elaborate* on their achievements so far; go into some detail about your attainments at school and college, including social interests and positions of responsibility you have held. Vacation employment should also be mentioned to indicate familiarity with the world of work (see Figure 4).

Mature applicants, by contrast, need to *condense* their career details (see Figure 5). Employers are more interested in your recent achievements than in your attainments of 20 years back. Only brief details of your educational attainments need be provided, though courses taken in recent years should certainly be mentioned to show that you are up-to-date in your field and still intellectually active. Similarly, employment in the early part of your career can be treated cursorily (unless it has direct relevance to the job currently being applied for), while the last two or three jobs held should be described in some detail, especially if the scope of the job is not apparent from the title.

COMPLETING AN APPLICATION FORM

Most people find the completion of application forms a terrible bore. However, many organisations prefer to have candidates' details in some standardised format to make comparison easier, and they may not be prepared to consider you if you don't return their form fully completed. So you have to make the best of a bad job. But beware: filling in a form is not a job that can be rushed.

1. Read it through carefully, making notes (alternatively make a photocopy of it and do a rough version on the copy).

2. Take a black pen and begin to fill it in with a copy of your CV at your side for reference (if you are a good typist, you might consider typing in the information, but not if the result will be messy; neatness is vital).

Curriculum Vitae

ANGELA SUTHERLAND
14 Epstein Close
Gainsborough
North Yorkshire
Tel: 01999-121212
Fax: 01999-121213

Born 16 May 1975 at Gainsborough. Unmarried. British nationality.

EDUCATION

1986–1991　Landseer High School for Girls, Gainsborough
　　　　　　GCSEs: History (C); French (C); English (C)
　　　　　　Maths (B); Art (B)
1991–1993　Sickert Commercial College, Leeds
　　　　　　RSA Diploma in Secretarial Studies

EXPERIENCE

1993–1995　Lowry and Lowry, Solicitors, 24 High Street,
　　　　　　Gainsborough:
　　　　　　Secretary
1995–1998　Whistler Estate Agency, 25 High Street, Gainsborough:
　　　　　　Secretary and PA to Manager
Since June　Turner-Constable Temps Agency, 26 High Street,
1998　　　　Gainsborough:
　　　　　　Secretary

INTERESTS

Ice Skating
Embroidery
Bridge

OTHER INFORMATION

I hold a full driving licence and a First Aid certificate
I have visited France, Germany and Switzerland
I am currently attending an evening course in German at Gainsborough
College of Further Education

Fig. 4. Specimen CV for a younger applicant.

Personal History
WILLIAM ALAN WORDSWORTH

Address: Shelley Cottage, Coleridge Walk, Tennyson Wells TE4 2TZ
Telephone: 01234 87654 extension 5 (daytime); 01234 98765 (home)
E-mail: waw@britnet.com
Date of birth: 28 February 1950
Marital Status: Widower
Place of Birth: Dundee

EDUCATION
1961-1966	Robert Burns High School, Land's End, Cornwall
	GCE O Levels in English Language, Greek, Mathematics, Physics and Swahili.
1966-1968	The Byron College of Further Education, Truro, Cornwall
	City and Guilds Certificate in Electronics
1975-1978	Yeats University, Sligo, Eire
	BSc in Computer Science

SUMMARY OF WORK EXPERIENCE
Electronics: Assembly and design of printed circuit boards
Information Technology: Computer programming and systems analysis
Management & Training: Supervision of IT projects and induction of client's staff

EMPLOYMENT RECORD
1968-1975	Eliot's Electricals, Browning Way, Cowperville: Apprentice, later Assistant Designer
1978-1979	Hardy Computer Services, Auden Square, Spenderbury: Computer Programmer
1979-1985	Milton Computers Ltd, Pope Street, Great Donne: Computer Programmer, later Systems Analyst
	During my time with Milton I was in charge of introducing and implementing major computer systems for foreign clients such as Hugo Chemicals in Paris, Dante Data Services in Turin, and Mörike Motor Work in Stuttgart.
1985-present	Shakespeare Computer Consultants, Johnson Row, Rochester: Senior Consultant
	I have designed and supervised a number of major projects, notably the installation of a computerised accounting system at Rochester District Council Headquarters and a computerised traffic control system for the Ras Al Khaimah Police Force.

INTERESTS
Ice-hockey, Judo and Ballroom Dancing
Treasurer of the Rochester and District Operatic Society
Member of Rochester District Council (1986–1989)

OTHER INFORMATION
Member of the British Institute of Management
Fluent in Swedish, Swahili and Urdu
Holder of a full and unendorsed British driving licence
Available to take up new position at three months' notice.

Fig. 5. Specimen CV for a mature applicant.

Particular points to note are:

- **Address** for correspondence. Make certain that this is likely to remain valid for the next six months. If not, choose one that will.

- **Contact telephone number**. Organisations are most likely to want to contact you during office hours. If you are difficult to get hold of, give the number of a relation or neighbour who can relay messages to you. A fax number or e-mail address is also acceptable.

- **Education**. If you are dealing with a foreign organisation that may not be familiar with the British educational system you may have to offer some explanation, e.g. 'GCSE – General Certificate of Secondary Education (an examination taken by 16 year olds)'; 'HND – Higher National Diploma (equivalent to . . . in your country).'

- **Work experience**. Fill in the details as required even though you may be duplicating the information on your CV. If there are any lengthy interruptions to your employment, you may have to account for them. If there is any information that you do not wish to disclose at this juncture (e.g. reasons for leaving a particular job), leave the space blank. Make sure that you have listed the jobs in the correct order. Some forms ask for chronological order, others reverse chronological order where your current or most recent job comes first.

- **Referees**. These need to be people who can vouch for your good character, your prowess at work, or your academic attainments. Make sure that they are willing and available to do this. If you know that one of your referees is about to go off on an expedition up the Amazon, find a substitute.

- **Salary requirement.** If the form asks you to state the level of salary you want, be careful. If you ask for too much, you are possibly eliminating yourself from the contest. One alternative might be to insert the words 'To be discussed at interview'.

- **Declaration**. At the end of many application forms you have to sign a declaration that the information you have provided is true. Check that this is so, since misleading information can lead to disqualification.

When you have completed the form look back over your handiwork, correcting any small errors that may have crept in and asking yourself what kind of impression it gives of you. Check if there are any vital details that have been left out, such as membership of a professional body or courses you have recently attended. If there are, try and include them somewhere on the form.

SENDING YOUR DOCUMENTS

Send your application as quickly as possible – to demonstrate your keenness for the job and to be ahead of the rest of the pack. Make sure you send off all the documentation required – the application form, your CV (whether requested or not), photocopies of your qualifications (if specified), passport size photographs (if specified) and a good covering letter (essential) – see Figure 6.

Before you finally send it off, stand back and ask yourself what effect all this information is likely to have on the recipient. If he receives a few dozen applications for the same post, is there anything that will make yours stand out?

If not, then something is wrong. Perhaps you need to redo the application, or at least make a mental note to try better next time. Perhaps the use of different paper – thicker or pastel-coloured – would make the difference between success and failure.

Always use first class post. If you are sending it abroad you might look into more secure or speedier ways of despatching it – Data-post, fax, e-mail or recorded delivery, for example.

Wait for a response

This is a period when your patience will be sorely tried – but don't keep telephoning to find out if your application has arrived or to persuade the organisation to get on with the recruitment process. Such impatience is understandable, especially if the job is one that you really want, but try and find something else to do in the meantime!

A wise applicant has plenty of irons in the fire. Do not assume that you'll get the post you have set your heart on. Instead, look round for other opportunities and fire off a volley of applications in other directions as well.

If the post is being advertised internationally, the wait will be even longer. A quick decision is a rarity in the case of recruitment for overseas jobs. Even if an advertisement includes the words REQUIRED URGENTLY you will be lucky to be bound for your foreign posting even two months after the date of its appearance.

Tel: 01999 121212
Fax: 01999 121213

14 Epstein Close
Gainsborough
North Yorkshire

31 December 200X

The Manager
Overseas Services
Rembrandt Recruitment
Rossetti Row
London SW51 8DD

Dear Sir

With reference to your advertisement in *The Guardian* for an English-speaking secretary in South Germany, I have pleasure in submitting an application.

You will note from my curriculum vitae that I have worked as a secretary
for a firm of solicitors and an estate agency. More recently, in order to broaden my experience, I have worked on a temporary basis for an English travel company and a French bank. These recent appointments have proved very enjoyable and have prompted me to look for a suitable position abroad.

I know South Germany well, having participated in the European Ice Skating Championships in Garmisch Partenkirchen on two occasions, and spent a holiday with my pen friend in Munich. I get on well with people of all nationalities, and having acquired a knowledge of German through attendance at evening classes I shall have no problems in communicating with your clients and their employees.

I do hope you will see fit to recommend me to your clients. I am, of course, willing to attend for an interview at any mutually convenient time.

Yours faithfully

Angela Sutherland

Fig. 6. Specimen accompanying letter.

PREPARING FOR TESTS AND INTERVIEWS

Coping with selection tests

Some organisations – governmental and intergovernmental ones in particular – subject candidates to a test as a preliminary to the interview. The test might be designed to measure intelligence, aptitude or personality, or to measure certain skills, such as drafting ability, linguistic ability, and so on. Normally you will be given some indication as to the form the test(s) will take in advance.

Don't regard the test as yet another obstacle along the path to finding a job; a good test might be better at measuring a candidate's competence than a badly-conducted interview.

Preparing for interview

Sooner or later you will receive a letter through the post either declining your services or inviting you for interview. If it is the latter, congratulations, but don't assume that it is downhill all the way from now on. After confirming that you are able to attend at the time and place specified, you need to embark on some intensive preparation:

- Read up about the job, the country and the organisation for which you will be working.

- Think hard about the qualities needed for the job and how you would measure up to it.

- See if you can get in some interview practice.

- Think of a few questions you would like to ask about the job.

- Try to envisage the type of questions the selectors are likely to ask and how you might answer them.

Possible interview questions

Why do you want a job outside the UK?
What attracts you to Ruritania/this job?
How well do you get on with people of other cultures/nationalities?
What experience do you have of working abroad?
What adjustments do you expect to have to make?
Why should we offer you this job?
What changes would you want to make to the organisation, if appointed?
Where do you see yourself in five years' time?
What are your strengths (weaknesses)?
What problems do you envisage having to overcome?

What sort of salary do you require?
What other jobs have you applied for?
How does your spouse/family feel about living abroad?

The interview itself

A lot of people dread interviews – not least some interviewers. Alas, the interview is by no means the most scientifically foolproof way of deciding whether a person is suitable for a particular job. If you are not offered a job after the interview, remember that this setback might not be a reflection on your ability, but rather reveal lack of discernment on the part of the selector(s)!

This is particularly true in the case of recruitment for posts abroad. If the selectors' expertise lies in recruiting people for jobs in the UK, there is a risk that candidates will be judged by inappropriate criteria. The person who fits in well at head office might not be the right type for a challenging post in Namibia.

While it helps if you can display knowledge of, and an interest in, the country concerned, remember that this may only be of minor interest to the recruiters, whose main concern is to fill a particular post. Your aim during the interview is to convey a good impression and convince the selector(s) that you are capable of performing all the duties connected with the job.

Dos and don'ts at the interview

- Do dress smartly.
- Do arrive in good time.
- Do try to establish some rapport with the interviewer(s).
- Do be polite.
- Do be as natural as you can.
- Do look at the interviewer(s).
- Do keep calm.

On the other hand:

- Don't sit down until invited to.
- Don't argue.
- Don't interrupt.
- Don't make jokes.

Tel: 01987 12345

Fax: 01987 23456

5 Vauxhall Drive

Morrisford

Austinshire AB1 2CD

14 July 200X

Roger Rover Esq

Personnel Director

Automotive International

Talbot Road

Morgantown

Dear Mr Rover

I am writing to say how much I enjoyed meeting you and other members of your firm when I came along for an interview yesterday.

I look forward to hearing the results of your deliberations.

Yours sincerely

George Riley

Fig. 7. A follow-up letter after an interview.

Tel: 01987 12345
Fax: 01987 23456

5 Vauxhall Drive
Morrisford
Austinshire AB1 2CD

16 July 200X

Roger Rover Esq
Personnel Director
Automotive International
Talbot Road
Morgantown MG20 1PQ

Dear Mr Rover

Many thanks for your courteous letter of the 15th regarding my application for the post of Regional Representative, Tahiti.

While I am naturally disappointed that I did not get the job, I would like to take this opportunity to thank you for giving my application such careful consideration.

I wonder if you are likely to have any similar vacancies in the future? If so, I would be very interested to hear from you.

My very best wishes for the continued success of your company.

Yours sincerely

George Riley

Fig. 8. A reply to a rejection letter.

- Don't run down your present or previous employer.

- Don't get on your hobby horse.

- Don't lie or make exaggerated claims.

AFTERMATH

After the interview there may well be another considerable wait, followed by either a telephone call or a letter. It may contain an invitation to a further interview. This is not a mistake or evilmindedness on the part of the organisation; obviously the first interview you attended was by way of an initial selection. Rejoice that you have been included in the final short-list and carry out the same procedures as you did before the original interview.

However, the letter may convey bad news: that you have not been selected. While this will obviously be a disappointment, *don't* despair. What you need to do is write back to the organisation that interviewed you to:

- thank them for meeting you, and

- express the hope that they will bear you in mind if a suitable vacancy arises in the future (see Figure 8).

Who knows, the appointee may decide not to take up the position, in which case you are once more a strong contender for it.

4

Coming to a Decision

You have now had the interview in which you should have learned more about the job, you have succeeded in landing the post, and you have been offered a contract. The ball is in your court, and you have to decide whether to take up the offer or not.

KNOWING YOUR EMPLOYER

If the job is with an organisation that is well known for dealing with its employees fairly, you need have few qualms about taking up the posting. However, not all jobs are with the likes of Shell or the Foreign and Commonwealth Office. You could be working for an overseas firm or government about which you know practically nothing except for some sketchy information with your job description. If you have any doubts about the credentials of the organisation, you would be wise to:

- Try to meet a former expatriate employee of the organisation.

- Consult a business directory dealing with the country concerned, such as *Kompass.*

- Ask your professional association or trade union if they have any details on the organisation.

- Check with the British Embassy or Chamber of Commerce in the country of operation.

- Check with an expatriate service organisation, such as Expats International.

- If you are being recruited by an intermediary, ask if they can supply comprehensive details. UK employment agencies are legally obliged to verify the credentials of their clients.

Although a good many employers of expatriates are reputable, there are, alas, some instances of employers who fail to honour their commitments to employees, and people have returned home considerably out of pocket as a result.

To take legal proceedings against them, particularly in a foreign court, can be complicated and costly, and there is no guarantee you will win; so look before you leap.

UNDERSTANDING THE SALARY PACKAGE

Many people are enticed into taking up positions overseas by the prospect of a higher salary. Even if you are not, as is the case with missionaries or volunteers, you need to be sure that the package on offer will be adequate to support you and your family, if you have one.

To think solely in terms of the salary figure on offer can be misleading. Usually you will be offered a **package** of benefits both in cash and in kind. This will consist of at least some of the following items. The more items on offer, the better the package:

- basic salary

- allowances:
  - overseas cost of living allowance
  - hardship allowance
  - accompanied spouse allowance
  - education allowance for children

- benefits:
  - pension
  - life insurance
  - medical cover

- free or subsidised housing or a rent allowance

- termination bonus

- paid leave at regular intervals

- fares and baggage allowance to and from the posting.

On this basis, for example, a job paying £30,000 with free housing and a pension contribution could well prove more attractive than one paying £40,000 with no extras.

There are also other points to remember. The total package may look fine, but is it all yours? Don't overlook the following which could affect your prosperity:

- Tax liability: is the package tax-free or do you have to pay income tax either at home or in the country to which you are posted?

- Social Security payments: what deductions are made to cover these?

- Extra expenses you are likely to incur by reason of living away from home (for example, maintaining two households).

Currency problems

For some postings, you might need to think about the currency you are to be paid in. If the company has suggested paying you in local currency, you need to find out:

- Is the currency convertible?

- How much of my salary can I repatriate?

- Is the salary tied to an international currency (e.g. the US dollar, sterling)? If not, you could lose out if any devaluation takes place against other currencies.

Even if you are paid in an international currency, be prepared for shocks. Recently British people whose salaries were paid in euros found that in sterling terms they lost out when the euros weakened against the pound.

Cost of living

Don't forget that there are likely to be differences in the cost of living between your home base and your foreign posting. Some capital cities – Tokyo, for instance – can be very expensive indeed. On the other hand, there are places where you can live like a lord on a relatively modest salary.

If you can, check that your pay level will be at least comparable to the rates offered to nationals of the country concerned, particularly if you are heading for high salary level countries such as the USA, Germany, Sweden, Switzerland or Japan. Is the organisation concerned after your skills and expertise, or merely cheap labour?

Salary differentials

International salary differentials can cause considerable bitterness. In overseas oil operations, for instance, where there is a mix of nationalities, the pay for executives and technicians from different countries often reflects their country of origin rather than their abilities.

A British employee may therefore find he is earning less than his counterparts from other parts of Europe and the USA. On the other hand, he could be earning several times as much as a highly qualified technician from India or the Philippines.

Many multinational employers are aware that this can be a very thorny subject and are starting to use remuneration and cost of living comparisons prepared by organisations such as Towers, Perrin, Forster and Crosby (TPF&C), Runzheimer, Business International, ECA International and *The Economist* Intelligence Unit. Most of these reports are quite expensive for an individual to buy, but if you have a chance to see one, you can judge for yourself whether you are being fairly remunerated.

Dual income families

Finally, dual income families could face a problem if one partner takes up a job abroad and the other who accompanies him/her is unable to take up salaried employment there. It is therefore vital to find out whether the earning partner's enhanced salary package will compensate for the other's loss of income.

THE JOB ITSELF

If the job is with an American or British organisation you can usually count on getting a detailed description of your responsibilities; however, organisations in other countries may regard such details as irrelevant. They may assume that if you are competent at your job then there is no need to spell out exactly what you have to do. You will be required to do what is necessary, no more and no less.

What can you expect?

People who have worked abroad before will have a pretty shrewd idea of what to expect, but a newcomer to the world of international employment really does need a proper job description; even if the job appears to be the same as the work you are used to in the UK, it will probably be different.

For example, if you are an executive posted to a Third World country, you may well be expected to spend part of your time training up your subordinates. You might also find that a significant part of your work is taken up with personnel matters.

The differences you will encounter will force you to look again at your methods and attitudes. According to David Wheatley, formerly of ECA International:

'the expatriate has to recognise, understand and adjust himself to unfamiliar styles of management and concepts of organisation. . . . What would be considered a dynamic and effective management style at home may now be perceived as quite unacceptable in the new environment.'

Your long-term future

Whether you are off on a short-term assignment or taking up a contract which will last several years, think about what will happen *after* this job finishes. Do you see your future life as a series of overseas contracts – which can be a precarious existence at times of world recession – or can you look forward to a long-term future with your employer?

If your assignment is a short one – six months or less – you ideally need to make sure that you have already secured your next job before you go. If you are off on a longer contract, make contact with organisations which could be useful when the time comes for you to move on – recruitment agencies, potential employers, and so on.

If you have landed a job which looks fairly permanent, don't assume that your future will take care of itself. In your distant outpost you might become the victim of the 'out of sight, out of mind' syndrome, which means that when promotions are discussed back at headquarters, you are not in the running.

Nobody wants to become forgotten, so you should look into ways of keeping your career pattern active while you are away. If you work for a large organisation, find out if they operate a mentor system whereby there is someone in head office looking after your career while you are out of the country.

FAMILY MATTERS

If you are single, you really only need to worry about whether you yourself are well suited to an overseas posting. But if you are married, and perhaps have a family, it's a different story . . .

At one time it was more or less taken for granted that a wife would follow her husband to his posting abroad, and this still tends to be the norm. But today other patterns are emerging; wife and husband may decide to go different ways for the duration of one partner's foreign posting, or it may be the wife who lands the job abroad and the husband who is the accompanying spouse.

In this chapter I am assuming that it is the husband who is posted to a foreign country and the wife and children who accompany him or not, as the case may be, for the simple reason that this is still the most common pattern. If you are the exception, please make allowances, and for 'wife' read 'husband' and vice versa.

Your spouse

Although the pattern of family life in this country has changed considerably over the past decades, with an increasing number of wives following careers of their own, relatively few postings abroad are able to cater for this interest, and a wife generally has to resign herself to being a non-working dependant. This is because many countries are keen to keep job opportunities for their own nationals, and are therefore unwilling to issue work permits for wives as well as husbands.

Many organisations prefer wives to accompany husbands and offer generous allowances for this. Their motives are not completely altruistic, however. The wife may be required to help her husband in his job – in entertaining visitors, for example. This is particularly true of wives of diplomats and senior businessmen. It is also generally true that a wife's presence boosts the morale of an employee, acts as a stabilising influence, and thus enables him to work more effectively.

Unfortunately, less attention tends to be paid to the morale of the wife, who may have more to adjust to than the husband. While the latter has a job which is probably not fundamentally very different from what he is used to, the wife has to get used to a completely new routine in a totally unfamiliar environment. And if she is used to a busy professional career, she may have difficulty adapting to her new life. Among the chief complaints of expatriate wives are:

- boredom – having nothing to do

- frustration – not being able to pursue their own profession or engage in useful work

- loneliness – particularly in places where the expatriate community is minimal or the husband spends a lot of his time away on trips.

She may also have problems adapting to the expatriate society where she is expected to socialise with women she would not normally get on with back home, or accept the 'pecking order' that sometimes exists in expatriate communities where the ambassador's or company boss's wife takes the lead and the others are expected to follow.

On the other hand, she may relish the life; in some countries, households employ servants who take over many of the household chores, and wives are able to use their time to develop new interests, to study, to meet new people, to travel, or to spend more time with the children.

An accompanying spouse ideally needs to be briefed on the country in question in as much detail as her husband, so that she can prepare herself accordingly, or – if the situation sounds very grim – opt to stay at home. Try finding answers to the following questions:

- What restrictions will there be on your movements? (In Saudi Arabia, for instance, women are not allowed to drive cars.)

- Will there be any expatriates in the area you will be able to turn to for advice? (In most capitals there is a well-organised British community; elsewhere you could be on your own.)

- How secure is the area where you'll be living?

- What is the attitude of the locals to European women?

- What sort of duties will you be expected to perform in connection with your husband's work?

- What kind of household assistance will be available, if any? And what do you need to know about handling help in the house?

- Is there any possibility of your taking up paid employment? (Probably not, except in Europe.)

- Are there any voluntary groups you might join?

- What type of leisure and study facilities are there?

The key to survival is to keep yourself occupied, and if you are going to accompany your husband, start planning your life at post *now*. Remember that you are going to have to give up a lot when you leave these shores; you will no longer be able to pop round for a chat with your friends, watch your favourite TV programmes, or attend club meetings. Your life may seem empty and meaningless unless you find ways of filling it.

Even worse, you will end up feeling morose and disconsolate, and start bombarding your husband with complaints. If a married employee terminates his contract prematurely, it is often because of his wife's failure to adjust rather than his own.

A Wife's Guide (Kuperard) looks at this matter in greater detail (see Further Reading).

The pros and cons of separation
Not all wives accompany their spouses to their overseas postings. They may have pressing reasons for remaining in the UK or they have no choice in the matter. A number of jobs, particularly in the Middle East, are bachelor status postings for any one of a number of reasons:

- there is no married accommodation available

- living conditions are difficult or hazardous

- lower ranking employees do not qualify for accompanied status

- the employer or host country prefers unattached people.

To compensate for the periods of separation, employees are often given frequent and generous leave entitlement – say, three months at post, one month off.

Although the majority of wives who have the option *do* accompany their husbands, there are some who do not, for a variety of reasons, such as:

● the wife needs to stay at home to look after the children

● the wife wishes to pursue her own career

● the wife suffers from poor health or cannot stand harsh climates

● there are elderly relatives to be cared for.

While a short period of separation is generally quite acceptable, prolonged periods away from home can cause problems for a marriage. Partners can become estranged or start to seek other emotional outlets, and from then on it is only a small step to marital breakdown. This may be less of a problem in well-established marriages or where a wife has a supportive family around her.

Remember that a foreign posting can put pressure on a marriage whether the post is accompanied or not. If your marriage is already in a fragile state, a job abroad – whether accompanied or otherwise – could prove the final nail in the coffin.

Your children
One of the joys of being a parent is watching your offspring grow up. Usually, younger children can live with their parents at a foreign posting, and this is the most popular option.

As they grow older, however, their education becomes a major factor and you may have to decide whether to rely on the local educational facilities or to put them into a boarding school in the UK or a third country. When coming to a decision, you need to bear in mind the character of the child as much as what is established practice in the country concerned. There are a number of options once children reach school age:

Children accompany parents to posting
This idea has always been popular with Americans and as a consequence there are American international schools or community schools in virtually every capital of the world. In Europe, the Gulf States and most Commonwealth countries, there are usually schools – both primary and secondary – for expatriate children which follow the British curriculum or prepare their pupils for the increasingly popular International

Baccalaureate. British military bases have schools run by Service Children's Education, which functions like any local education authority in the UK.

As soon as you receive news of your posting abroad, the onus is on *you* to make enquiries as to what educational provision there is for expatriate children at your destination. The British Embassy or Corona Worldwide should be able to advise you.

The Directory (European Council for International Schools) is a useful handbook in this regard if you cannot find details from other sources.

Once you have ascertained that a suitable school is available, make contact with the principal immediately to find out more details and then to secure a place for your child. Virtually all these schools are independent organisations with only a limited number of vacancies, and they may not be in a position to accommodate last-minute applications.

If you find that there are no suitable schools locally or it is too late to register, that does not rule out the possibility of your children accompanying you to your posting abroad. They could, for instance, study by correspondence; alternatively you or your wife could teach younger children yourself with the help of the Home School Service of WES – Worldwide Education Service. No teaching experience is necessary.

For children up to the age of 11 the Service offers:

- a detailed programme of work based on the UK curriculum suited to a child's age and ability

- advice to the parent-teacher on what and how to teach the child

- a weekly timetable indicating the time to be allocated to each subject

- the support of a WES tutor who will advise the parent in the role of teacher, and assess the child's progress on a regular basis

- support in setting up and managing a home school

- all books and materials required to support the curriculum.

Mercers College provides a complete tuition service by correspondence for children living abroad with their parents from the pre-school stage up to the age of 18. It prepares them for such examinations as GCE A Level, GCE Overseas O level, GCSE and the Public Schools Common Entrance Examination.

Children are educated in Britain

You may have reservations about taking your children abroad, in which case you need to explore other options. Talk things over with their teachers or seek advice from an independent educational consultant, such as Premier Education, who can provide information on schooling options and perhaps provide support for your children while you are abroad.

Boarding education is still a popular choice for families who move around from country to country at regular intervals, and has the merit of avoiding disruption to a child's educational career. Many employers offer allowances which will partly offset the fees.

The least expensive option if you normally reside in the UK is to send your children to a state (maintained) boarding school. These are listed in a DfES directory and details are also available from the State Boarding Information Service (STABIS). Most boarding education, however, is provided by the independent sector and you would be wise to consult an advisory service such as Gabbitas Educational Consultants or ISIS (the Independent Schools' Information Service).

If your child attends a day school, and is either reluctant to leave it or at a crucial stage of his or her education, you could look into alternatives. Perhaps he or she could be boarded out with relations or family friends who live close to the school. Or, if your offspring are exceptionally mature and responsible, you could leave them in charge of the house. Generally speaking, however, parents are reluctant to leave their children unsupervised to this extent!

Some parents may have qualms about breaking up the family in this way, but it has to be said that a number of children – particularly older ones – enjoy living away from their parents. In any case, families are usually together for the school holidays.

One idea you might consider is to appoint a guardian for your children while you are away who would visit them at school, monitor their progress, look after their travel arrangements and perhaps invite them to his/her home for half-term holidays. If you have no relation or friend who can take on this role there are a number of organisations who can offer such a service, including Corona Worldwide and Universal Aunts.

For further information, see the *Directory of Maintained Boarding Schools* (Department for Education and Employment); *Internet Guide to UK Boarding Schools:* http://www.darch.co.uk; *The Parents' Guide to Independent Schools* (SFIA Educational Trust); *The Directory* (ECIS); *Independent and Boarding Schools World Handbook* (Nexus Business Communications).

Spouse remains behind to look after children

Sometimes this decision is made for you, as in the case of bachelor status posts abroad. But there may be other strong reasons for choosing this particular option – for example, if a child has crucial examinations in the near future, you may be anxious that his or her studies should be disrupted as little as possible. It is not a sensible policy to switch schools when a child is in the middle of a GCSE or A Level course, and there is a lot to be said in favour of one parent remaining behind to maintain a stable home background and offer advice and encouragement.

Such a decision is not an irrevocable one. In some cases it may mean the wife remaining at home for only a matter of months before joining her husband at post. However, if the children are still a long way short of their teens, there is probably little point in following such a course for the children's sake alone. Indeed, living abroad can be more enriching educationally for them than staying in suburbia.

Elderly relatives

An increasingly important factor is the plight of elderly relatives – usually mothers or fathers – especially if they form part of your household and are dependent on you. Even if they do not live with you, those who are single or widowed may well depend on regular visits from you to keep their morale up, and for shopping or other services.

In some cases they represent a problem, particularly if they are disabled; you may be faced with the prospect of having to put them in a residential or nursing home or sheltered housing, or of one of you staying behind to keep an eye on them. In others they represent a solution to a problem; able-bodied ones may be able to provide a home base for your children, enabling them to continue their education at schools with which they are familiar; or they may be keen to move off to foreign climes with you.

Obviously, every situation is different and has to be judged on its merits. But if you have elderly dependants, their welfare during your absence is certainly one matter that needs to be gone into. Organisations such as Help the Aged or Age Concern may be able to offer advice.

ADAPTING TO YOUR NEW ENVIRONMENT

Will you fit in? This is the final – and perhaps the most important – consideration. Your qualifications may be impeccable and you may be regarded as an expert in your field, but this will not necessarily be enough.

An alien environment is bound to affect you in one way or another. Some people flourish in it, while others find living abroad a stressful experience. If you are going to be posted to a place for some time, it needs to be a place where you can feel at home. You cannot divorce your job from the context in which you will be performing it.

The physical environment
This is an important consideration, particularly for people who are not in the best of health.

- **Climate and altitude**. Most people are able to adapt to different climates without difficulty. However, hot climates can be trying for some – particularly if accompanied by high humidity. Of course, if you have access to modern comforts such as air conditioning, life will be eminently more bearable.

  If possible you will need to adjust your lifestyle to suit the climate – perhaps by doing as much work as you can in the morning and taking an afternoon siesta. Also, remember that high altitudes can be hazardous for people who are not physically fit.

- **Health considerations.** Medical science has made tremendous strides in the past century and places which were once regarded as extremely hazardous need no longer be approached with fear and trembling. Provided you take simple precautions – like boiling drinking water, cooking food, having the prescribed vaccinations – there is no reason why you should not live as healthily as at home; in any case, you may well be required to take a medical before you take up your posting.

The socio-cultural environment
'No man is an Island, entire of itself; every man is a piece of the continent, a part of the main.' Donne's words also have relevance to the expatriate. When you are posted abroad you cannot cut yourself off from your social environment, however strange. In the past, the British expatriate often found himself in a powerful position where he could impose his own customs and norms. This was true whether you were a colonial administrator or a missionary. The locals were expected to conform to your standards, whether they liked it or not.

The world, however, has moved on since then. Independent nations no longer have a foreign elite who dictate to them how to manage their affairs. They like to do things their own way, and they expect foreign nationals to respect and adjust to their customs and values rather than try to replace them. As the International Committee of the Institute of Personnel and Development notes:

'Cultural awareness, role flexibility and the ability to communicate effectively across cultures have become prerequisites for successful expatriation.'

This awareness is needed even if you are posted to a country which is part of the Western world. For instance, a British person who goes to work in the USA will find that Americans have different tastes and attitudes. Marmite and black pudding are unknown over there and British pastimes, such as cricket and pantomimes, are regarded as mildly eccentric. The USA – like Australia, Canada and New Zealand – has its own distinctive culture, which you need to understand properly in order to be 100 per cent effective in your job.

If you go to a European country, the differences are likely to be much more striking than in English-speaking countries. As well as the people speaking a different language, their laws are different, and so are their institutions, their food, their etiquette, their way of conducting business and their family life.

A further problem arises if you are working in a foreign country as part of a multinational team (e.g. within a European Union institution, in an international agency, in an international development project, in a UN peace-keeping operation). Misunderstandings and tensions can occur between people of different nationalities working together particularly in times of stress, and an understanding of the attitudes and motives of your colleagues is every bit as important as getting to grips with the country in which you are residing.

Identifying cultural values

How can you prepare for these differences? The key is to begin by understanding one's own system of values and perceptions, and then set those of other cultures against this. Geert Hofstede's study of national differences among large numbers of employees in more than 40 different countries might be a useful starting point (*Culture's Consequences*, Sage, abridged edition 1984). Hofstede identifies four key dimensions that provide maximum differentiation between national cultures:

- **Individualism** – favouring independent rather than collective action. The USA, Australia, Britain and the Netherlands, for example, clearly favour the individual. Pakistan, Guatemala, Taiwan and Indonesia, by contrast, tend to be extremely collectivist in their attitudes.
- **Masculinity** – how dominated is society by male values? In Japan, Germany, Mexico and Italy, Hofstede found that traditional male values were very well entrenched. In the Netherlands, Chile, France

and Sweden, male dominance was much less pronounced.

- **Power distance** – the extent to which inequality is accepted. Countries such as Nigeria, Malaysia, Panama and India showed high rates of acceptance of inequality. Israel, Denmark, New Zealand and Britain, on the other hand, were more strongly egalitarian.

- **Uncertainty avoidance** – concern for order and security. People from Portugal, Uruguay, Belgium and Japan were very concerned that order and security be maintained. In Singapore, Denmark, Hong Kong and Britain, people were found to have more relaxed attitudes to law and order.

Fons Trompenaars warns us not to make the assumption that 'universal' management solutions can be universally applied. 'In every culture such phenomena as authority, bureaucracy, creativity, good fellowship, verification and accountability are experienced in different ways. That we use the same words to describe them tends to make us unaware that our cultural biases and our accustomed conduct may not be appropriate or shared' (*Riding the Waves of Culture*).

The woman in a man's world
A woman planning to take up a position abroad needs to pay particular attention to cultural attitudes, because while men in the Western world are prepared to see women as professional equals (however grudgingly), this is not true elsewhere. In the Third World, for instance, you will have to accept that you will not be as free to act as you are at home, and you will probably need to seek social diversions within the expatriate community rather than outside it.

Life for an expatriate woman overseas can be frustrating at times. You may be expected to adopt Victorian modes of dress and behaviour, and your response to male colleagues and acquaintances will probably have to be cool and guarded in order to prevent misunderstandings.

In order to assess your 'survivability ratio' it makes sense to find out from other women expatriates how they have fared in these situations, and ask them if they have any tips for you. Then ask yourself if you will be able to tolerate the restrictions you may be placed under. *Travelling Alone: a Guide for Working Women* offers useful advice.

SOURCES OF INFORMATION

Decisions on whether or not to take up a position abroad are often made on the basis of insufficient information. Ideally, a comprehensive briefing should form part of the decision-making process, but in practice this rarely happens until after the contract has been signed – if at all. It may therefore be up to you, the employee, to take the initiative. You could begin by:

- reading up about the location of your posting
- contacting people who have experience of the place.

Even if you have a good idea of what to expect, your landing at a foreign posting will feel much softer if you and your family are properly briefed before you arrive; and it is certainly in your employer's interest to ensure that you make the transition to your new environment as smoothly as possible. ECA International points out:

'Insufficient briefing is one of the most significant causes of failure in expatriate personnel. Lack of adequate briefing for the spouses and other members of the family also indirectly affects the performance of the organisation that employs them.'

Premature repatriation can prove an expensive business, but even so only a few employers brief their staff adequately before despatching them to another part of the world. Of course, if you have travelled the world before, any form of briefing may seem superfluous. However, if you have not lived in the country of your forthcoming posting, take nothing for granted. Indonesia is not the same as Singapore; Senegal is quite different from Zambia.

If no mention is made of a briefing session, it is a good idea to ask for one. A number of organisations have staff who are knowledgeable about the country to which you are to be posted, and it should be easy enough to arrange a meeting between you and them.

Some companies and organisations arrange their own briefings. Others will arrange for you to make a preliminary visit to the country before you commit yourself irrevocably. If the posting is to a European country this is an easy matter to arrange. If you are heading to Vanuatu, however, your employer might balk at the added expense.

Briefing centres

Not all organisations have facilities to conduct proper briefings, and you may be offered the chance of attendance at a **professional briefing centre** (addresses in Chapter 20). Among the best known in the UK are:

Farnham Castle International Briefing and Conference Centre.
This is the Rolls Royce of briefing centres – an independent, non-profit-making organisation, which has been in existence for more than 40 years.
It has an ongoing programme of residential briefing and communications skills courses, each of which covers one of five regions:

- the Middle East
- Asia
- Africa
- Latin America, the Caribbean and the Pacific
- North America.

The courses last up to four days and consist of lectures and discussions led by people who have recent experience of working in the countries concerned, experts on the area, and nationals of the countries. There are also opportunities to meet others on an informal basis and to experience some aspects of the country's or region's culture, e.g. its cuisine. The courses are normally based around the following themes:

- understanding the region and its people (historical, political and economic factors, religion, art, music, education, and so on)
- the country itself (geography, climate, politics, infrastructure, customs and social conventions)
- the working environment (economic and human resources, business methods, working relationships, and so on)
- the social and domestic environment or international negotiation skills.

The Centre also has an excellent bookshop offering a mail order service with a wide range of materials available of interest to people going abroad. Its resources centre contains an extensive range of published material (books and videos) on virtually every country in the world as well as reports on living conditions in a number of places written or recorded by former participants.

ECA International is a non profit-making information and advisory service for companies employing expatriates or local nationals away from their home base. Apart from advising its members on terms and conditions of service, it publishes reports on living conditions in various countries and provides one-day intensive briefings for company staff due to take up assignments abroad as well as more specific briefings for couples. These courses are designed to teach the skills necessary to be effective as a foreign national. They include:

- basic preparation (documentation, contract, health requirements, and so on)
- children's education at home and abroad
- financial matters and taxation
- the changing role of the spouse
- the host country (national aspirations, value systems, customs)
- cultural awareness
- coping strategies
- planning ahead – the reintegration process
- language tuition can also be provided.

Howell & Associates offers in-company courses in understanding and working with other nationalities developed in association with the Institute for Training in Intercultural Management in the Hague (ITIM).

ITIM courses seek not only to improve the effectiveness of those who need to work with foreign customers and in a foreign environment, but also to improve working relationships within international organisations or companies. By demonstrating how to accommodate national differences ITIM endeavours to build people from a number of different countries and backgrounds into cohesive and effective multicultural multinational teams.

School of Oriental and African Studies (External Services Division) offers 'tailor-made' briefings on various countries in Africa, Asia and Eastern Europe – the latter in collaboration with the School of Slavonic and East European Studies. A language training component can form part of the course, if required.

Women's Corona Society. This organisation started out as a dining club for the wives of Colonial Service officials. Its role has expanded greatly and it now has branches all over the world whose members are ready to help new arrivals settle down in their new environment. As Corona Worldwide it offers:

- bi-monthly one-day seminars on living abroad
- individual briefings either face to face or by telephone
- in-house briefings for companies
- escort services for children and elderly relatives
- briefing notes (see below).

Objective Team Ltd organise safety courses for anyone planning to work in difficult or dangerous locations.

Communicaid, Canning, Frost and Sullivan, Robertson Languages International, **Culture Shock Consulting** and the **Arab Orientation Consultancy** are also involved in cultural briefing.

It is not always possible to arrange a full-blown briefing session before you leave, however desirable this may be. In such cases you will have to rely on other sources of information such as embassies or high commissions, bi-national cultural associations (such as the Anglo-Austrian Society or the Society for Anglo-Chinese Understanding), the Commonwealth Institute, university departments specialising in particular regions of the world, and the national tourist offices. (See Country Directory.)

Written information
Briefings and visits need to be supplemented by notes on living conditions in the country to which you will be posted. Some embassies in the UK provide notes or booklets along these lines, while certain organisations, such as the FCO and the British Council, produce such information for their own staff and appointees – but it may not be easy for members of the general public to get hold of these. However, there are alternative sources:

Expat Network publishes a series of inexpensive *Location Reports* which contain information on living conditions, health service, transport, work opportunities, laws, customs, entertainment and expatriate meeting places.

Notes for Newcomers published by Corona Worldwide (Women's Corona Society) is a series of briefing notes for over 100 countries. In addition to information on living conditions there are sections on education, employment opportunities for spouses, and sample price lists. The Society also produces a useful booklet entitled *Living in a Moslem country.*

ECA International publishes *Country Profiles for Expatriates* which covers social customs and business practices, the economy, services, housing, health and hygiene, immigration and customs formalities, education, travel and hotels, money matters, etc., and provides addresses and sources of information for 75 different countries.

Culturegrams: the Nations Around Us, a two-volume set of cultural profiles of some 150 countries, has been prepared by the David M. Kennedy Centre for International Studies of Brigham Young University.

The Economist publishes a series of Business Travel Guides which offer useful information about specific countries.

Another worthwhile source of information is *Working Abroad*, (Kogan Page) which contains reports on over 40 different countries.

The Culture Shock series published by Kuperard/Times Publications deals with a more extensive range of countries. There are also several How To Books publications on how to live and work in America, Australia, Canada, Belgium, France, Germany, Italy, Hong Kong, Japan, New Zealand, Portugal, Saudi Arabia, the Gulf, Spain, etc.

The Travellers' Bookshop in London publishes country fact-sheets with information on passport and visa requirements, customs allowances, climatic and weather information, health requirements, business and social hints. The Department for Education and Employment has free fact-sheets on EU countries which are available at Job Centres.

Other useful publications are: *Mind Your Manners* by John Mole (Nicholas Brealey Publishing), which deals principally with different business cultures within Europe, and *Dos and Taboos around the World* by Roger E. Extell (John Wiley).

The Department of Trade and Industry publishes a range of booklets on different countries entitled *Hints to Exporters*. Although not ostensibly for expatriate employees, they include some useful information on the countries in question.

CONTRACT CHECKLIST

Overseas employment contracts can be formidable documents and there is no standard format. You are advised to read through your contract carefully and, if necessary, take legal advice before signing. Generally speaking, a comprehensive set of terms and conditions is preferable to a short agreement which offers scope for different interpretations or misunderstandings. British employment legislation does not cover British people working in foreign countries; you are subject to the laws of the land you are working in. The following checklist may prove useful, although it does not claim to cover every eventuality:

- What is the name and address of my employer?

- Where precisely will I be working?

- What is my job title?

- What are the responsibilities of the job?

- Who am I directly responsible to?

- What is the commencement date and duration of my contract?

- Is the contract renewable (in the case of fixed contracts)?

- What is my net salary and how frequently is it paid?

- What other remuneration may I receive (e.g. overtime pay, bonuses, gratuity)?

- What hours will I normally be expected to work?

- What provision is there for paid leave?

- What provision is there for absence due to sickness?

- Do I have to work for a probationary period before being confirmed in the post?

- What are the accommodation arrangements (rent allowance, free housing, none)?

- How much notice does either side have to give to terminate the contract?

- What arrangements apply in the event of the premature termination of the contract by either side?

- What extras can I expect (fares paid to and from post, family allowance, company car or transport, and so on)?

- Which country's laws is this contract governed by (UK, USA, the country of employment)?

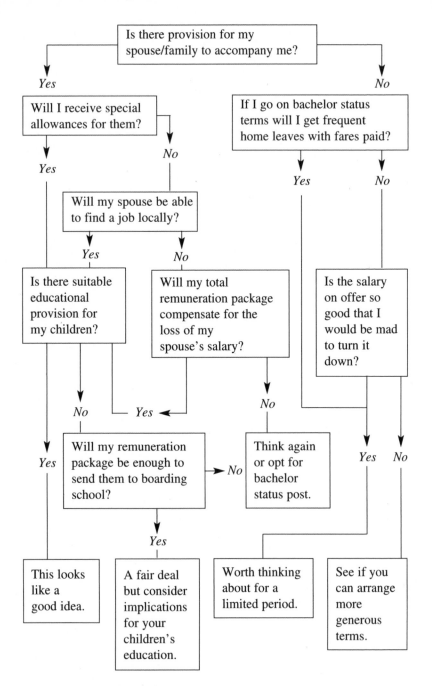

Fig. 9. The decision-making process for a married person.

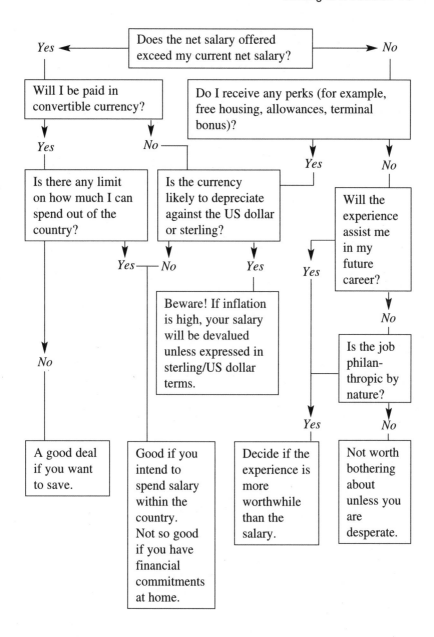

Fig. 10. The decision-making process for a single person.

PART THREE: PREPARATION AND ACCLIMATISATION

5

Preparing to Leave

If all you have had to prepare for in the past has been a holiday by the sea, the length of this particular chapter may seem daunting. Yet, just as you have to prepare for a holiday by the seaside with care – especially if a whole family is involved – so you cannot perform all the groundwork necessary for an extended stay in foreign parts in just a few hours.

The shorter the time you will spend abroad and the fewer dependants who accompany you, the less preparation you will have to make. So I would suggest that you first skim through the chapter, make a note of all matters that will concern you, and jettison those that you can safely disregard. Then work out a timetable for the weeks between now and your date of departure.

While much of the information in this chapter is directed specifically at UK citizens, nationals of other countries will find they will need to adopt similar procedures.

BANKING

Will you need a bank at your overseas posting? If so, it could save time on arrival if your own bank provides you with a **letter of introduction** to one in the country concerned. Whatever the case, you will need to visit your bank to:

- inform the bank that you are leaving the country

- leave a contact address

- obtain foreign exchange or travellers' cheques, both for your journey and to tide you over for the first few days in your new posting. Can you obtain cash with your credit card or charge card?

- transfer money

- make arrangements for the payment of bills and other financial commitments

- obtain financial advice (alternatively, you may prefer to approach an independent financial adviser who is not connected with your bank; see the section on Finance).

It makes sense to keep your current account open, even if you are planning to be abroad for many years. But if you are going to be non-resident for a lengthy period now could be the time to investigate off-shore bank accounts. Most British and Irish high street banks run off-shore operations – notably in the Isle of Man and the Channel Islands – which are used to handling money for expatriates. Bear in mind that many off-shore banks charge a fee to operate such an account, whereas most current accounts in UK-based banks do not charge private customers whose accounts are in credit.

This matter is also discussed later in this chapter under **Financial Planning: Investing your savings.**

YOUR CAR

It always helps to have your own transport if you are going to be abroad for a long time, especially in a place where public transport is poor.

Begin by finding out if your employer will provide you with a company or official car at post, and, if so, whether the vehicle will be available for your own personal use. If the answer to both questions is 'no', then you should look into the following possibilities:

- **Buying a car** (either new or second-hand) **in the country of your posting**. This is perfectly feasible in certain countries, but you need to find out about the state of the local car market before you leave! If on arrival you find there are no bargains to be had, it may be too late to opt for alternatives.

- **Taking your own vehicle**. This is quite sensible if your vehicle is in good condition and does not contravene any of the country's legislation, e.g. with respect to emission controls, and so on. The manufacturer or local agent should be able to put you wise on this. The position of the steering wheel might prove a problem for some people in countries which drive on the right, though the difficulties are not really as bad as some people would claim.

- **Buying a new vehicle and shipping it out**. This can be a sensible idea, since you can buy one free of VAT and may also be able to negotiate a discount. However, first you will have to find out about freight charges and import duties.

  When you choose a model, make sure that it will be suitable for the country you are going to. There is no point in buying a low slung sports saloon if you are going to a country where the roads are little more than tracks. Find out, too, which are the most popular makes of car in the country and which manufacturers are represented, so that you can obtain spares if necessary.

While on the subject of cars, it is also a good idea to apply to a motoring organisation for an international driving licence. While some countries accept a British licence – notably European Union countries – there are others that do not. *The Traveller's Handbook* has details, and motoring organisations can advise.

CLOTHING

If you are going to live in a country where the climate is markedly different, you will have to make changes to your wardrobe. Bear in mind that your clothing needs to be:

- *Comfortable*. In warmer climates this means lightweight outfits, short-sleeved shirts, lightweight shoes, sandals, etc. If you are likely to spend a lot of time out-of-doors under the blazing sun, headgear is essential.

- *Appropriate*. In many countries people dress more formally than in Britain, with suits commonly worn even in hot countries. In certain parts of the world women should avoid short dresses and skirts, and short-sleeved dresses and blouses, as these may offend.

- *Sufficient*. In tropical countries, for instance, people tend to change their clothes more frequently, and you can never have too many items of underwear, shirts, dresses, pairs of trousers, etc. In cold climes, where the temperature may reach -25°C or lower, you will clearly need plenty of warm clothing.

Should you buy your clothes before you go, or wait until you get there? Clothing in the UK tends to cost less than in many other countries of Europe and shops offer considerable variety. However, in many Asian countries, for example, where wage rates are lower, you may well be able to have clothes made to measure more cheaply than in Europe.

Generally speaking it is easy to buy ready-made clothing in Europe, North America and Australasia. Elsewhere it is sometimes difficult to find garments in your particular size, particularly if you are well built. This is less of a problem for children.

ARRANGING EDUCATION FOR THE CHILDREN

By now you should have decided on what provision you are to make for your children's education. If they are to move from their current educational establishment, you will need to search for appropriate schools either at home or abroad and send in an application as quickly as possible. If you delay, you may find the school is unable to accommodate them (see Chapter 4).

FINANCIAL PLANNING

Money matters are a very big topic, particularly if you are being offered what seems like a very good salary. But in order to benefit to the full from your time abroad you must keep two objectives in view:

- Minimising tax liability.
- Maximising the return on your investments.

Tax

The people that recruit you may be able to give you a general idea of your liability to tax, based on past experience. However, you need to do your own homework. Taxation is a complex matter and your liability for tax – either in the UK, or abroad – depends on a number of factors such as:

- how long you will spend abroad
- whether you will be abroad for a complete financial year
- where your employer is based
- taxation practice in the country of your posting.

In order to find out your precise tax position in the UK, the best course of action is to:

- Contact the **Inland Revenue** – either the local office or the Claims Branch, Foreign Division – for information. The IR publishes a number of leaflets of relevance, notably Booklet IR 20 *Residents and Nonresidents – Liability to Tax in the UK* which sets out the rules governing the taxation of income from jobs overseas.

● Read **up-to-date books** on personal finance for expatriates, such as *The FT Guide to Working Abroad*, D.Young (Financial Times Business Information), and articles in expatriate journals. A number of expatriate finance advisers, including banks, also produce booklets which explain the expatriate's tax liability, such as *The Allied Dunbar Expatriate Tax Guide*.

● Seek **advice**, preferably before you go. A good adviser may be able to suggest ways of modifying your compensation package in order to reduce liability to tax. Make sure, however, that your adviser has experience in advising expatriates. Many such advisers advertise in the various expatriate magazines. Chapter 20 lists a few.

Remember: good advice is likely to save you money in the long run.

Investing your savings

Many people find that they are able to put away money during an overseas assignment. If this is the first time in your life that your earnings will exceed your expenditure, you will want to find a sensible way of investing the surplus. You need to think along the following lines:

Short-term investments

You need to have some reserves in ready cash in case of emergencies, and this generally means an investment account with a building society, bank or other reputable financial institution. Go for an account which offers a high rate of interest. Currently some of the best rates are available from Internet banks.

If you are planning to be abroad for more than a year and will not be liable for UK income tax, ask for your interest not to be taxed at source. Some banks and building societies may suggest you open an account with one of their branches in an offshore tax haven, such as the Channel Islands.

Long-term investments

If you reckon that you will have cash that will not be needed for a few years, it will probably be worth your while to invest it in equities. This is, of course, riskier – but the rewards can be much greater, and this definitely holds true the longer you keep your investment. In any case, risks can be minimised by achieving a spread of investments – in unit trusts, investment trusts, ISAs or managed currency funds, for instance. Investment in property, commodities, and individual companies is not to be recommended to a beginner. The exception is if you are buying your own home, but you need to make sure that it is fully insured and looked after in your absence (See **Your Home**).

Getting investment advice

Unless you are already a sophisticated investor, you should ideally get advice on investments right from the start rather than pick them out with a pin. The reason for this is that individual needs differ, and an investment package which is ideal for a bachelor in Bahrain might be inappropriate for a married couple in Malawi.

People heading abroad for the first time do not usually begin considering investment until they have already built up reserves, and this is perfectly understandable. But rather than rely on local expertise, try and find an investment adviser either based in a country where the financial services industry is tightly regulated (such as the UK, Jersey, Guernsey or the Isle of Man) or who is associated with a firm of international repute. It is important to understand the difference between an independent adviser and one who is tied to the products of a particular company:

- An **independent** adviser is committed to offering a client the best buy over a whole range of competing products and therefore needs to be particularly knowledgeable.

- The '**tied**' adviser will only offer you the products of his particular company. Many of the banks in the UK, for instance, only offer their own range of investment plans.

Outside the UK one needs to beware of offshore investment companies that claim to be independent, but tend to recommend the products of the company offering them the best commissions, regardless of whether these products are also the best on the market for their clients. One needs also to beware of so-called 'telephone salesmen' who sell non-existent shares to expatriates.

It is better to be safe than sorry, so my advice is to **check the credentials** of any investment adviser or firm before you take the plunge. Approval by the Financial Services Authority is a good sign, and the *Financial Times* listings specify which offshore funds have FSA authorisation.

PROTECTING YOUR HEALTH

To be beset by poor health for the duration of your tour is no joke, but with careful preparation you can avoid such problems. For, while in many countries health standards are as high as they are in the British Isles, in others they may leave much to be desired. Here are a few suggestions for UK residents:

- Obtain a copy of the *Health Advice for Travellers* leaflet free from the Department of Health, a pharmacy or a post office. If you will be travelling through an EU country you should also obtain Form E111; if you will be living in the EU you need Form E121.

- Make sure you are fit and properly equipped; have a dental check, a sight test (or a spare pair of spectacles made), a chest X-ray, and a medical check up. Several employers insist on this as a condition of employment. Even if they do not, it may be wise to consult your GP as to your general state of fitness.

- Have a prescribed course of vaccinations. Smallpox vaccinations are no longer required, but for certain parts of the world you will need to be vaccinated against:
  - cholera (two injections at least ten days apart)
  - yellow fever (a single injection)
  - typhoid (two injections a month apart)
  - infectious hepatitis (a single injection just before you leave).

For details of which vaccinations you need you should consult:
Health Advice for Travellers (Department of Health)
The Traveller's Handbook (WEXAS).

Medical Advisory Services for Travellers Abroad Ltd (MASTA) can provide details of your vaccination and other medical requirements on its website. (See Useful Addresses.)

Your general practitioner will probably be able to vaccinate you, but you may find it more convenient to use a travel clinic. British Airways has two clinics in London and there are MASTA associated travel clinics throughout the UK which can provide information on immunisation requirements, vaccinations and medical items. (See MASTA website.) Boots the Chemist now operates travel clinics in some of its larger stores.

- Arm yourself with a first aid kit and useful medicines, such as:

anti-diarrhoea pills	sun lotion
indigestion pills	antiseptic cream
travel tablets	insect repellent

anti-malarial pills   basic dressings
aspirin   prescribed drugs

Advice on which you will need is given in the literature mentioned above. If you are on medication take a list of the drugs you are taking certified by your doctor to show to customs and any doctor you may consult abroad.

- Buy a book on how to keep healthy. Examples are:

Travelling Abroad, Y. Holt (Self Publishing Association).
Travellers' Health, Dr Richard Dawood (OUP).
Preservation of Personal Health in Warm Climates (Ross Institute).
The Tropical Traveller, John Hatt (Pan).

YOUR HOME

If you are going abroad for only a brief period, your main concern about your house will be to ensure that it is properly looked after while you are away. These days, alas, it is inadvisable to leave a house empty for any length of time because of the possibility of break-ins and worse; so if possible, ask a neighbour or friend to keep an eye on it for you, contact a caretaking agency such as Homesitters Ltd, Animal Aunts or Universal Aunts, and perhaps inform the local police that the residence will be empty.

If you are going to be away for a year or more, there are two options that you might think about:

Finding a tenant

Many expatriates plump for this solution, since it ensures that the house is occupied and it provides income which will cover the rates, mortgage repayments, upkeep, and so on. It also provides a base that you can return to.

However, remember that some tenants are far from perfect; they can cause damage, withhold rent, and may try to stay put when you return. Also beware of letting agents; whilst most are fine, not all of them are reliable. You should find out exactly what services they offer, how much they charge, and – if possible – contact one of their current or recent clients to check that they are as reliable as they sound.

It is essential to clarify your tax situation with the agent and the Inland Revenue (Financial Intermediaries and Claims Office – FICO) before you leave, since normally tax has to be deducted quarterly from letting income. (See Leaflet IR 140).

Take out a legal protection insurance policy if you have qualms about letting your house.

Selling the house

If you do this, you are at least spared the worry of what may be happening to your property, and can invest the proceeds. In the past, however, people have usually found that the rise in the value of their investments has not kept pace with house price inflation. So whether you benefit or lose on the deal is very much a matter of timing.

INSURANCE

There are four types of insurance that you need to consider:

1. **Health and accident insurance** – this is particularly vital if there is little social security provision in the country where you will be working and your employer does not provide it. There are a number of organisations specialising in expatriate health care, among them:
    - BUPA International
    - Healthsearch Ltd (impartial advice on healthcare plans)
    - Europea IMG
    - Exeter Friendly Society
    - PPP International
    - Expat Healthcare Plan (see Expat Network).

    See Useful Addresses in the UK.

2. **Personal effects insurance**. Loss or damage to personal effects.

3. **Car insurance**, if appropriate. Note that your current insurer may not be equipped to provide cover for you on some distant shore and you may either have to look for one that does or use a local insurance company.

4. **Life insurance**, if you have dependants. The basic 'no frills' type (which has no investment element) is quite adequate.

For all of these it pays to consult a good financial adviser or broker who specialises in insurance for expatriates. Many advertise in expatriate magazines. See also Useful Addresses in the UK.

LANGUAGE LEARNING

If you are going to a country where English is not widely spoken you may find it frustrating that so few people understand you. One solution is to try and learn the local language before you arrive. There are various ways of doing this:

Teaching yourself

You can buy a **language teaching manual**. Increasing emphasis is put on the spoken language these days, and many manuals are accompanied by cassettes, videos and CD-Roms. If you cannot find a suitable course at your local bookshop, try an academic bookshop or one which specialises in a wide range of languages (including some of the less common ones), such as Grant and Cutler or LCL.

The following publishers and distributors have language books and supporting material for a wide range of languages:

- Audio Forum
- BBC Books
- Hugo Language Books
- Hodder (Teach Yourself Books)
- Linguaphone
- Routledge (the Colloquial Language series).

Taking a course

Many local colleges provide part-time and open access courses in the more common languages. In London and other large centres the range of languages taught is quite considerable. If you have difficulty finding the course you need, contact the Learn Direct database of the DfES or the Languages National Training Organization (BLIS Professionals). (See Useful Addresses in the UK.)

A number of universities and HE colleges have their own language centres which offer facilities for casual students. Central London, for instance, is particularly well served with such organisations as

- City Literary Institute
- School of Oriental & African Studies (SOAS)
- University of Westminster
- King's College Language & Communication Centre.

Countries like Austria, France, Italy, Spain and Germany have their own cultural institutes in London and elsewhere which offer language tuition (see Country Directory) and there are many private language schools which offer courses as well. They include:

- Berlitz

- Linguarama

- Inlingua.

However, there are several smaller language training organisations dotted around the UK which can provide a tailor-made service, including the Centre for International Briefing and Robertson Languages International. Your local *Yellow Pages* will offer details of the ones nearest to you.

Alternatively, you could consult *Where and How*, an international guide to language centres published by the Wie und Wo Verlag, Postfach 2464, D-5300 Bonn 1, Germany.

The National Institute of Adult Continuing Education, 19B De Montfort Street, Leicester LE1 7GE, Tel: (0116) 2551451, publishes a list of residential language courses in the UK.

Finding a tutor

Many colleges can put you in touch with private tutors while private language schools may be able to provide one-to-one tuition on their premises which may form part of an open-learning package. You could also contact:

- Association for Language Learning

- Institute of Linguists.

Language learning is treated at length in *How to Master Languages* (How To Books), which includes a directory of training providers.

SENDING LUGGAGE AND PERSONAL EFFECTS

If you are travelling by air you will normally find that you can't take everything with you, unless your employer happens to be remarkably indulgent. Some of your luggage can probably be sent by air-freight in advance – which is much cheaper than the excess baggage rate – while the rest may have to be sent by sea or overland – which works out even cheaper.

Don't forget that however good your planning is, there is little likelihood of you and your personal effects all arriving at the same time. So make sure that you take with you essential household items and clothes which will keep you going for the initial period.

If you are planning to take a good many household items with you, you need to contact a reputable international removal company whose representative will come to visit your home, note what you plan to take, and eventually provide an inventory and a quotation (not an estimate). If you find that your employer is reluctant to foot the whole of the bill, you may either have to sell off surplus goods or put them in storage.

In Britain many of the established companies are affiliated to BAR Overseas – the British Association of Removers (Overseas Group) – which operates a bonding scheme, FIDI (the Federation of International Furniture Removers), and possibly also OMNI (the Overseas Moving Network Inc). Unless you receive contrary instructions from your employer you should opt for a door-to-door service which includes packing, insurance, collection and delivery, and customs clearance (where necessary). Normally household goods are shipped in containers, 20ft long or more. If you have fewer items they might be sent in tea chests that are around five cubic feet in volume.

NATIONAL INSURANCE

Will you have to make National Insurance contributions while you are abroad, or will you be expected to contribute to the social security fund of the country in which you will be working? You will have to find out before you go.

The best plan is to contact your local Social Security office, stating where you are going and for how long. The Department will then give you the relevant leaflets, such as leaflet NI 38, *Social Security Abroad.*

If you are going to work within the European Union, Leaflet SA 29 explains your social security and pension rights. There are other leaflets dealing with individual countries with which Britain has reciprocal social security agreements. In most cases you have the option of making voluntary contributions to the British scheme to preserve your UK pension entitlement and other benefits.

PASSPORT

Make certain that your passport is still valid. If it isn't, get an application form from your local post office, but remember that you and your dependants who are accompanying you will each need a full passport. If the passport expires in a matter of months it is sensible to renew it anyway. Time may be pressing, in which case to avoid delay you may have to pay a visit to your regional Passport Office. (See Useful Addresses in the UK.)

PENSION

Is your job pensionable? In the case of many contract posts it probably isn't, but you will receive a gratuity at the end of your term in lieu of a pension contribution. You should therefore consider taking out a personal pension scheme which offers maximum flexibility with payments. Whether it should be a UK-based scheme or an international plan will depend on how long you are likely to remain abroad. As for your state pension, you can continue to make contributions on a voluntary basis (see National Insurance Leaflet NI 38).

If you are a permanent employee in a company pension scheme, you may wish to continue the arrangement. However, you need to find out whether this is your best option when discussing the terms and conditions of your posting abroad. Not all company schemes cover expatriate employment – particularly extended assignments – and in some circumstances you could benefit by opting out of the company scheme and making your own pension contribution arrangements.

You should look for the following features when assessing expatriate pension plans:

- **Security**. You require a reputable insurer and fund manager.

- **Contributions**. There should preferably be no limits at all with maximum flexibility to increase, reduce or stop contributions.

- **Build up**. This should be gross of tax on investments – preferably 100 per cent or with major relief.

- **Benefit design**. Complete flexibility is required with 100 per cent cash or annuity/cash options. Provision for irregular payment is useful.

- **Tax on benefits**. Ideally there should be some relief on benefits.

- **Investment choices**. Although a wide range of choices is useful, some people prefer the security of a *with profits* or *guaranteed* fund.

- **Charges**. These should be as low as possible, but it is unrealistic to expect none.

If you are looking for high quality independent advice on pension planning matters, you will need to take great care in selecting an adviser. The following questions for your adviser may help you to distinguish genuine specialists in retirement planning:

- Does your firm work for employers as well as for individuals? If an adviser is working for an employer that is a good sign.

- Does your firm employ or have access to actuaries? The actuary does not have to be employed directly by your adviser – but his willingness to call on one is an important test of his quality.

- How large or long established is your firm?

- Can I pay fees? In retirement planning it is a good sign if you can pay fees for professional advice, usually with a rebate of commission.

- Does your firm employ expatriate financial planners? What is their experience? You need to be sure that your adviser combines a pension capability with general expatriate financial planning.

Clearly it is not always possible to track down a firm which fulfils all these criteria. Nevertheless, a financial adviser is not a person to be chosen lightly, otherwise you could be the loser.

SHOPPING

Some prospective expatriates go on a wild shopping spree before they leave as if they are going to a remote corner of the world where shops do not exist. When they arrive, they realise that a good many of their purchases were not really necessary and that some of the items are actually cheaper abroad.

A seasoned expatriate, on the other hand, finds out what he *really* needs to buy before he takes the plunge. There are basically three reasons for buying items before you go:

- They are unavailable or in short supply in your adoptive country.

- They are much more expensive there than at home.

- They are going to be needed immediately upon arrival.

To avoid unnecessary purchases, it makes sense to find out about the availability and price of goods at your posting if possible. Consult someone who has recently returned from the country, or the lists that may be available from the Women's Corona Society, the British Council, DFID, and the relevant diplomatic missions.

If you are buying expensive items, you will probably be able to get them free of VAT provided you deal with a store which is au fait with the tax-free export scheme. Certain items, such as cameras, radios or cassette players, could be purchased en route at an airport duty-free shop. But do make sure that you will not be subjected to hefty customs duties on entry, otherwise your bargains may not seem such bargains!

Below is a rough list of items which you might find useful but which are not always readily obtainable abroad, and may therefore be worth taking with you:

- corkscrew/bottle opener
- mug and plate
- clothes line and pegs
- electric kettle/boiling jug
- torch
- knife, fork and spoon
- portable radio capable of receiving short-wave broadcasts
- thermos flask
- electric plug adapter
- universal bath/washbasin plug
- can opener.

TRAVEL PLANNING

Most overseas employers will provide you with an economy class air ticket, and many will also provide tickets for your dependants. If your employers are reluctant to do this, ask for the fare equivalent in cash and contact an IATA bonded agency which sells fares at a discount. Many of them advertise in the classified columns of national dailies, on Teletext or the Internet.

Other modes of travel, i.e. by sea or overland, are normally out of the question, except in the case of Europe and perhaps North Africa – unless you have plenty of time at your disposal. In Europe sea and rail travel have one advantage over air insofar as you can take much larger amounts of luggage with you, at little or no extra cost.

If you have a car, car travel is another very sensible option within Europe. Even distant locations such as Turkey can be reached easily in a few days. But if your insurance policy is limited to the British Isles, inform your insurance company; either you will need a green card before you go, or long-term alternative arrangements for your insurance may be necessary.

Advice on safety in around 80 countries is available on BBC Ceefax 564-567 and from the FCO Travel Advice Unit, www.fco.gov.uk.travel.

VISAS AND WORK PERMITS – ARE THEY NECESSARY?

In most cases – even if you are only planning to do casual work – you need to get a work visa before you go. The main exception is if you are a citizen of an EU country (e.g. Britain, Ireland) going to work in another country of the European Union. (See Chapter 10.)

Obtaining a visa can take weeks or even months, so it makes sense to find out well in advance exactly what you have to do to get one. Generally speaking, you will have to use one of the two following procedures:

System 1: You take your employment contract or a letter of appointment from your employer to the consular section of the appropriate embassy together with your passport and several passport size photographs. You may also need some or all of the following:

- birth certificate

- marriage certificate

- educational documentation – diplomas, certificates, and so on

- a certificate of good conduct (not UK residents)

- a medical certificate.

In order to avoid a wasted journey, ring the consular section in question to enquire precisely what is needed. This process can be a lengthy one if the embassy has to contact the immigration department or labour department back home.

System 2: Your employer applies for the work permit which he sends to you. You take this to the consular section with other relevant documentation for processing. Theoretically, this is a much speedier method, but do not count on it!

If you have any sort of official status (for example, if you are going to be employed directly by the government of the country or an international organisation there), the visa application is little more than a formality.

If you plan to travel overland or stop en route, check whether you will also need visas for the countries you pass through. *The Traveller's Handbook* (WEXAS) contains information on this score. If you have any problems getting visas for travel, your travel agent may be able to assist you for a fee. (See also Useful Addresses.)

FINAL CHECKLIST

- Cancel the milk, newspapers, subscriptions, and so on.

- Pay the water, telephone, electricity, and gas bills and inform the companies of what is happening. Do you want to be disconnected?

- Make your will.

- Arrange for the redirection of mail – by the Post Office (for a fee) or by your tenants.

- Ensure that you have made provision for your pets. The local RSPCA may be able to advise. If you are planning to take them with you, contact a specialist animal shipper and the Department of the Environment, Food and Rural Affairs' website or PETS helpline for advice on pet passports and export regulations. Pets need to be vaccinated well in advance of their travel date and a miniscule microchip inserted under their skin.

- Inform your next of kin, bank manager, solicitor, tenants, insurance company and other interested parties of your new address.

- Get plenty of passport photos made of yourself and your dependants.

- Confirm arrival arrangements and ask for contact telephone numbers at your destination in case of emergency.

- Buy a phrase book, guidebooks and maps of the country. *The Traveller's Handbook* (WEXAS) is useful if you will be travelling around.

- Prepare an inventory of your personal effects for customs.

- If you are not taking your car with you make arrangements for storage with a friend or garage. If your car is licensed in the UK and it will be off the road for some time, inform the Driver and Vehicle Licensing Authority and ask for a refund of the car tax.

- Ask the Electoral Registration officer of your local district council for an 'absent voter' application form.

- Do you pay local taxes? If so, inform the local council office of your movements.

- Inform credit, debit and store cards companies where to send their bills, or arrange for these to be paid by direct debit.

- Cancel rental agreements for TVs, videos, cable TV, etc. You may be able to get a rebate of your TV licence fee.

6

Settling In

Your first few weeks in your new posting are crucial ones, and will set the tone for the rest of your stay. It is a time of hectic activity when you are busy making arrangements and meeting new faces. Not only are you getting to grips with your new job, but you are also trying to adapt to new social and domestic arrangements. It's not surprising, therefore, that it is also a time when less seasoned expatriates experience a measure of stress!

Stress caused by a sudden change of location is often described as **culture shock**. However well you prepare for your overseas assignment, the sudden change of environment could well have unpleasant repercussions, albeit temporary ones.

FACING CULTURE SHOCK

Culture shock can take a number of forms:

- **Strain**. Adapting to your new environment often involves considerable effort.

- **Sense of loss and deprivation**. You miss familiar faces, places and objects and suffer from a sense of anonymity. You feel homesick.

- **Feeling of rejection**. You reject your new environment or the new environment seems to be rejecting you. You refuse to learn the language or adapt to local customs.

- **Confusion**. You are confused as to your identity and how to behave in a culture with different values and customs from your own.

- **Anxiety, disgust and indignation**. As you develop awareness of the cultural differences, you react negatively to the way people behave. You get angry about bureaucratic delays.

- **Feelings of impotence**. You feel unable to cope with your new environment and shut yourself off from it.

Culture shock can manifest itself in the form of headaches, lassitude and even rashes, but it should eventually pass. However, it is no use expecting your bout of shock to disperse of its own accord. It is up to *you* to make a positive effort to come to terms with your new surroundings.

Adaptation: a five-phase process

It is not uncommon for newcomers to go through five phases before they begin to feel at ease:

1. **The honeymoon stage**. The beginning of your tour is rather like a holiday. You are fascinated by the novelty of your new surroundings and are enthusiastic about the people you meet.

2. **Crisis and disintegration**. After a while the initial euphoria wears off and you may start to feel inadequate and depressed.

3. **Reintegration**. You regain your self-esteem, but only by rejecting or finding fault with the surrounding culture.

4. **Autonomy**. As you develop an ability to cope with the new culture socially, and perhaps linguistically, you become more relaxed and empathetic.

5. **Independence**. You feel at home in your new surroundings, and accept the differences.

CREATING A FRIENDLY PERSONAL ENVIRONMENT

To counter or overcome the worst effects of culture shock you need to concentrate from the outset on creating a friendly personal environment. You will find that you settle down more easily if you strive for:

- a comfortable home base
- a satisfying job with good interpersonal relationships
- good companionship
- a full range of leisure interests.

Let's look at these one by one.

The right accommodation

Many people are put up in hotels on arrival, but hotel life – even if you are put in the best – tends to jar after only a short time. The best plan, therefore, is to move into more permanent accommodation as soon as possible, if your stay is to be an extended one, and especially if you are accompanied by your family.

Some people can choose their accommodation; others have no choice. Instead they are allocated housing, perhaps in a company compound, which will vary from the luxurious to the downright seedy. It has to be admitted that housing standards depend greatly on the location; while in one country you might have a villa with a swimming pool, in another you might have to be content with a small flat. If you are dissatisfied with your accommodation, find out what the normal standard is for expatriates in similar jobs to yourself before you complain.

If you have to find your own accommodation, so much the better. However, it is a good plan to ask fellow expatriates for advice on the most suitable areas to live, and then proceed with care. That elegant residence you take a liking to at first sight could prove to be a nightmare when it rains, when the water pipes run dry, or at night when you find your residence is in the red light district. Points to check are:

- How safe is the area?

- Where are the nearest shopping facilities?

- (If you have children) How far is it from an expatriate school?

- How easy is it to get to your workplace?

- Are the utilities good – are there likely to be any power cuts, water cuts, and so on?

- What is included in the rent – furniture, telephone, and so on?

- What extras do you have to pay for – for example, night watchmen, or a concierge?

- How good is the heating/air conditioning?

- Is it large enough to entertain visitors in?

- Is the area liable to flooding or other environmental hazards?

If possible, get your employer to sign the contract and pay the rent direct to the landlord. Otherwise, you could find yourself having to pay a hefty premium in order to secure the house or flat.

The main consideration is: **do you feel comfortable and at ease in the accommodation?** At times you will need a refuge from the pressures you have to face – a place where you can relax and be yourself. Make an effort to select the right sort of accommodation first time round. If you keep on chopping and changing your residence, as some expatriates do, you will never feel at home.

Your job

Starting work in a foreign environment has certain similarities to starting a new job in a new organisation at home. Your first objectives therefore must be to find out:

● how the organisation works

● who is responsible to whom

● the extent of your responsibilities

● what support is available to you

● when and how you are to be paid.

Sooner or later, however, you will recognise that there are differences – sometimes subtle, sometimes glaring – between the way the foreign organisation operates and what you would regard as normal practice back home. So in order to start off on the right foot you need to get rid of any preconceptions you may have, and apply yourself to learning the ropes.

In some organisations, you will experience a happier landing than in others; you may be offered an induction period as a matter of course. On the other hand, you could find yourself tossed into the hurly-burly right from the start with little or no explanation of how things work and what is expected of you. If you are in a senior position, your subordinates may well assume that you know it all, and so no induction is considered necessary.

Unless you *do* happen to know everything, try to find someone who can put you into the picture. If, for example, there are other expatriates in the outfit who have been through the same process in the past, you may be able to turn to them for advice. Not all the advice you get will necessarily be helpful, since some individuals may have particular axes to grind. So you should not rely too much on the opinions of just one person but instead seek out a number of sources before coming to your own conclusions.

If you are the only expatriate in the organisation, you may feel you have no one to turn to. Local staff are often hesitant to provide the information you really need until they have got to know you well, and it takes time to build bridges between cultures. But you will build your bridges more quickly and effectively if you approach the task in the right way.

ECA International offers seven useful tips designed to facilitate cross-cultural communication, which will also apply to any accompanying dependants trying to fit in:

- **Communicate respect**. Demonstrate a positive regard for the country and its people, be encouraging and show interest in them.

- **Be non-judgemental**. Don't make moralistic, value-laden, evaluative statements.

- **Personalise knowledge and perceptions**. Recognise that values, perceptions and knowledge (including your own) are relative rather than absolute.

- **Display empathy**. Try to understand the other person's point of view by putting yourself in his or her position.

- **Practise role flexibility**. Try to reach your goals in a manner and time-scale appropriate to the other culture.

- **Demonstrate reciprocal concern**. Take turns in talking and thus promote circular communication.

- **Tolerate ambiguity**. Accept a degree of frustration in order to deal with different circumstances and culture.

Companionship

Human beings are social animals, and few people set off abroad intending to live the life of a hermit. The luckiest people are those who have a partner or family that they can take with them, as they will have someone to confide in, and share their experiences with.

An unattached person, on the other hand, needs to find companionship. However, if you have lived in the same locality for years you may have lost the knack of striking up new friendships. So what do you do?

The answer is to build on existing relationships if you can. Normally if you spread the word at home that you are off to Helsinki or Honolulu, someone you know is bound to recall that he has a cousin three times removed who has been living there for years, and will suggest that you look him up. Don't hesitate. Take his address and contact him at the earliest opportunity.

Making casual visits may sound out of keeping to anyone brought up on the principle that an Englishman's home is his castle. However, you will probably find that in foreign climes most British people drop their reserve and positively welcome visitors, while many other nationals are used to spontaneous fraternisation as a matter of course. Strike up a few acquaintances and it will not be long before you find yourself on the party circuit.

Your first friends are likely to be expatriates, just like yourself, and you are most likely to meet them:

- at work
- in local hotels
- in clubs
- at church.

Even if you do not have strong religious feelings, you may well find that expatriate life revolves around the church, and the local parson may be a useful contact or, if needed, a source of comfort. The church may also provide a welcome for newcomers. For example, if you have Anglican leanings, you could contact the Overseas Resettlement Secretary at Church House, Westminster, and he or she can provide a contact for you at your destination. The Intercontinental Church Society publishes a *Directory of English Speaking Churches Abroad.*

The local expatriate community can be tremendously supportive, but try not to restrict yourself to expatriate circles and remain aloof from the world about you; life will be more rewarding if you can strike up friendships with local people as well. However, it is wise to study local etiquette first of all to avoid making any embarrassing *faux pas.*

Some people go to the other extreme and 'go native', dressing up in national costume and trying to emulate their hosts' lifestyle to the letter. Such behaviour seldom finds favour with other expatriates or, indeed, with the local people themselves. Far from being flattered that you are trying to adopt their ways, they might turn suspicious or give you the cold shoulder.

One of your best plans is to make contact with local people who have lived or studied in Britain. Most will be able to observe their country through British eyes and will therefore be well placed to help you adapt to your new circumstances. They will be keen to hear of the latest trends in Britain and be only too happy to regale you with their own experiences.

Don't be so eager to establish friendships that you throw caution to the wind. In camp type situations, especially, you need to be circumspect. There is usually a bad apple or two who can cause problems, for example through borrowing money from all and sundry and then disappearing on leave with his debts unpaid.

Women abroad
Many countries of Southern Europe and the Third World have not really come to terms with the idea of the liberated woman yet, so women –

especially single women – need to be careful in their relationships with the opposite sex. Perhaps the two most important or basic tips are:

- Dress modestly.

- Avoid looking men straight in the eye.

If you can, find out from other expatriate women with experience of the country exactly how you should behave to avoid trouble. You may find it safer to stick with the stuffy expatriate community than embark on adventures of your own. One compensation in expatriate communities is that single women are much in demand at parties. *Travelling Alone – A Guide for Working Women* by Roberta Bally (Macdonald Optima) has some useful general advice for women.

Leisure interests

Some people never get beyond the second or third phase of culture shock. For them an overseas posting is a penance, and they spend long hours wishing they were back home.

It's true that not every job abroad is a dream posting, but even if it is dull and tedious, there are usually some benefits to be derived from the experience. If you have plenty of leisure time at your disposal – and this is especially valid for accompanying partners – make sure you do not waste the opportunity. By keeping active mentally, physically and socially your posting abroad might turn out more rewarding than you ever imagined it could be. Here are a few suggestions as to how you might use your spare time:

Get to know the country
Travel around it, read about it, attend lectures and cultural events. There are plenty of good guidebooks on the market these days including the *Fodor, Baedeker, Insight* (Harrap), Footprint (TTP) and *Rough Guides* (RKP) series. Lonely Planet and Bradt Enterprises publish a selection of books on off-beat destinations.

Learn the local language
There are usually language courses on offer for expatriates, at least in the capitals. Otherwise you should be able to find a private tutor. Not only will this help you to communicate effectively, it will keep the little grey cells working.

Do a course
This could stand you in good stead in the future. Contact distance learning organisations such as the Open University or Association of Correspondence Colleges in the UK to find out what is available. Alternatively, you may find that there are part-time courses in institutions in the country to which you have been posted.

Join a club
There are all kinds of clubs from ubiquitous British Clubs with their own premises (that have usually seen better days) to international clubs and special interest clubs with no premises of their own. Dramatic societies, choral societies and Rotary Clubs seem to exist everywhere.

Take up a sport or other outdoor activity
It is important to keep fit and active, and there are sporting opportunities even in the most unpromising circumstances. You will come across improvised golf courses in the desert and tennis courts with barely a passing resemblance to Wimbledon. A number of expatriates use the opportunities afforded by their surroundings to take up hobbies such as bird-watching or archaeology.

KEEPING IN TOUCH

Fortunately, life is much easier than it was, for example, three generations ago. Even if you are in a very remote spot you are not cut off completely from the world outside – that is, unless you want to be. Communications have improved. No longer does mail take months to reach you – except perhaps in the case of St Helena – and telecommunications have progressed in leaps and bounds. However, international telephone calls may turn out to be more expensive than you expect, and for instant communication you should consider fax and e-mail.

You can buy British newspapers and magazines in many of the larger cities or you may prefer to have them sent to you direct (some addresses are listed in Chapter 22). In remoter areas, given suitable equipment, you can access the websites of many publications and broadcasting organisations, such as the BBC.

Many expatriates tune into the broadcasts of the BBC World Service, Voice of America or Radio Australia, all of which can be received on short wave transistor radios. The BBC and CNN transmit TV programmes by satellite to parts of the world and other English-language programmes can be picked up in most of Europe. BBC World Service programmes are listed in *On Air*. Many BBC programmes are also available on the Internet. (For address see Chapter 20.)

ATTENDING TO THE PAPERWORK AND OTHER DETAILS

There will be plenty to do shortly after arrival, and it is sensible to make a checklist of all the matters that you will need to attend to. This is likely to include some of the following:

- register with the embassy/consulate in case of a future emergency and to secure your voting rights at home

- arrange banking facilities

- register your children with a school

- notify the police/local authorities of your place of residence, if required

- obtain a residence visa/work permit

- register your car (if imported)

- obtain a directory of local services

- enquire about language course facilities.

Your employer should be able to advise you on bureaucratic matters. If not, try other expatriates, the embassy or your landlord.

Experienced expats recognise the benefit of expending plenty of effort in the initial stages in order to get their affairs straightened out quickly. If you manage to launch yourself successfully, you will find that your life will turn out to be relatively trouble-free. You are less likely to be troubled by culture shock . . . or dipsomania!

WHEN THINGS DON'T WORK OUT

Dissatisfaction with the job

This book has tried to help you avoid the pitfalls associated with employment abroad, urging you to do some soul searching and to look closely at what is involved *before* you take up a position. Yet however much care you exercise as you prepare, you have to face up to the possibility that things will not turn out as planned.

Your duties may prove to be very different from what you had been led to expect. Your employer may not seem to be fulfilling some of the clauses in your contract. Your accompanying spouse may find it impossible to come to terms with the new environment. You may have reservations about how the organisation is run. What should you do in circumstances like these? You have certain simple choices:

- Carry on regardless.

- Walk out.

Clearly, if you find your work a thankless chore, you are unlikely to give of your best, and a period of stagnation is not going to help your career. On the other hand, breaking a contract can prove costly, both from your point of view and from that of your employer. At worst you might have to forfeit your salary, pay your fare home and face a compensation claim.

Try, instead, to find a solution to these problems. Contact the people that recruited you, or your boss at home (if you are on secondment), explain what is wrong, and ask if they can mediate on your behalf. If the answer is 'no', then you will have to go it alone – not always an easy task.

This means talking matters through with a person in authority and attempting to reconcile your differences. If you have been genuinely misled as to the nature of the work, you may well be given a sympathetic hearing. If, on the other, you complain about terms and conditions that are not even mentioned in the contract, then you will find yourself on less firm ground.

If you do decide to leave your post prematurely, make sure you have reasonable grounds for doing so. These would include:

- ill health

- failure by the employer to honour the terms of your contract

- job is not compatible with your experience or status

- domestic problems.

Try, above all, to have the contract terminated by **mutual agreement**, if only to avoid costly litigation procedures.

Coping with dismissal

The fact that you are working abroad is no guarantee that sooner or later you will not lose your job, whether you are on contract or have a 'permanent' position.

All firms periodically reorganise their staffing structures to achieve greater efficiency, and this sometimes means slimming down the organisation and making people redundant; and firms – particularly newly established ones – sometimes go bust.

Such occurrences can be particularly worrying when you are working in an unfamiliar environment far from home. Most importantly, you will probably expect some form of compensation – and ideally terms should be mentioned in your contract. If, on the other hand, the company or organisation for which you are working goes into receivership, you may find no payment at all is forthcoming.

Another eventuality you have to face up to is that your employer may be dissatisfied with you for some reason. Common grounds for dismissal are:

- absenteeism

- professional misconduct

- insubordination

- poor workmanship

- activities incompatible with your status.

If you believe you have been unfairly dismissed, you may well want to take the matter to court. Keith Edmonds of Expats International recounts how an EI member working in Libya was dismissed by his Libyan employer and took his case to the local People's Court. He conducted his own case against the employer, using an interpreter, and won, though Edmonds admits he was very lucky; don't assume that all court judgements decide in the employee's favour. Indeed, employment legislation in some countries is heavily weighted in favour of the employer, and so you would be wise to seek advice before embarking on costly litigation.

If you are a UK national, the local British Consulate will be able to provide you with a list of English-speaking lawyers, but will not be able to offer legal advice itself or institute legal proceedings on your behalf. Members of Expats International and the Expat Network should contact these organisations for free advice on problems of this nature. You might also try your trade union or professional association back in the UK to see if they have a sister organisation in the country that can help you.

If possible, try to leave your ex-employer on reasonably friendly terms. You may require a reference from him in future or in certain countries a letter of release from his employ.

Other problems

In a foreign location problems often seem more complicated to resolve than they do at home. This might be because you are unfamiliar with the way things work, because there is a language problem, or because you feel isolated from the people and institutions you know best.

If something serious happens, it is vital to inform the nearest British Consulate which should be able to advise you or offer assistance (citizens of other countries should contact their own national consulate). Such help can be invaluable in the following situations:

- **Entanglement with the law**. If you are arrested on any charge, you should insist on the British Consulate being informed.

- **Civil disturbance and war**. It is advisable to register with the Consulate on arrival. Then, if violence breaks out, the Consulate can try and keep you informed of the situation and, if necessary, arrange for your evacuation.

- **Death or accidents**. The Consulate can arrange for the next of kin to be informed and advise on procedures.

- **Financial emergencies**. Consulates can offer advice on the transfer of money, cash a sterling cheque supported by a banker's card and – as a last resort – make a repayable loan for repatriation to the UK.

- **Theft.** This should be reported to the police and a statement obtained. If your passport is lost or stolen, report the loss to the Consulate right away so that an emergency passport can be issued.

- **Illness**. The Consulate can provide a list of local doctors and hospitals. However, it is in no position to reimburse medical costs.

- **Voting**. Under the Representation of the People Act 1989 UK citizens may register as overseas voters in the constituency in which they or their family were registered before leaving the UK. The qualifying period is up to 20 years and the Consulate will have forms and an explanatory leaflet.

The consulates of other countries may provide similar services to the above mentioned for their citizens.

It might well be a good idea to get hold of a leaflet entitled *Consular Assistance Abroad*, published by the Foreign and Commonwealth Office.

PART FOUR: SURVEYING THE OPPORTUNITIES

7

Working Holidays and Work Experience

CONSIDERING SHORT-TERM WORK

Not every reader of this book will be thinking of working abroad on a long-term basis. However, there are opportunities to go abroad for a short period just for the experience. And contrary to the impression you may have gained so far, not all these jobs require qualifications beyond A Level or the equivalent.

For instance, tens of thousands of people from Britain, especially students, do holiday jobs abroad. These range from working in hotels and restaurants, conservation and picking grapes to running children's summer camps. While the majority of participants are students who enjoy the advantage of long vacations, there are also opportunities for people who are longer in the tooth.

A year off is becoming a popular option for young people, notably in the Gap Year between school and university. A number of specialist organisations have been established to address the needs of this age group and fortunately red tape is usually kept to a minimum for younger people.

There are also various opportunities for more experienced people who want to avoid undue upheaval. Most are designed to extend your experience rather than make you rich. They range from professional exchanges to short-term consultancies – often in the voluntary sector.

This chapter focuses on the types of opportunities available.

Why consider a short-term assignment?
As mentioned above, many of the short-term foreign assignments do not pay well. Indeed, you may have to make a contribution to the costs and find yourself out of pocket as a consequence. So what is the point?

To use a well-worn cliché – the world is getting smaller. National boundaries are starting to disappear, particularly in Europe, and to be successful in your job you may need to have a well-developed international outlook and be able to operate effectively anywhere in the world.

Whether you are on the threshold of your career or well advanced in it, international exposure can prove beneficial. It can also be character building. You learn how people in other parts of the world live and react.

It is also an option for people who may have retired, but who do not wish to turn their backs on the world of work entirely. Mention to your former employers or your other contacts that you are interested in short-term assignments abroad, and there is a chance that they will bear you in mind if something crops up.

Looking for short-term jobs

Some of the best short-term jobs are found through **personal contact** rather than through advertisements. If you have business or professional contacts abroad, ask them to keep an eye open for you. Alternatively, find out if your locality has any twinning scheme with a town or region in another country. Such schemes usually operate an exchange programme and may foster business and employment links as well.

For 16–25 year olds who are interested in volunteering, **Worldwide Volunteering for Young People** has a comprehensive database of projects lasting from one week to a year which is also obtainable in directory form. The organisation can match an individual's requirements to a suitable vacancy.

VACATION JOBS

If you are in your teens or early twenties there are a number of schemes designed to enable you to travel and live in other countries for a short while without having to go through masses of red tape to gain entry to them.

Many are vacation jobs, but not all of them pay well, if at all. Indeed, you may well have to make some financial contribution yourself. These are jobs where the experience you gain is regarded as of greater import than financial reward.

The **Central Bureau for International Education and Training** publishes leaflets with plenty of suggestions on holiday jobs for young people. It also publishes an annual guide entitled *Working Holidays*. **Vacation Work International** publishes and distributes some relevant handbooks: *Directory of Summer Jobs Abroad*, *Summer Employment Directory of the US* and *Emplois d'Été en France*.

If you have access to the **Internet** you might try a few relevant websites, such as www.summerjobs.com. The organisation **Worldwide**

Volunteering for Young People (mentioned above) may also be able to help. (For address see Chapter 22.)

Here is a brief survey of the type of opportunities available.

Hotels, tourism and catering

During the holiday season hotels, restaurants and holiday centres in the major European resorts take on extra staff as kitchen assistants, cleaners, waiters, bar staff and chambermaids. This can be hard work, requiring long hours, and the pay may be poor, but tips or bonuses could compensate for the drudgery.

If you turn up in a European resort 'on spec' early in the holiday season there is always a chance that some establishment will take you on.

Otherwise you should try:

- looking in vacation work directories

- contacting local tourist boards who can supply you with the names of establishments which take on extra staff in the summer

- contacting temporary employment agencies, such as Manpower or Adecco

- contacting government employment agencies, (UK Job Centres can help)

- applying to advertisements in foreign and overseas jobs papers

- approaching establishments listed in the *FT World Hotel Directory*

- accessing the websites of holiday firms and hotel groups, many of which have a recruitment section.

For more extended stays see the Seasonal Work section and Chapter 17.

Farm work

At harvest time farmers need to take on casual staff for fruit picking and other agricultural work. The work is often hard and the accommodation basic, but you are likely to find yourself working with people from all parts of the world.

While it is certainly possible to turn up 'on spec' in the hope that there will be jobs going, it might be more sensible to arrange everything in advance. If you are interested in harvesting grapes in France, try the *Guide to Vineyard Employment in France* (World Publications, UK).

If you are interested in going to Israel there are opportunities to work on a kibbutz or a moshav. *Kibbutz Volunteer* by John Bedford (Vacation Work) gives details of agencies which can arrange such holidays.

Among the organisations that can arrange placements are the **British Universities North American Club** (BUNAC). Temporary staff agencies and government employment agencies (e.g. Job Centres) are also worth contacting and you should also delve into the vacation work directories mentioned above.

Work camps/international voluntary projects

'International work camps are a form of short-term voluntary service providing an opportunity for people of different racial, cultural and religious background to live and work together on a common project providing a constructive service to the community,' according to the Central Bureau.

Normally they are for young people aged 16+ and the work can include building, gardening, decorating, conservation, constructing adventure playgrounds, and providing roads and water supplies to villages in the Third World.

There are opportunities in places as far apart as Canada and Cap Verde, Bulgaria and Bangladesh. A typical work camp will have between 10 and 30 volunteers from several countries and participants usually have to arrange and pay for their own travel.

British-based organisations that organise or recruit for work camps include:

- BTCV

- Concordia

- International Voluntary Service

- Quaker Work Camps

- United Nations Association International Youth Service

- Earthwatch Europe

- Kibbutz Representatives

- Tear Fund.

Children's holiday camps

Opportunities arise for camp leaders/camp counsellors and support staff at children's holiday camps. Such camps are particularly popular in the

United States and a number of organisations exist which can fix you up with a job there, make your travel and visa arrangements, and provide orientation courses. They include:

- BUNAC

- Camp America

- Camp Counselors USA

- Concordia

- PGL

- Village camps.

Working in children's holiday camps can entail an exhausting 7-day week with long hours and you will be expected to remain cheerful at all times. Although little or no experience is required for most jobs, which include cooking, cleaning and washing up, people with secretarial and nursing skills are particularly welcome.

Au pair work
This involves looking after children and doing light household duties. Although most au pair arrangements last for six months or longer, there are also holiday au pair posts where the au pair accompanies the family on their vacation.

This type of employment is treated in greater depth in the Gap Year section overleaf.

Other opportunities
There are all kinds of jobs available if you are prepared to look for them. If you are a citizen of a European Union country (e.g. British, Irish) there are no barriers, apart from language, and you could turn up in the country of your choice and try the local job centres and newspapers. If you are qualified (or partly qualified) you could look round for a job in your particular field.

EU citizens planning to venture outside the European Union can encounter immigration problems. To overcome them in the case of the USA you can enlist the help of a sponsoring organisation which can arrange all the documentation. You are then at liberty to make your own working arrangements. They include:

- BUNAC (Work America Programme)

- Camp Counselors USA

- Council Exchanges (CIEE).

If you are interested in working in the Third World you could approach organisations which normally arrange longer-term placements. They include:

- missionary organisations
- voluntary organisations
- Teaching & Projects Abroad Ltd
- i to i International Projects.

Other suggestions are offered in the Seasonal Work section following.

SEASONAL WORK

If you are available for months rather than weeks, you might consider seasonal work. The **hotel, catering and tourism** industries, in particular, take on many extra staff during the holiday season ranging from waiters and chambermaids to resort representatives and camp site staff. Some of the jobs require maturity and experience.

While you can always keep your eye open for such jobs in the relevant trade journals and some overseas jobs papers, the best idea is to approach organisations (hotels, tour operators) direct and offer your services. Ideally this should be before the season begins, but it is also worth trying later on as the season becomes busier.

The holiday season is not restricted to the summer. Many tour operators have extensive **skiing** programmes during the European winter and recruit so-called chalet girls and boys to look after the guests. This involves cooking meals, cleaning the chalets and generally ensuring that the holiday goes with a swing. There are also jobs for resort representatives, skiing instructors, nannies, etc.

Working at a holiday resort is not the same as being on holiday yourself, and while chalet personnel do manage to find time to get onto the ski slopes, the work is by no means easy. Resort reps tend to get better salaries, but have much less free time.

It may even be possible to arrange that you have **two seasonal jobs** to keep you occupied through the year – at ski resorts in the winter and at summer resorts for the rest of the year.

Do not imagine Europe is the only place for seasonal work. It is possible to pick up work on a casual basis in places like **Australia** at harvest time or to work in hotels and restaurants for part of the antipodean summer – which is winter in the northern hemisphere. This is particularly suitable for young people on a working holiday visa.

Further details are given in the respective sections of Chapter 17, Job opportunities by profession.

GAP YEAR EMPLOYMENT

Taking a year off between school and university is an option which attracts a sizeable number of young people these days. Some use the time to build up funds to sustain them through their course, while others see this as a chance to travel and broaden their experience.

A large number of organisations have been set up in recent years to provide opportunities for students wishing to make the most of their Gap Year, some of which are excellent, others less so. If you have any doubts about the credentials of a particular organisation, you should contact the Year Out Group, a body which seeks to maintain good standards in this sector. (Details in Chapter 20.)

Tailor-made schemes

Several organisations cater specifically for this need. Among the best established are:

- Gap Activity Projects
- The Project Trust
- Student Partnership Worldwide.

GAP Activity Projects offers work placements to some 1,200 school-leavers in more than 30 countries around the world. In recent years its volunteers have worked at a Cheshire Home in India, at an orphanage in Ecuador, on a farm in Australia, at a school in Mexico and in many other places besides. **The Project Trust** covers similar ground.

Student Partnership Worldwide concentrates on the Third World, notably Africa and India. It offers teaching and social programmes where a person works as an English teaching assistant in a local school helping with English teaching and extra-curricular activities as well as programmes which concentrate on environmental issues.

For most of these work experience schemes some cost is involved, typically around £2,000, which would normally cover administration and travel. In return participants receive board and lodging and usually a small allowance.

Au pair work

Although most au pairs tend to be single women aged between 18 and 25, equal opportunities legislation now makes it possible for the male of the species to undertake this kind of work in certain countries.

The primary purpose of this arrangement is to enable a young single person to live with a family in another country in order to study their language and way of life. In return for doing certain household chores you are offered accommodation and pocket money.

There have been high profile cases of au pairs who have clearly been exploited rather than treated as a member of the family. However, such instances are the exception, and normally such arrangements work well. An invaluable guide to the ins and outs of these arrangements is given in *The Au Pair and Nanny's Guide* by Susan Griffith and Sharon Legg (Vacation Work Publications).

For some girls au pair work might prove ideal. Many au pair posts can last for six months or a year. If you like children, are prepared to cope with light domestic chores and possess a certain amount of maturity, you could find the experience well worth while. But first read *The Au Pair and Nanny's Guide* mentioned above.

Other opportunities

Several organisations which cater for all age groups also attract Gap Year students and may organise placements for you. They include:

- **BUNAC**

- **Teaching and Projects Abroad Ltd** (teaching conversational English, journalism, conservation, business)

- **i to i** (teaching conversational English in Sri Lanka, India, Russia and Turkey)

- **Coral Cay Conservation** (coral reef surveys, etc.)

- **Frontier** (conservation)

- **Gap challenge** (World Challenge Expeditions)

- **Gorkha HED scheme.**

Missionary organisations, such as **AIM** and **Interserve**, offer similar opportunities, as does **Kibbutz Representatives**. The charity **Worldwide Volunteering for Young People** operates a computerised enquiry service covering hundreds of volunteer organisations which cater for would-be volunteers aged 16 to 25. (See Useful Addresses in the UK.)

Visas and other matters

A number of young people decide to strike out on their own and hope to make their own work arrangements along the way. If you are a resourceful, outgoing person you may succeed, but it is not as easy as it sounds, especially because for some of the more popular destinations you need to obtain a work visa in advance.

Australia, Canada and New Zealand all issue a special category of visa which enables young people to have an extended working holiday of up to one year. In order to facilitate matters you could contact an organisation like **BUNAC**. Under its Work Australia, Work Canada and Work New Zealand programmes it offers:

- travel and insurance arrangements

- orientation before departure

- help in finding a job

- full backup on arrival

- help with accommodation.

Further reading

For a more comprehensive view of Gap Year opportunities try the following books:

- *A Year Off* (CRAC/Hobsons)

- *Jobs in the Gap Year* (Independent Schools Information Service – ISCO)

- *The Gap Year Guidebook*, Rosamund McDougall (Peridot Press).

- The website www.gapyear.com also offers advice and contacts.

A YEAR OUT AS AN UNDERGRADUATE

Once you are enrolled as a student the number of options increases enormously. For example, you become eligible for a number of other **BUNAC** schemes, notably Work Jamaica and Work South Africa. Once you have graduated, Work Ghana and both Teach in Jamaica and Teach in Ghana are open to you. (See also the following section.)

EXCHANGE SCHEMES

The purpose of exchange schemes is to broaden the experience of people who are studying for qualifications and those who are already qualified.

The countries of the European Union are particularly keen to foster education, cultural and work exchanges with the **Socrates** and **Leonardo da Vinci** schemes. In Britain these programmes are overseen by the **Central Bureau for Educational Visits and Exchanges**.

There has been an explosion in recent years of **undergraduate courses**, notably in business studies, which include a work placement of up to a year in another European country. Clearly these are designed to train the international executives of tomorrow.

In other instances you may need to take the initiative yourself. Here are some of the organisations which could help you.

The Central Bureau
This organisation has two well-established exchanges:

- **Language Assistant Exchange Scheme**. This is a scheme whereby students (usually modern language students) and young teachers are sent abroad to work in schools and colleges in Europe and certain countries in South America and Africa.

- **Teacher Exchange Scheme**. This arranges exchanges for experienced teachers for one, two or three terms in various European countries and the USA. The positions in Europe are usually for modern language teachers. More recently opportunities have arisen for specialists in other subjects in Eastern Europe.

The League for the Exchange of Commonwealth Teachers
The League arranges post-to-post exchanges for qualified teachers in all subjects with Commonwealth countries.

The Royal College of Nursing
The Royal College operates the ICN Exchange Programme which enables its members to gain experience abroad.

National Agricultural Centre
There are two schemes for young people organised from this centre: the International Farm Experience Programme and the International Agricultural Exchange Programme. (See Agriculture, Chapter 18.)

International Association for the Exchange of Students for Technical Experience
Founded in 1948, the IAESTE offers short-term course-related work in three broad categories:

- scientific

- professional

- manual.

Participants must normally be nominated by an institution or sponsored by a company.

Association Internationale des Etudiants en Sciences Economiques

AIESEC specialises in exchanges for students studying business (e.g. accountancy, marketing, finance).

Council on International Educational Exchange

CIEE operates a number of exchanges with Canada and the USA which enable undergraduates and recent graduates to take up placements (internships) relevant to their chosen field.

British Universities North America Club

BUNAC's Overseas Practical Training Scheme offers an opportunity to do an internship (traineeship) in the USA in a limited number of fields for up to 18 months. Its Work Spain programme gives British graduates up to 3 months' experience in the Spanish tourism industry.

Voluntary Service Overseas

- *World Youth Millennium Awards:* This new initiative offers young people aged 17–25 an opportunity to work in community projects first in the UK and then in a developing country in Africa or Asia for a total of six months.

- *Youth for Development* (formerly *Overseas Training Programme* and *Youth Action):* Ten- to 12-month placements for motivated and semi-trained young people to gain practical work experience in an international setting.

- *Youth for Youth:* A regionally based programme which does not accept direct applications.

For further details on these organisations please turn to the Recruitment Directory (Chapter 18).

8

Contract Work

The majority of people who go to work abroad do so on contract terms. This may sound a risky business, particularly if you have grown up to believe that you should aim for a job which lasts a lifetime. Actually, 'jobs for life' are becoming thin on the ground these days, and (if it makes you feel better) there is a good chance of your contract being renewed, provided you acquit yourself well in the job.

Indeed, some people succeed in building a career out of a succession of contracts in the same way as an actor does. But there is an inherent insecurity in this way of life, and as a consequence people with growing families often prefer a position offering greater permanence and security.

What type of jobs?

In the following sectors a high proportion of the jobs on offer are on contract terms:

- **Education**. A very high proportion of teaching and training jobs are on contract terms – and this is particularly true in the field of teaching English as a Foreign Language.

- **Construction**. Construction projects by their very nature are temporary. Teams of people are recruited for a particular project – the Channel Tunnel, for instance – and while some of the top managers may well be permanent members of their companies, the majority of jobs, even the high ranking ones, are contract posts.

- **Technical co-operation**. Virtually every job connected with aid programmes, whether you are working for one of the voluntary organisations or as a technical expert with the UN, is of finite duration.

- **Healthcare**. There are opportunities for doctors, nurses and others involved in the medical field throughout the world, e.g. administrators, paramedics, medical technicians, etc.

- **Oil and gas industries**. This is a very wide field which includes exploration, production and refining both on land and offshore. A wide range of disciplines is needed.

- **Mining**. This is another important sector employing a wide range of skills, though the opportunities – certainly at the tradesman level – have diminished.

- **Maintenance**. This is a term which covers a wide field from water supply to electricity generation. Many countries in the Third World employ qualified engineers to ensure that utilities installations run smoothly. Others are employed to run airports or maintain aircraft.

- **Hospitality**. Opportunities arise for managers and senior catering personnel in international five star hotels, on contract catering projects and on cruise ships.

SHORT-TERM CONTRACTS

These last a matter of weeks or months and are usually to cover a short-term need. They are ideal for people who do not want to go through the business of relocation or who find they have time to spare before taking up a more permanent post.

In some cases people are able to take time off from their usual job or obtain secondment by their employer. Clearly it is unwise to embark on such a contract if you have no job lined up to follow on from it.

Relief work

A number of relief organisations require skilled professionals, often at comparatively short notice, to assist with disaster relief operations, perhaps only for a matter of months, sometimes in remote and underdeveloped parts of the world. A landslide in Armenia, an earthquake in Afghanistan, a famine in Africa – all require resourceful people with the necessary skills.

The British Red Cross indicates the qualities that are needed in such situations: 'Candidates must be over 25. They must be adaptable, flexible and mature in judgement, should possess initiative, diplomacy and have the ability to live and work in a team, usually under arduous and sometimes dangerous conditions. Sound mental and physical health is essential. Supervision and training of local staff is an integral part of most assignments. All personnel must be computer-literate; they must fully accept the fundamental Red Cross ethic and principles and be prepared to acquire an understanding of the Movement and its ideals. A First Aid certificate is desirable.'

Here are some of the organisations which recruit for such emergencies and the kind of skills they need:

- **British Red Cross Society**. The Red Cross needs experts in the areas of health, engineering, logistics, development work, etc.

- **International Health Exchange**. This is not a recruitment agency as such but maintains a candidate register and acts as a clearing house for various relief agencies that need medical personnel at all levels. Many of the posts on offer are at mission hospitals. The Bureau also offers medium-term opportunities and publishes a bi-monthly newsletter.

- **Oxfam**. People are needed for emergency relief operations and as advisers in community health, agriculture, engineering, social studies, etc. Contracts are usually from 3 to 6 months.

- **Save the Children Fund**. The chief need here is for medical personnel.

- **RedR (Engineers for Disaster Relief)**. RedR maintains a register of experienced engineers in all fields who can be called upon at short notice to fly out to a disaster area to provide technical support for relief agencies. Contracts are from 2 weeks to 6 months.

   'RedR engineers must be adaptable to tough living conditions and ingenious in their approach to problem-solving,' observes the organisation's brochure. 'They must have proven patience and tenacity and be sensitive to other people's different attitudes and cultures.'

- **International Rescue Corps**. This is an organisation which sends out rescue teams to victims of natural disasters.

- **Médecins sans Frontières**. This is the world's largest emergency medical aid organisation.

- **MERLIN.** Medical Emergency Relief International is one of the newer medical charities.

Short professional assignments

Short assignments tend not to be advertised, since it is not particularly cost-effective for an organisation to do so. Besides it may well have a network of contacts or a register of candidates to fall back on. So it makes sense to send details of your experience and availability to a number of these, or approach an agency that specialises in the recruitment of temporary staff for abroad.

Computer personnel, nurses, doctors and secretaries are in particular demand for short-term placements. There are plenty of opportunities for experienced people to undertake short-term consultancy work. Developing an educational curriculum in the Third World, advising on the rescheduling of debt, drawing up a rural development plan – these are the kind of projects that need consultants just for a matter of weeks rather than years.

Here it is often a matter of being in the right place at the right time – or on someone's candidate register or database. Check whether your professional association keeps such a register.

If you have experience of the Third World, you should make sure that **public organisations** such as the Department of International Development, the British Council, the Commonwealth Fund for Technical Co-operation, Crown Agents and relevant UN agencies are aware of your availability and expertise. (See later in this chapter.)

British Executive Service Overseas is also worth contacting. This is a voluntary sector organisation that sends retired businesspeople on 2–6 month assignments to developing countries to advise small and medium-sized businesses. The organisation, which is funded by DFID, industry and commerce, pays all expenses plus a small allowance.

UNISTAR, the private sector arm of United Nations Volunteers, also recruits executives who wish to work on short volunteer assignments.

LONGER CONTRACTS

Most contracts tend to be for between one year and three years. The length of the contract is determined by a number of factors, including the following:

- **The living conditions in the country**. If the country is at war, for instance, staff may not be prepared to stay long.

- **Immigration regulations**. Some countries only issue work permits lasting one year. Others tend to be more relaxed.

- **Whether the task has a finite life**. For example, the employer may be under contract to an organisation or government, and the agreement is renewed on a yearly basis.

There is nothing sinister in being offered a shortish contract. This no reflection on your ability or sticking power. A short contract can benefit both parties. If the job does not come up to your expectations, you may be relieved it is not for longer. But once you have proved yourself in the job, future contracts could include some guarantee of renewal.

Private sector contracts

It would be an impossible task to list all those companies which offer overseas contracts, though some of the most important are noted in Chapter 17: Job opportunities by profession.

As Chapter 2 pointed out, some firms recruit direct, and their advertisements appear in the press. But a substantial amount of recruitment is done through intermediaries – employment agencies, recruitment consultants, executive search consultants and the like.

But if you do not see any jobs that appeal, you should get in touch with agencies which specialise in your particular field and ask to be put on their candidate register – if they operate one. The Recruitment Directory in Chapter 18 will help you to identify some of the firms which could be interested in you.

There are some organisations which could be described as hybrid; they are a division of a larger firm and recruit for that firm as well as other organisations – often foreign companies with which they have ongoing relationships. One example is **Kvaerner**. Clearly, in such circumstances you need to establish at the outset who is going to be your employer: the firm which recruits you or some other company.

Do not be put off by the outward appearance of an organisation. An oil company operating abroad needs not only engineers and drilling personnel, but also accountants, personnel officers, catering staff, admin officers, trainers – even lawyers.

Take the example of **British Aerospace**, whose chief activity is making aeroplanes – or so one would suppose from its name. Some years ago BAe won a contract to supply fighter planes to the Saudi Arabian Air Force, but included in the deal was a training and maintenance package.

This meant that the company had to provide English and technical teachers, pilot instructors, maintenance engineers, etc. to support the contract – people it does not employ in the normal course of events. It has therefore set up a special organisation to recruit contract staff for the project.

Public sector organisations

While jobs with private companies represent the lion's share of the opportunities available, there are also plenty of interesting contracts available in the public sector. Many of them involve postings to Third World countries. Here are some of the main UK ones.

- **Department for International Development (DFID)**. Formerly the Overseas Development Administration, this is the government department which administers Britain's aid programme. In some cases its recruits direct but more often than not it gives financial support to other organisations which recruit on their own behalf.

When the DFID recruits direct, it is usually looking for experienced people for advisory positions. If you are on its candidate database it may contact you when suitable positions arise.

- **Crown Agents**. Crown Agents are a statutory public corporation providing supply, financial and technical support services to overseas governments and public sector bodies, for the most part in the Third World. These include ports authorities, railways, central banks, electricity authorities, broadcasting corporations and police forces. Most contracts are for two or three years. In addition to advertising vacancies, the Crown Agents maintain a 2,500 strong candidate database.

- **The British Council**. The British Council is funded jointly by the Foreign and Commonwealth Office and the Department for International Development and is involved in cultural diplomacy and education overseas. For example, it operates libraries and organises tours by leading British artists, and runs English-language teaching programmes.

  From its **London office** it recruits hundreds of English (TEFL) teachers a year to teach on its courses. These teachers are directly employed by the Council.

  From its **Manchester office** it recruits a wide range of experts – from curriculum advisers to health education officers. The contractual arrangements vary from post to post. Some of the posts are funded by DFID, while for some of the others the British Council is acting as a recruitment agency.

International organisations

Opportunities arise in the following:

- **European Union institutions**. While most of the posts in the European Commission and the other institutions of the European Union, such as the European Parliament at Strasbourg and the Central European Bank in Frankfurt, tend to be permanent, contract and temporary jobs do exist, notably in research establishments and on development projects.

- **Commonwealth Secretariat**. The Commonwealth Fund for Technical Co-operation recruits for development and other projects.

- **The United Nations and its agencies**. In addition to its permanent staff, the UN has ongoing requirements for technical experts for assignments mainly in Third World countries. Such assignments are on a contract basis offering good conditions of employment and tax-free salaries. Highly experienced personnel are needed, normally aged 35 or older. The requirements are as follows:

– **United Nations**. Opportunities arise in the following fields: economics, mineral resources, public finance, statistics, transport, electric power, housing, town and country planning, public administration, data processing, social welfare, community development, tourism. Very occasionally specialists in energy conservation, cartography, land surveying, museums and libraries are required.

– **UNIDO** (United Nations Industrial Development Organisation). Experts are needed to assist in all stages of industrial development over a wide range of basic and manufacturing industries.

– **ILO** (International Labour Organisation). Experts are required in the fields of manpower planning and utilisation, labour statistics, social security, vocational training, management development, organisation of co-operatives, work study, personnel management, etc. There is a constant demand for specialists in apprenticeship training, vocational training and instructor training.

– **FAO** (Food and Agricultural Organisation). Highly qualified personnel are needed in agriculture, irrigation engineering, forestry, fisheries, nutrition, economics and statistics who are able to plan and execute work independently, train local personnel and advise national authorities.

– **IAEA** (International Atomic Energy Agency). Vacancies occur in such fields as the application of radio-isotopes, reactor physics and engineering, beta and gamma spectrometry.

Other UN agencies which recruit staff on a contract basis are the **World Health Organisation** (WHO), **UNICEF**, **UNESCO** and **UNOPS** (United Nations Office for Project Services). You will find a special section devoted to the United Nations in the Recruitment Directory (Chapter 18).

Non-governmental agencies

These differ from the volunteer organisations mentioned later in that contract employees are paid a salary, rather than a volunteer's allowance. Most of the opportunities are contract posts but there are usually a limited number of permanent staff posts as well. For all positions, qualifications and experience are vital.

There are a large number of these agencies, some of which concentrate on just one country. The following organisations are fairly representative.

- **ACORD** (Agency for Co-operation and Research in Development). This is an international consortium of 11 European and Canadian non-governmental organisations which recruits experienced and qualified professional development workers for agricultural, training and rural development projects in Africa. It offers 2-year contracts.

- **Oxfam**. One of Britain's largest NGOs, Oxfam offers contracts of 1 to 4 years in relief and development work.

- **Save the Children Fund**. SCF is involved in community health programmes, medical care for refugees, nutrition and feeding programmes in addition to disaster and famine relief.

- **World Vision**. This is an interdenominational Christian humanitarian organisation operating in 70 countries through local churches and community leaders in co-operation with the UN and international relief agencies. Medical staff, engineers, logistics experts and vocational instructors are the main categories in demand.

Voluntary organisations

Developing countries often require outside expertise but do not have funds to pay high salaries. This has led to the growth of organisations which recruit people on contract and pay them normally at the local rate for the job – which is inevitably much lower than the salaries they can command at home.

In the early days, most of the volunteers were young and not particularly experienced, but all that has changed. Today most countries require highly motivated people with good qualifications and experience in their particular field, and so the average age of volunteers has crept up to above 30. Some are in their 50s or 60s.

Volunteering is not an option for everyone, particularly people with heavy responsibilities and financial commitments at home. 'Every volunteer . . . often leaves secure employment in the UK with little anticipation of any real material reward for the two years' tough and unpredictable experience ahead,' warns one voluntary organisation in its brochure.

In order to carry out their work a number of agencies receive public funds. In the UK the following organisations are supported by the Department for International Development and other sponsors.

- **Voluntary Service Overseas (VSO)**. This is the largest of these agencies. It recruits about 1,000 people a year (including 400 teachers) to work in more than 40 Third World countries, and some 1,300 volunteers are at post at any one time. Opportunities exist in a wide range of sectors:

  - agriculture
  - forestry and fisheries
  - education and librarianship
  - health
  - business and commerce
  - technical trades
  - crafts and engineering
  - community and social development.

  Accommodation and payment based on local rates are provided by the community, organisation or government requesting volunteers. VSO for its part provides training and pays for air fares, National Insurance, medical insurance and equipment grants. It recruits for posts in Africa, the Caribbean, China, SE Asia and the Pacific.

  VSO also recruits on behalf of United Nations Volunteers (UNV) based in Switzerland and sends volunteers to Eastern Europe and former Soviet Union countries.

- **Skillshare Africa**. This is run along similar lines to VSO and concentrates on southern Africa.

- **United Nations Association International Service (UNAIS)**. This, the volunteer programme of the United Nations Association, recruits mainly for Africa and Latin America.

- **International Co-operation for Development (ICD)**. Also supported by DFID, ICD is particularly involved with rural development schemes.

A number of countries have their own government-sponsored organisations which send volunteers abroad. The Irish equivalent of VSO is the **Agency for Personal Development Overseas**, Canada's is **CUSO** and the United States' equivalent is the **Peace Corps**.

Other volunteer organisations include:

- ATD Third World

- Concern

- Teaching and Projects Abroad Ltd

- Volunteer Missionary Movement.

The organisation **Christians Abroad** provides an advisory service about openings overseas – mainly in Third World countries – through voluntary secular and Christian recruitment agencies. It publishes a jobs bulletin *Opportunities Abroad* which lists current vacancies on offer. **Returned Volunteer Action** publishes a useful guide entitled *Thinking About Volunteering*. The *Third World Directory* lists organisations which offer opportunities for voluntary work overseas.

Missionary organisations

These days it is difficult to draw a distinction between the work of volunteer agencies and that of religious groups. In most of the organisations mentioned below volunteers are recruited for their practical skills rather than their missionary prowess.

These organisations recruit for a wide range of disciplines, including teachers, doctors, paramedics, agricultural experts, engineers, healthcare experts and technical instructors. Here are some examples:

- Crosslinks (teaching, health)

- Christian Outreach (primary healthcare)

- Concern Worldwide (teaching, etc.)

- Interserve (health, agriculture, engineering, teaching)

- Medical Missionary Association (medical)

- Missions to Seamen (spiritual and moral assistance)

- Quaker Peace and Service (health)

- Tear Fund (health, agriculture, technical training)

- Voluntary Missionary Movement (teaching, technical).

For a fuller list of missionary societies turn to the section on missionary work in Chapter 17: Job opportunities by profession.

LOOKING BEYOND THE END OF THE CONTRACT

A person on a contract has the best of both worlds. If the posting proves tiresome and unpleasant he or she knows that it will all be over after a certain time, and there could be a carrot in the form of a terminal bonus to look forward to if you can stick it out.

On the other hand, if you enjoy your work and the location, there is usually a possibility of extending it – often on enhanced terms and with greater responsibility.

Some people manage to build their careers on a succession of contracts, and if you have a much sought after specialism you will be presented with an extensive choice of locations and jobs as one contract draws to a close.

However, there are certain matters to be faced up to if you opt for this type of career. You need to take responsibility for upgrading your knowledge and skills, since contract posts rarely offer in-service training. You also need to make provision for your future – arranging a pension for yourself and insuring yourself against illness and loss of salary.

The latter point is certainly worth bearing in mind. At some time in the future you could suffer a period of unemployment – and loss of income – between one contract and the next. However, your successful completion of a contract or two can lead on to a more permanent type of engagement.

Alternatives to renewal

On the other hand, for various reasons your contract may not be renewed or you may not wish to extend it. Bear in mind that you have a range of options.

Find another job in the same country

During your time in your current posting you should have made many useful contacts and be extremely familiar with the local economy and jobs market. If you keep your ear to the ground you might hear of opportunities that you could have a stab at.

Do not be deterred by the fact that the job is in a slightly different field or your qualifications are lower than those specified for a particular vacancy. Such deficiences are compensated for by your knowledge of local conditions and the local language, which an outsider could not possibly have.

Find another job abroad

If you enjoy the expatriate life, but feel the need for a change, this could be an excellent idea. There is much to be said career-wise for gaining experience in a completely different part of the world – perhaps moving from South America to Japan, or from Africa to Europe.

However, from the personal point of view, a move like this means considerable upheaval, and you will have to come to terms with a new way of life and experience culture shock once more. Fortunately, you should be better able to cope with this second or third time round. For instance, when you are briefed on your new location you will know exactly what sort of questions to ask.

Set up your own business abroad

In certain countries this is a possibility, though in many countries this involves having a local partner. Some expatriates solve this problem by marrying a local, though one does not necessarily have to go to such extremes.

Make sure, however, that you are aware of all the legal implications. In certain countries the red tape that would-be foreign entrepreneurs have to cope with is horrendous. And you have to reckon with the fact that if your chosen country is politically unstable you risk having your assets seized.

Find a job back home

On the other hand you might decide that your roving days are over – at least for the time being – and opt to return home. It is sensible to make plans at least six months before your contract terminates – and start looking through the job adverts in newspapers or surfing the Internet for jobs.

When you are on home leave, you should spend time visiting organisations and agencies that might be interested in your experience or would be able to assist you. Or send off your CV with a covering letter asking to be put on their candidate database.

If you have not fixed yourself up with a job before your return, there is no need to panic. If you have followed this advice you should have made some contacts by now and perhaps received invitations for a few interviews.

Have a sabbatical

If you have spent the past few years in an isolated spot you may find that you have lost touch with some of the latest advances in your particular discipline, and need to catch up. Or you may decide that you want to change career direction. In either case a period of study is to be recommended.

If you do not feel you can manage a full-time course, remember that there are various alternatives: a correspondence course with the Open University, a part-time university or college course (at Birkbeck College, London University, for instance) or even courses on the Internet.

British Council offices around the world have plenty of useful information on educational courses such as these, and the librarian or educational adviser should be able to help you.

9

Permanent Jobs and Self-employment

If you have lived and worked abroad for a while – on contract or as a volunteer, for instance – you should have gained a good idea as to whether or not you could regard this way of life as a long-term option.

While it is possible to have a career which consists of a succession of contracts, there are disadvantages. Such a plan cannot guarantee continuity of employment, and like an actor, you may find yourself 'resting' for long periods between one contract and the next. Another problem is that you will miss out on perks, such as company pensions or training.

A job which offers security of tenure is therefore a great attraction. Here you need to decide what kind of job you want:

- a UK-based job with opportunities for short visits and postings abroad

- a career where you may be seconded to a foreign location

- a career where for a substantial amount of time you will be based abroad

- permanent relocation – emigration, working for an international organisation or company, or setting up your own business abroad.

A HOME BASE WITH VISITS ABROAD

The idea of being based in your own country will appeal to many people who are interested in foreign countries but do not relish the prospect of uprooting themselves completely.

If you are part of the international sales force of a company you will be accustomed to making business visits. Consultants and highly qualified specialists in a variety of fields are often sent off on a succession of international assignments which take them away for a time, though never long enough for them to get homesick.

A second trend, thanks to improving communications, is the increasing number of people living in one country and working in another. Some

British people, for instance, work on the European continent during the week and spend weekends and public holidays at home in the UK.

The weekly routine would thus be similar to that of a person who divides their time between their office in the metropolis and their weekend cottage in the country, or between a North Sea oil-rig and a home on the mainland. Obviously, such a plan is not feasible if your work is thousands of miles away and would involve lengthy journeys and high cost.

Admittedly, in both cases you would not enjoy all the perks of expatriate life – allowances, tax-free salaries, and so on. On the other hand, if you are a 'dual-career' family, your spouse will not be obliged to sacrifice her or his career and salary in order to follow you to the ends of the earth – a move which could result in financial loss overall. It will also mean less disruption to the rest of the family.

SECONDMENT ABROAD

Secondment is likely to happen in a firm which has subsidiaries, partners or clients abroad. It is also possible within the public sector. For example, civil servants in Britain's Department for International Development may be posted to one of the department's regional offices around the world. Police officers are sometimes seconded to train overseas police forces.

Secondments can turn out to be quite lengthy – for up to five years in some cases – and they generally fulfil one or more of the following purposes:

- to fill a vacancy where no local staff are suitably qualified

- to train local nationals

- to create an international cadre of managers

- to increase understanding between head office and subsidiaries

- to set up a new venture

- to exercise control over an overseas operation

- to create a development opportunity for a high-flier

- to increase mobility within the organisation.

Secondment is very similar to going abroad on contract terms, and it is essential that you are adequately prepared for the relocation, properly remunerated, and given guidance on overseas removal, personal taxation, house-letting, etc. A special contract may need to be drawn up to cover your period abroad.

Not all secondments work out successfully. So you and your employer should consider very carefully whether you are really suited to a lengthy assignment in another country. Although you may have enjoyed a successful career until now at home, there is no guarantee that you will be able to replicate this success in other parts of the world. If you do not have the right personal qualities (the questions explored in Chapter 1 should help you to decide), it might be better for both sides in the long run for you to opt out, even though this might mean turning down a promotion.

The Chartered Institute of Personnel and Development makes another valid point: 'Communication with the home base is particularly important for secondees overseas. Because they may be in frequent contact on business matters, the need to maintain general contact with the UK organisation may be overlooked. This can be achieved through:

- the regular despatch of journals and company newsletters

- meetings with visitors from the UK

- frequent contact with UK-based line personnel or career managers where appropriate.'

The CIPD Secondment Code also emphasises the importance of planning for your return well in advance.

A HOME BASE WITH POSTINGS ABROAD

Although there is a distinct trend away from the career expatriate who spends the greater part of their working life abroad, there are still certain sectors that offer truly international careers where perhaps only a third of an employee's working life is spent in their own country. Periodically they find themselves transferred to some new location, where they are able to gain new vistas and enjoy new experiences.

The public sector has a number of organisations where an employee must be prepared to spend a substantial part of his or her life in an overseas location. This is true of the Diplomatic Service and the British Council.

However, it is also true in the missionary field and with some non-governmental organisations, and in industry and commerce. At one time a company with extensive overseas interests might have posted an executive to a foreign location virtually for life. Nowadays, such a person is more likely to be changed around on a regular basis.

Certain companies are more likely than others to send people abroad – particularly if their activities tend to be based overseas. This is true, for instance, of British overseas banks, international mining companies and oil firms.

Potential drawbacks

Such careers normally offer good remuneration, free accommodation and ample allowances. But these advantages have to be set against potential disadvantages:

- **Rootlessness**. Your life is not as settled as that of your contemporaries back home, and at times you may have to relocate at a moment's notice.

- **No choice of destination**. You may be posted to a place which you find uncongenial. However, you have to grin and bear it in the hope that your next posting will be more satisfactory.

- **Family disruption**. If your children follow you to different locations there is a chance that their education will suffer. Boarding school is sometimes the only solution despite the periods of separation it entails.

- **Potential loss of income**. This could be true of dual career marriages where the accompanying spouse has no chance to pursue an uninterrupted career of her/his own.

- **Getting out of touch**. If you have a succession of two or three postings abroad you may find you get out of touch with your home base and developments in your field.

It is often helpful to see a career of this nature in terms of a succession of contracts or secondments. No two postings will be the same, and each time you land in a different place a large measure of personal adjustment will be needed, not least when you are posted back home.

Returning home

As a permanent employee you have one advantage over the contract expatriate: your job and salary do not terminate when the posting abroad comes to an end. Yet the advantage does not lessen the problems of what is technically known as 're-entry' – your return home.

For one thing your outlook will be broader than that of many of your colleagues, and you have to face the fact that you are no longer a big fish in a small pool. A new head office position may well not have the same status and autonomy as the overseas posting.

Clearly, the problem of readjustment is more pronounced for people whose contracts have lasted several years. Some companies and organisations have schemes for reintegrating expatriate staff, but many more still need to address themselves to this problem.

Whether you are to gain help with 're-entry' or not, the International

Committee of the Chartered Institute of Personnel and Development has some useful suggestions. The key is to think ahead and consider the problems you could face.

- **Take time to disengage properly**. Don't rush things. It will take time to acclimatise yourself and find your feet. A holiday or a training course might be sensible options.

- **Assess and review the change in yourself and those at home**. The likelihood is that the Britain you knew has changed. The topics of conversation are different; the fashions have altered; a new political climate may have emerged.

- **Smooth the way for re-establishing relations with friends, relatives and professional contacts**. People you once knew may regard you as a stranger and may have formed new friendships. They could be startled if you appear as a bolt from the blue.

- **Plan long- and short-term goals along with the strategies for achieving them**. These could include setting up a new home, improving your qualifications, or changing career direction.

- **Accept that there will be a degree of reverse culture shock**, particularly of an organisational, financial and psychological nature. Your income is likely to go down, you will have to face the horrors of the British climate, and the outfit you have worked for may have changed out of all recognition.

(The key points are the CIPD's; the comments are the author's.)

PERMANENT RELOCATION

Since the days of the Pilgrim Fathers people have left Europe in search of a better life elsewhere. Some realise their dream and end their days in their chosen location, while others drift back home in a mood of disillusion. They find that their new life is no better than the one they left behind.

As I have already indicated, going abroad on a short assignment is quite different from shooting off for a two-year contract. Uprooting yourself completely belongs to yet another category, and a good deal of soul searching is essential before taking such a step, particularly if you have no experience of living outside your own country.

To be a successful emigrant requires a number of qualities, notably:

- a sense of adventure

- a belief in yourself
- unbridled optimism
- a will to succeed.

No matter how strange and inhospitable your destination turns out to be, you must see it through rose-coloured spectacles – recognising the opportunities it offers and disregarding the drawbacks. The fainthearted either find it impossible to tear themselves away from their home and origins, or having disengaged themselves moan about their new environment and suffer heavy bouts of homesickness.

Admittedly, it is more normal nowadays for people to test the water before committing themselves irrevocably to spending the rest of their days in a far-off clime. If you start off with a contract posting and find the place is not to your liking, you know that at the end of the contract you will receive an air ticket home.

There are two main options for anyone deciding to reside permanently overseas:

- emigration
- a job with an international organisation.

Emigration

The days of mass emigration, when countries like Australia and Canada opened their doors wide to everybody, are long since past. Most countries have restrictions on entry which discriminate against the unqualified and unskilled. They prefer to let in people who have skills which are needed or are in short supply. Computer specialists, nurses and engineers, for instance, are generally welcomed with open arms.

If you have close relations residing in the country in question, it may well prove easier for you to gain entry. The same is true if you plan to set up a business in the country and have sufficient capital to invest.

Australia, Canada, New Zealand and the USA are populated for the most part by immigrants and the descendants of immigrants. And their attraction has not diminished even though one may be subjected to a lengthy wait before one's application is approved or rejected.

However, that is not to say that there are no others.

A large number of countries, in fact, accept immigrants – usually according to a quota system – provided certain criteria are met. If you possess much needed skills or have money to invest, you stand a good chance of being granted the necessary visas to start off.

If you are a citizen of the European Union, there are no immigration restrictions if you wish to settle in a member country. British people can go to live and work in France, just as French people cross the Channel in the other direction.

A job with an international organisation

If you get a job on the permanent staff of an international organisation, you will find that you are exempt from immigration restrictions. You become a citizen of the world, as it were, while retaining your original nationality.

The United Nations, for example, has offices and regional offices in a number of locations. The UN Secretariat is in New York, and the organisation has offices in Geneva and Vienna. In addition, there are the various UN agencies and sister organisations. Several of these are listed in Chapter 17, Job Opportunities by Profession section.

The European Commission and the other institutions of the European Union also offer long-term careers in Brussels, Strasbourg, Luxembourg and elsewhere.

THE ULTIMATE OPTION: WORKING FOR YOURSELF

This handbook has concentrated on looking for jobs, applying for jobs and getting jobs with companies and organisations. But there is another option which you might also consider: working for yourself.

History abounds with people who have gone off to foreign climes and set up thriving businesses: shops, consultancies, trading companies, schools, estate agencies, restaurants, pubs, law firms, brokerages, newspapers, travel agencies . . . The list is endless.

One advantage is that countries with the most draconian immigration restrictions often have a healthy respect for businesspeople – provided the business is completely above board. They reckon that if you have managed to create a job for yourself, you will probably in time create work for others. Since you will not be taking jobs from local people, they will be prepared to let you in to prove yourself.

If you have plenty of funds to invest, they will be even more interested in you, particularly if technology transfer is involved. People with large amounts to invest may benefit from tax and other concessions. However, if you have little cash but plenty of knowhow, there is no need to be deterred. You might consider a joint venture with a local company or individual with ample funds.

Have you sufficient experience?

This is essentially an option for people who have some experience of working for themselves. Entrepreneurship can be a hazardous business even in familiar surroundings. In a foreign environment it carries even greater dangers.

Before you even contemplate such a move, you need to acquaint your-self thoroughly with business practices within the country concerned, and understand how company law and labour law operate there. Assume that everything is quite different from the UK unless proved otherwise.

Contact chambers of commerce and commercial attachés of embassies and high commissions. Track down businesspeople who have first experi-ence of the country concerned. Read any handbooks you can find about doing business in the country: your nearest business reference library should be able to help. In particular, find out about tax rates and the legal position: they differ from country to country.

If you are determined to press ahead, remember there may be other obstacles to overcome. If you want to operate in a country for which entry visas are mandatory you will need to satisfy the relevant embassy or high commission on a number of counts before the visa is issued.

Here are the type of questions they are likely to ask:

- Do you have a minimum amount of capital to invest in your project?

- Can you demonstrate that you have proven business skills?

- How viable a proposition is your project?

- Would it endanger the livelihood of existing locally owned business-es?

- Do you have sufficient resources to cover your living costs until you begin to derive profits from your business?

- What benefit would the business bring to the country?

Vague answers are unlikely to impress. Make sure you have a clearly thought out business plan before you start. This means thorough prepara-tion gained through visits to the country beforehand. Enlist all the help you can, but expect some of the advice to be contradictory. If you have doubts, then there is no shame in withdrawing at this stage.

A long term aim

An alternative plan would be to regard self-employment as a long-term aim. For instance, you might start off working under contract. Later when you are well established in the foreign location, you branch out on your own.

Long-serving teachers break loose and become private tutors or open their own schools. Insurance company representatives set up their own bro-kerage firms. Journalists decide to go freelance or set up their own press agencies.

Such people will have become knowledgeable about the country and its people and developed a number of useful contacts along the way. With luck they will have saved sufficient funds to keep them going until the profits roll in. Even if you are new to the business world, you will benefit greatly from having such firm foundations on which to build.

PART FIVE: THE REGIONS OF THE WORLD

10

Europe

Opportunities for employment in Europe have increased enormously during the last decade or so. This is a result of two important political developments:

- the development of the European Single Market

- the dismantling of the Iron Curtain between Western and Eastern Europe.

The first development means that – for citizens of member countries of the European Union, at least – restrictions on taking up employment in another member country have been lifted.

The second development means that Eastern Europe has opened up considerably to the outside world, and as the economies of the countries of this region develop exciting opportunities are arising for the international job seeker.

THE EUROPEAN UNION

One of the most positive features of the twentieth century – certainly for the international job seeker – is the way that barriers have come down all over Europe. If you are a citizen of a member country of the European Union, you are free to seek employment anywhere in the area without the need to get an entry visa or work permit.

The European Union comprises Andorra, Austria, Belgium, Denmark, France, Germany, Greece, Ireland, Italy, Luxembourg, the Netherlands, Portugal, Spain, Sweden and the UK (including Gibraltar). To these we should add Norway, Iceland and Liechtenstein which together with the EU countries form the European Economic Area. A conspicuous absentee is Switzerland.

In the coming years more countries are likely to join the European Union, notably Cyprus, the Czech Republic, Hungary, Poland, Slovenia and possibly Turkey. For the moment these are considered in the Rest of Europe section.

A single market for jobs

If you are a national of any of these countries you have the right to go to another member state and take up employment there. The only provisos are that you comply with the laws or regulations on employment there and have a valid passport or national identity card. You are then entitled to the same treatment as nationals of the host country in matters of:

- pay
- working conditions
- vocational training
- income tax
- social security
- trade union rights
- unemployment benefit.

However, you must bear in mind that these benefits vary from country to country, and Italy, for instance, may not offer exactly the same kind of benefits as the UK.

The Treaty of Rome established the principle of freedom to work any-where in the community. In 1992 the European Community established a single 'common' market – 'an area without internal frontiers in which the free movement of goods, persons, services and capital is ensured in accordance with the provisions of the Treaty'.

Admittedly some countries have been somewhat tardy in implementing the decisions of the European Commission. For example, some govern-ments have resisted opening up jobs in the government sector to foreigners. However, the Commission seems to be taking a tough line on such matters and forcing member governments to comply with its directives.

Will my qualifications be accepted?

Not so long ago the professional qualifications of one country carried little weight in another. Now the European Commission has decreed that where the education and training for a profession is substantially the same as that in the host country, the qualifications will be recognised as equivalent. This directive applies notably to:

- doctors
- dentists

- nurses
- midwives
- vets
- pharmacists
- architects.

The qualifications for these professions have been co-ordinated at EU level.

For other professions where the education and training are substantially different from provision in the host state, such as:

- teaching
- the law
- engineering
- psychology

you must first apply for recognition of your qualifications. Within four months the authorities have to let you know the result.

If they consider your training to be significantly different, you may be required to undergo one of the following:

- an aptitude test – designed to assess your ability to pursue your profession in the host country
- a period of supervised practice not exceeding three years
- further training.

In Britain the National Academic Recognition Centre can advise on the recognition of academic qualifications and the Department of Trade and Industry (Kingsgate House) on professional qualifications.

Legislation already exists to make it easier for people to meet vocational training requirements in other member states, though this is restricted to certain jobs and trades. Certificates of Experience facilitate recognition of your skills by the authorities of other member states. To obtain one you should apply to the European Division, Department of Trade and Industry.

The opportunities
Although some of the countries have experienced recession in the 1990s, there are signs everywhere that the European economy is resurgent, and if

you have expertise in science, technology, finance, electronics or IT you should have few problems in finding suitable opportunities.

There is a demand for teachers, too, particularly English (TEFL) specialists as Europeans attempt to surmount the many language barriers. There is a requirement for translators and technical authors, the latter particularly in the private sector, since manuals and technical documents all have to be rendered in clear English for export markets.

A large proportion of the UK's trade is with Europe, and many large firms maintain permanent offices in several of the European capitals. This does not apply only to manufacturing firms, however. Banks, accountancy firms, law firms, insurance companies, management consultancies, advertising agencies, and so on are becoming familiar sights on the continent, and their number is likely to increase rather than diminish. However, the majority (if not all) of the staff are likely to be recruited locally.

There are also plenty of permanent opportunities in the public sector – in the institutions of the European Union, European research establishments, the Council of Europe, NATO and the different agencies of the United Nations located in Europe. Here there are opportunities for specialist staff, administrators, translators and interpreters as well as secretaries.

Generally speaking, employers are on the lookout for marketable skills. However, in some of the wealthier parts of Europe it is still possible to land semi-skilled jobs, notably in construction and the hotel and catering trades – but normally you will need to speak the local language.

Finding a job in the European Union

If you decide to go to a country of the European Union to look for work, your first port of call should be the government employment agency. You will find the addresses of these in the Country Directory in Chapter 19.

Most continental countries do not have the range of private employment agencies found in Britain, and in some cases the state employment agency still enjoys a monopoly. Elsewhere temp agencies, such as Manpower and Adecco, are starting to spring up.

It is also worth looking at job advertisement columns of the local papers. A number of large cities also have English-language papers which advertise jobs suitable for expatriates. Some of these are mentioned in the Country Directory.

Do not overlook the possibilities for self-employed individuals. If you have specialist skills and/or cash to invest, you might well consider the possibility of setting up on your own in some European location. The possibilities are endless, but like any potential businesspeople at home, you must first do a feasibility study and be prepared to spend much time and effort in getting your show off the ground. You should also bear in mind that legal requirements differ from country to country.

The European Commission has produced a booklet entitled *Working in another Country of the European Union,* with accompanying factsheets. Job Centres in the UK can provide factsheets on individual countries.

THE REST OF EUROPE

If you are planning to work in other European countries, you will find immigration restrictions in place. Generally speaking you need to obtain a work visa if you want to take up employment in any of these countries. You cannot normally arrive in one of these countries in order to look for work, but need to arrange your job in advance.

They include Cyprus, Malta, Switzerland and Turkey. The first three are similar in every other respect in terms of opportunities to the countries of the European Union.

Turkey stands a little apart, being right on the edge of Europe. (In fact, 97 per cent of it is in Asia.) Perhaps you should regard it as a halfway house between Europe and the Middle East, since away from the main cities there are areas which remain relatively undeveloped. Salary levels are considerably lower than in the countries mentioned so far, though the cost of living is also lower.

Western Eastern Europe and the Baltic States
Czech Republic, Hungary, Poland, Slovenia, Estonia, Latvia, Lithuania

During the Cold War, opportunities for outsiders were few and far between in the former Communist block countries, but the area has opened up to the West and these countries have made rapid strides in developing market economies.

They have been helped by injections of expertise from the West (including the European Union and the British Government's Knowhow Fund), and consultants in finance, banking, advertising, management and a whole range of technical skills have made their mark. There has also been a thirst for education: English (TEFL) teachers have been in particular demand. However, in general, salaries tend to be lower than in Western Europe.

Now they are approaching the economic standards of Western Europe, and the first four countries listed above are strong candidates for membership of the European Union in the near future. As trade develops, Western firms will need to have their own staff strategically placed in different centres in order to benefit from opportunities as they arise.

Eastern Eastern Europe

Albania, Belarus, Bosnia, Bulgaria, Slovakia, Macedonia, Moldova, Romania, Russia, Ukraine, Yugoslavia

These states are still engaged in the painful transition from Communist to Western-type market economies and the anticipated prosperity is proving elusive. In some cases the economies are volatile and old attitudes are proving hard to shift. Virtually all the countries in this section are receiving aid in one form or another.

There is another reason why some of these countries are lagging behind the others. Three of the former states of Yugoslavia have been through extremely nasty conflicts which could break out again. However, prospects look reasonable for Croatia as its tourism industry recovers. Political unrest could easily erupt once more in Albania which has the unhappy distinction of being Europe's poorest and least-developed country.

The economies of Russia, Belarus and Ukraine are struggling. Yet these countries can hardly be described as underdeveloped since they have well-educated populations, even though Russia's economy is smaller than Indonesia's. While a minority have benefited enormously from the changes, large sectors of the population, especially civil servants and those in state-run enterprises, are living at subsistence level. Other economies of the region are little better.

For this reason anyone planning to work in these countries must be prepared for disappointments, frustrations, even hardships. Some of the people you will come across may seem demoralised and regard new methods with suspicion. In some countries crime, once ruthlessly suppressed, has reared its ugly head. You therefore have to be very security conscious and steer clear of trouble.

On the positive side, this part of Europe offers plenty of scope to anyone who enjoys a challenge.

People and language

It is merely stating the obvious to mention that the European continent is not part of the English-speaking world. While English may be used for international communication, within the country itself you will find everybody talking to one another in the national language. This contrasts strongly with parts of the Third World where English is very much the lingua franca.

So the first cultural barrier you will need to surmount is the linguistic one. While your colleagues at work may be able to communicate with you in English, for most of the time they will address each other in their own language. In order to participate more fully in their deliberations you need to get down to learning their tongue, particularly if it is a major one, such as German, French, Spanish or Italian.

If your posting is away from the cosmopolitan atmosphere of the capital, the need to come to grips with the language becomes even more self-evident.

There are other differences to be taken account of as well. Although we inhabit the same continent, each nation can differ quite markedly in **temperament and outlook** from its neighbour.

The **Germans** have a reputation for being thorough and professional, though their legendary dedication to work is less evident these days. For instance, they have the longest holidays of any Europeans. They are tough negotiators.

They observe a degree of formality in their personal relationships. For instance, they tend not to be on Christian name terms with colleagues. To a great extent men still rule the roost, but that is changing. You will encounter considerable differences in attitude between the confident West Germans and the less confident Germans from what was formerly East Germany.

The **French** are proud of their culture, food and language, and if you want to curry favour you cannot do better than praise items one and two in the third. Status is important, and who you are or where you have studied is more important than your actual accomplishments. They tend to dress well but conservatively, and attach great importance to good manners. French people never mix business with pleasure, and so you should avoid discussing business at meal-times. The pace of life in the provinces tends to be more sedate than in Paris.

Status is also important to **Italians** who often behave in an autocratic way with subordinates. Italy seems somewhat disorganised, nepotism is rife and endless red tape can be a problem. **Spaniards** tend to be formal in personal relationships and place great stress on personal honour. However, there are considerable variations between the various regions of Spain.

Turkey represents a blend of East and West. Although it is regarded as part of Europe and European attitudes and styles predominate among the educated classes, most of the population are followers of Islam and a good many may disapprove of alcohol, women's lib and other aspects of Western life. Turks are hospitable people but Turkish society is somewhat autocratic and male-dominated.

In **Eastern Europe** you will find countries with a strong sense of nationalism as they search for a new identity after years under Communism. In some cases this may manifest itself in a strong dislike of neighbouring states or intolerance of minorities, such as gypsies.

Each country of Europe is distinctive, and your life abroad will prove more congenial and rewarding if you make an effort to familiarise yourself with national characteristics and attitudes and blend in with your surroundings. Fortunately there are plenty of handbooks on the market dealing with life in individual countries.

FURTHER INFORMATION

Working in . . ., a series of factsheets on each of the member states of the EEA, is available at Job Centres in the UK.

The European Commission publishes a number of useful free booklets for job seekers, including:

> *Europe Direct: Routemap for job seekers in the EU.*
> *Working in another country of the EU.*

There are also fact sheets on:

- right of access to employment

- looking for work

- recognition of diplomas

- right of residence

- social security

- welfare benefits

- taxes

- cross-border workers

- national education systems.

This information is also available on the Internet: www.europe.eu.int/citizens.

Europages: European Business Directory (Euroédit SA).

What's What and Who's Who in Europe (Cassell).

Networking in Europe: a Guide to European Voluntary Organisations (National Council for Voluntary Organisations – NCVO).

Contact addresses for individual countries are listed in the Country Directory (Chapter 19).

11

The Arab World

The Arab World stretches from Morocco in the west across North Africa and the Arabian Peninsula to Oman in the east. It embraces a diverse range of countries, some poor, some rich, some backward, some sophisticated. The common denominator is that the residents of all these countries, for the most part, regard themselves as Arabs.

It is a region that the international job seeker cannot ignore. Several Arab countries employ expatriates extensively – notably Libya and the other oil-producing countries on the Arabian Peninsula (Kuwait, Qatar, Oman, Saudi Arabia, UAE).

However, not all Westerners feel at ease in this region. There are substantial cultural differences between Middle Eastern society and the West, and anyone planning to work in the area would be well advised to develop an understanding of and respect for the region's traditions. This chapter aims to help you understand it.

THE OPPORTUNITIES

After the oil price rise in the mid-1970s, the oil-producing countries of the Middle East offered boundless job opportunities for expatriates in a variety of different fields. While the best jobs initially were in the oil and gas industry, as the oil money flowed in, these countries, for the most part, were keen to develop their infrastructure, which meant plenty of openings in construction, education and healthcare.

When oil prices fell in the late nineties prosperous countries like Saudi Arabia – the biggest employer of expatriate labour in the Middle East – found themselves running up budget deficits and decided to rein in costs. So they began to make greater use of local labour or Asian workers who were willing to work for much lower wages.

'1999 saw scores of expatriates having to either return to the UK due to lack of work, or take what existing work there was on less than favourable terms' observes recruitment consultant Neil Dawes. 'However, one sector of the skills pool managed to avoid all this bother, namely those who had language skills with local experience to match.'

As this edition of *Getting a Job Abroad* goes to press, there are signs of an upturn in oil prices. It is too early to say whether this will lead to a corresponding increase in jobs for Western expatriates. Even if it does, employers are likely to continue to be more selective with regard to the people they recruit.

For people with qualifications and experience the main opportunities are in the following areas:

- the oil and gas industry
- construction (of buildings, roads, etc.)
- education and training (including military training)
- the medical sector – hospitals and clinics
- banking and financial services
- telecommunications
- utilities management
- IT
- hotels and catering.

A number of expatriates are involved in the aid sector, notably in Egypt (which is a major recipient of aid), Yemen and the West Bank and Gaza. In the major cities there are plenty of expatriates involved in the service sector.

Prospects are not completely rosy. There is still a good deal of tension in certain countries. Algeria can be dangerous for both Algerians and expatriates alike. However, on a happier note, Libya's relations with the outside world have improved considerably and this can only be of benefit to the large expatriate workforce in the country. Plans to improve the infrastructure of Jordan and Mauretania may well boost job opportunities there in the near future.

THE INFLUENCE OF ISLAM

While there are a significant number of Arab Christians – among the Lebanese, Palestinians and Egyptians – the majority of Arabs and Iranians are Muslim.

Islam is more than just a religion, it is a way of life, which affects people's behaviour and attitudes. You need to be aware of the following matters:

- **Prayer times**. The call of the muezzin summons the faithful to prayer five times a day, and the very devout may well prostrate themselves facing towards Mecca. In Saudi Arabia shops close at prayer time.

- **Weekends may be centred on Friday**. This is the holy day for Muslims, many of whom attend the mosque at midday.

- **Fasting from sunrise to sunset** takes place during the month of **Ramadan**. However, many people stay up for part of the night eating and merry-making, and this can mean frayed tempers and lack of attention the following day at the workplace. You should avoid eating or drinking in view of a Muslim during daylight hours.

- **Abstinence from alcohol**. Many Muslims abstain from alcohol, and in certain countries (notably Kuwait, Libya and Saudi Arabia) it is prohibited.

- **Abstinence from pork and pork products**. Pork is regarded as unclean, and is usually unavailable in Arab countries. Even if you manage to obtain some, you should avoid serving it up at a meal attended by Muslims.

- **The subordinate position of women**. Some of the more traditional Arab societies are very much male-dominated. Social contact between the sexes is discouraged, and in some countries women may not be allowed to work, drive a car or leave the house unaccompanied.

There are two main branches of Islam – **Sunni** and **Shia** – and a number of sects. Conflicts sometimes arise between these different groupings, and nowhere is this more evident than in Lebanon. Arabs tend to be Sunnis, while most Iranians are Shiites. In Iraq, however, the ruling class is Sunni while the majority of the population is Shiite.

The Wahabbis are a puritanical Sunni sect whose influence is felt particularly in Kuwait and Saudi Arabia, and there are Islamic fundamentalist movements in many countries with a strongly traditionalist (and often militant) outlook – in Egypt and Algeria, for instance.

POLITICAL ATTITUDES

It is best to avoid discussing politics in the Middle East, unless you happen to be talking to someone you know well. Politics has strong emotional overtones, and your observations, however well-meant, are likely to be regarded as criticism.

The Arabs are inheritors of a civilisation which flourished for eight centuries and then went into decline. For the following five hundred years they came under the rule of the Ottoman Empire, and later individual countries came under French, Italian or British control.

Now the Arab countries have regained their independence, there have been attempts to create a single Arab nation which could restore their civilisation to its former pre-eminent position. However, past attempts (such as Nasser's United Arab Republic) have usually ended in failure. Indeed, there is considerable hostility between certain states – Iraq and Syria, for instance – and you need to be aware of such tensions. Nevertheless, there is still a sense of Arab nationhood, and an outsider is unlikely to be thanked for pouring scorn on the concept.

Democracy in the Western sense has not really taken root in the Arab world, and there is a tendency to see the regimes of the region as authoritarian and led by hereditary rulers or generals who are liable at any moment to be brought down by a *coup d'etat*. Yet this picture does not necessarily reflect modern realities.

While it must be admitted that strong leadership is often preferable to a state of anarchy, the Arab World is undergoing a gradual transformation. The emergence of younger, more enlightened leaders could have a very positive impact on the nations they govern.

ISRAEL AND THE PALESTINE PROBLEM

The creation of Israel in 1948 caused consternation in the Arab World, and has been a cause of tension in the area ever since. If there was one cause which united the Arab states it was opposition to the Jewish homeland.

Israel's existence is at the root of any anti-Western feeling you come across. In Arab eyes, the West requisitioned a portion of Arab territory and gave it to the Jews displacing the Palestinian Arabs.

The country, rightly or wrongly, is regarded as a bastion of Western imperialism, and was at one time blamed for all the Arab World's problems. Until recently, no Arab state was prepared to recognise the existence of Israel, and when Egypt did so the country was ostracised.

Many Arab countries operate a blacklist of firms that trade with Israel. If you wear St Michael clothing, for instance, it is a sensible precaution to cut off the labels before you go to the Arab World as they could be confiscated by the customs officials.

Considerable international efforts have been made to solve the conflict, and one consequence of the Peace Agreement brokered by President Clinton is that the Palestinians in Gaza and on the West Bank enjoy a certain measure of autonomy. However the peace remains fragile, and since the beginning of the new millennium relations between Israel and the

Palestians have worsened resulting in increased tension.

Israelis see themselves as surrounded by hostile neighbours and there-fore have something of a siege mentality. But they too are divided among themselves in a country which represents three distinct traditions: the Ashkenazi Jews from Eastern Europe who predominate in the urban areas, the Sephardic Jews whose origins lie on the Iberian peninsula, and the Middle Eastern Jews.

Whatever your views regarding the creation of Israel, you need to be aware that for Arabs this is an extremely sensitive subject, and you would be wise to steer away from it if it crops up and refrain from comment.

You will encounter Palestinians throughout the Arab World. Many of the educated ones work in the countries of the Gulf which lack a profes-sional class.

DEALING WITH MIDDLE EASTERNERS

Some of the Arabs you come into contact with will have been educated in Western countries, and are distinctly cosmopolitan in their outlook. Others will expect you to adapt to their norms. Here are a few tips on good etiquette:

- Be patient, and don't expect quick decisions, particularly after only an initial meeting. Arabs like to build up a relationship with people and that takes time.

- Accept a flexible approach to time. People may be late for appoint-ments and be unwilling to agree to deadlines.

- Observe social niceties before you get down to business. Accept offers of coffee or tea and converse generally before turning to business matters.

- Enquire about the health and progress of the male members of the family, but do not ask after the womenfolk (unless you are a woman).

- Be prepared for interruptions to meetings and the presence of other people during your deliberations, however confidential you may regard them. An official or the director of a firm sits in his office and holds court, often dealing with a number of matters at the same time.

FINDING JOBS

The countries of the Middle East are not easy places to enter without a proper work visa, and it is therefore best to arrange your job in advance.

This does not present any problems since there are numerous recruitment agencies (some featured in this book) which handle jobs in the area. Alternatively you could approach international construction, oil or hospital management companies. Opportunities are widely advertised in the national and specialist press, and overseas jobs papers (e.g. *Nexus*).

FURTHER INFORMATION

Middle East & Mediterranean Business Directory (Owen's World Trade Ltd, Tridon House Industrial Estate, Thame OX9 3XB).
The Arabian Year Book (Owen's World Trade Ltd).
Major Companies of the Arab World (Graham & Whiteside).
UK Firms with Offices in Arab Countries (Arab British Chamber of Commerce, 6 Belgrave Square, London SW1X 8PL. Tel: (020) 7235 4363).
Middle East Economic Digest (21 John Street, London WC1N 2BP).
The Arab Mind, R. Patai (Charles Scribner's Sons, New York).
The Arabs, P. Mansfield (Pelican).
The Arab Way, Dr Jehad Al-Omari (How To Books).
The Gulf Directory, (Telegulf Director Publications).

Addresses
Committee for Middle East Trade, 33 Bury Street, London SW1Y 6AX. Tel: (020) 7839 1170.
Middle East Association, address as above. Tel: (020) 7839 2137.
Anglo Arab Association, 21 Collingham Road, London SW5 0NU. Tel: (020) 7373 8414.
The Arab British Centre: address as above.
School of Oriental & African Studies, see Useful Addresses in the UK (Chapter 20).
Centre for Arab Gulf Studies, Old Library, University of Exeter, Prince of Wales Road, Exeter EX4 4JZ.
Centre for Middle Eastern & Islamic Studies, University of Durham, South End House, South Road, Durham DH1 3TG.
Arab Orientation Consultancy, PO Box 17, Tetbury, Glos GL8 8ZD. Tel: (01249) 655275.

Contact addresses for individual countries are listed in the Country Directory (Chapter 19).

12

Asia

It is impossible to describe Asia in just a few words, since it is a vast continent – both in area and population – and comprises a diversity of ethnic groups and cultures. It is a continent of contrasts: some of the countries – like Nepal, Burma and Bangladesh – belong to the Third World; while others – South Korea, Taiwan, Hong Kong, Singapore, not to mention Japan – have flourishing economies and living standards on a par with those in the West.

For the purposes of this book Asia has been divided into four regions:

● Central (or Western) Asia

● the Indian Subcontinent

● South East Asia

● the Far East (including China).

CENTRAL ASIA

Afghanistan, Armenia, Azerbaijan, Georgia, Iran, Kazakhstan, Kyrgyzstan, Tajikistan, Turkmenistan, Uzbekistan

Most of these countries appear in this handbook for the first time. In the past there was little point in including those which were part of the Soviet Union, since they offered no opportunities to the international job-seeker.

Now the situation has changed completely for those states which were formerly part of the Soviet Union and they can look forward to an exciting future. The reason is the oil reserves around the Caspian Sea which have already attracted a number of international oil companies.

Much of the oil is in Kazakhstan which also has natural gas, gold, uranium, copper and other valuable minerals. Turkmenistan, the southernmost state of the group, is particularly rich in natural gas. However, all of the states expect to benefit from the oil bonanza, and could develop quite rapidly as the oil-producing countries of the Gulf did. At present Azerbaijan seems to be leading the field.

Apart from jobs in the oil industry, there are likely to be a wide range of infrastructure projects: pipeline construction, improvements to telecommunications, the building of roads and railways, technology transfer, etc. There will also be opportunities for trainers and teachers (notably TEFL experts). Companies and agencies with experience of recruiting for the Arabian Peninsula are now turning their attention northwards.

There are some caveats. This is a region in transition from a Soviet-style economy to a private enterprise one. Such changes are seldom achieved without pain and conflict, and there have been some local difficulties. Few of these countries pretend to be models of stability.

However, most have made surprisingly good progress – with the exception, perhaps, of Turkmenistan and Uzbekistan. On the other hand, there are some hangovers from the past: corruption is rife, and there is a danger that some of the regimes will follow the example of Nigeria and squander the nation's oil wealth. This is a fascinating area to work in, but you must be prepared for frustrations. It could be dubbed 'the last frontier'.

Of the other countries in this area, Iran, another oil giant, is slowly emerging from its Islamic extremist cocoon and developing friendlier relations with the outside world. A few opportunities are likely to develop in the coming years.

There is little hope, however, for impoverished and backward Afghanistan which has endured political turmoil for two decades. The only discernible opportunities here are in the aid sector, and these are only for the intrepid.

THE INDIAN SUBCONTINENT

Bangladesh, Bhutan, India, Maldives, Nepal, Pakistan, Sri Lanka

Britain's involvement with this part of the world reaches back to the eighteenth century, and it is still possible to see vestiges of the British Raj in many of the institutions of these countries and the attitudes of their peoples.

Nowadays countries like India and Pakistan have plenty of indigenous expertise, so much so that they export their expertise to other countries, notably the oil rich countries of the Gulf. Opportunities for expatriates are relatively few, though foreign companies with investments in the area will bring in their own executive staff. In addition, given the relative poverty of many countries, there is plenty of work for aid organisations.

In recent years India and Sri Lanka have become popular countries for Gap Year students to gain work experience, notably in teaching. A number of missionary groups are active here running hospitals, orphanages and other schemes for the less fortunate.

The people of this region are proud of their cultural traditions and anyone working here should show respect for their religious practices in particular. The leading religions are Hinduism, Islam and Buddhism (notably in Sri Lanka) and there are important Sikh, Christian and Jainist minorities. Occasionally religious conflicts erupt and, more seriously, border differences arise between India and Pakistan.

But on the whole, the people of the region are a fairly tolerant lot and most foreigners develop an affection for the area. However, the poverty you come across, especially in the cities, can be distressing. One advantage is that English is readily understood throughout the region. India has several times more English speakers than Britain itself!

SOUTH EAST ASIA

Brunei, Burma (Myanmar), Cambodia, Indonesia, Laos, Malaysia, Philippines, Singapore, Thailand, Vietnam

Described by George Coedès as 'the Indianised states of South East Asia', the countries of this area are coming together into a political and economic grouping known as ASEAN. However, their differences (religious and historical) are every bit as great as their similarities.

Burma, Laos and Cambodia are the least developed of these countries as a result of past and continuing conflicts and inept government. The most obvious opportunities here are in the aid sector.

At the other end of the spectrum are the former British possessions of Malaysia and Singapore, which have prospered since gaining independence. The latter, an island state with a largely Chinese population, has become an important financial and commercial centre and boasts a very cosmopolitan workforce. Predominantly Muslim Malaysia with its large Chinese, Indian and Dayak minorities is developing a strong industrial structure to complement resource-based industries such as tin and rubber.

Thailand has grown in prosperity – particularly the Bangkok region – though there are plenty of pockets of poverty in the countryside. So while Thailand attracts foreign investors and trading firms, there are numerous aid projects and Bangkok has a large UN representation.

Indonesia, the most populous country of the region, has a thriving oil industry and many of the expatriate jobs are directly or indirectly connected with this. The Philippines with its well-educated population is at last coming out of its economic torpor.

Vietnam is regarded as a country with considerable potential and has attracted a number of foreign companies. But its Communist legacy, particularly in the north, is acting as a brake on progress. There are a number of aid projects designed to modernise the country employing expatriates.

Brunei has little need of aid, since it has plenty of oil deposits and is a prosperous place. The main employer of expatriates here is Shell.

Until 1997 countries like Thailand, Singapore, Indonesia and Malaysia enjoyed some of the highest economic growth rates in the world. However the Asian recession of the late 90s had a devastating effect on the region. Currencies were devalued and companies went under.

Fortunately three of these countries have well developed infrastructures and educated workforces, and are starting to regain their former prosperity. However, Indonesia has experienced mixed fortunes in recent years and there are doubts over its long-term stability.

Expatriate involvement in the region in such areas as mining, oil exploration and drilling, education and services looks set to continue.

THE FAR EAST
China (including Hong Kong), Japan, Korea, Taiwan

Most of the countries of Eastern Asia have highly developed economies and can no longer be termed part of the Third World. Many of the opportunities for expatriates lie in the education field and as representatives for foreign companies that need a presence there.

China is the exception. However, the Chinese economy goes from strength to strength and is attracting a large amount of foreign investment – often in joint ventures – which necessitates a considerable expatriate presence. Foreign companies and governments are also helping the country to develop its infrastructure, notably telecommunications and management. The new industrial zones on the coast are proving particularly successful.

After Hong Kong was incorporated into China a few years back, there were doubts as to whether this former British Crown Colony would continue to play such a pivotal business role. These doubts have now been dispelled, and this small territory continues to attract large amounts of foreign investment and offer good job opportunities to expatriates.

Taiwan has long ceased to be a developing country. Its economy seems to be stronger than most of the others in the region and opportunities for expatriate employment seem to be mainly in education and training.

Of the Koreas, North Korea has until recently pursued an isolationist role despite a succession of natural disasters, and opportunities for foreigners have been virtually nil. South Korea, by contrast, has had a very buoyant economy until recently and there were plenty of opportunities for business people and teachers. It is currently sorting out its economy and should eventually regain its old prosperity. Better relations with North Korea will be regarded as a bonus.

Japan has grown into one of the world's leading industrial powers, but during the 1990s its economy, too, has been in recession. As a consequence a number of foreigners working in the country have not had their contracts renewed. It is doubtless only a matter of time before this major economy is back on its feet again.

UNDERSTANDING DIFFERENCES

Historical and religious differences

Many of the Asian peoples adhere to religions and cultural traditions that differ markedly from our own. Buddhism, Confucianism, Hinduism and Islam have shaped attitudes over the centuries, and in some areas these are tinged with animist beliefs. It is not unusual for a country to have a multiplicity of religions rather than a predominant one.

Islam is strong in Pakistan, Bangladesh, Malaysia, Brunei and Indonesia and many of the countries of Central Asia. Afghanistan and Iran are subject to a particularly fundamentalist strain, but in most other countries more benign attitudes prevail.

Hinayana Buddhism is the predominant religion in Thailand, Sri Lanka, Burma, Cambodia and Laos. Korea, Japan and Vietnam are predominantly Mahayana Buddhist, while the Chinese tend to be Buddhist or Confucian. The predominant religion in the Philippines is Christianity, while India, as mentioned above, is home to all the world's main religions.

There have also been Western colonial influences at work, which should not be underestimated. Britain once controlled the Indian Subcontinent, Burma, Malaysia, Singapore, and Hong Kong. Cambodia, Laos and Vietnam were once French possessions, Indonesia was a Dutch colony, and the Philippines came under Spanish and American control. If Central Asia still feels a bit like Russia, this is no coincidence.

Many of these countries have significant racial minorities. Immigrants from China play an important role in the commercial life of several South East Asian countries. In some (e.g. Thailand) they have integrated well with the local populace and often intermarried, but in others (e.g. Indonesia) this has not happened and violent conflicts erupt from time to time.

There are substantial Indian minorities, too – particularly in Malaysia, Singapore and Burma.

Cultural differences

Asians often have value systems and manners which some foreigners find strange or irritating. Here are a few pointers which will help you appreciate the differences and adjust your behaviour accordingly.

- *Avoidance of confrontation*. People exercise tact. Arguments are to be avoided at all costs.

- *Fatalism*. People accept that they are powerless to change the world.

- *Superstition*. People often believe in the supernatural and often do not embark on an enterprise without consulting an astrologer beforehand.

- *Submission to authority*. It is unthinkable for a person to contradict their boss even if they know the boss is wrong.

- *Respect* for age and education.

- *Passivity*. People are not as demonstrative as Westerners. Excessive shows of affection, for instance, are often frowned on.

- *The concept of face or status*. This is very important. You must take care not to humiliate a person either directly or indirectly.

- *Politeness and discretion*. You will give offence if you go about criticising people and speaking your mind.

- *Collectivist mentality*. People prefer to do things in groups rather than individually.

FURTHER INFORMATION

Asian Oil and Gas, Publishing Resources Ltd, 12th Floor, 200 Lockhart Road, Hong Kong.
Far East Economic Review, Centre Point, 181 Gloucester Road, Hong Kong (weekly).
All Asia Guide (annual – published by *Far Eastern Economic Review*).
Asia Mining, 7514 Bagtikan Street, Corner Pason Tano, Makati, Metro Manila, Philippines.
Far East Expatriate, Hilal International, Regal House, London Road, Twickenham, Middlesex TW1 3QS (monthly).
Indonesia – Malaysia – Singapore – Brunei Business Directory (Utraco Pte Ltd, Colombo Court, PO Box 782, Singapore 9117).
Languages of Asia and the Pacific, C. Hamblin (Angus & Robertson) – a phrase book covering 25 languages.
Dun's Asia & Pacific: Key Business Enterprises (Dun & Bradstreet).

Addresses
School of Oriental & African Studies: see Useful Addresses in the UK.
Centre of South Asian Studies, University of Cambridge CB2 1TN.

Centre for South East Asian Studies, University of Hull HU6 7RX. Tel: (01482) 46311.

East Asia Centre, University of Newcastle upon Tyne NE1 7RU. Tel: (01632) 328511.

Asian Studies Centre, St Anthony's College, Oxford OX2 2JF. Tel: (01865) 59651.

Contact addresses for individual countries are listed in the Country Directory (Chapter 19).

13

Africa

Africa south of the Sahara consists of 47 countries, 2,000 tribes and 750 languages. Many of the countries are artificial entities whose boundaries cut across ethnic and tribal groupings – a consequence of the 1884 Conference of the Great Powers in Berlin which partitioned the continent among the different European governments. When conflicts break out, e.g. in Rwanda and Burundi, it is often because tribal loyalties outweigh national ones.

Sub-Saharan Africa is very much part of the Third World, with a large proportion of the population living at subsistence level or below. The figures speak for themselves. At least 45% of Africans live in poverty and only 15% live in 'an environment considered minimally adequate for sustainable growth and development' – to quote the World Bank. In 1999 average economic growth on the continent was 2.5%, less than the rate of population growth. In some African countries 20% of the population is infected with AIDS which has a devastating impact not only on society but also on economic life. Unless the overall situation improves, Africa would appear to be on a downward spiral, its population doomed to become larger, poorer, less educated and probably more desperate.

As a consequence, the continent is a major recipient of aid. Virtually all the major aid agencies and volunteer agencies are active here, and there is a substantial input from missionary groups as well.

Many of these bodies are involved in education, health, rural development, small industries and agriculture. In an effort to make Africa self-sufficient in food production, agriculture is receiving top priority these days, and agricultural advisers are much in demand. In addition there is considerable private sector involvement in mining, oil, agriculture-related industries, utilities and telecommunications.

For convenience I shall divide the area into four:

- West Africa

- Central and East Africa

- Southern Africa

- South Africa.

WEST AFRICA

Benin, Burkina Faso, Cameroon, Chad, Gambia, Ghana, Guinea, Guinea Bissau, Ivory Coast, Liberia, Mali, Niger, Nigeria, Senegal, Sierra Leone, Togo

The best opportunities for British people tend to be in former British territories, and for the French in parts of what was French West Africa. However, a few British firms have operations in Francophone Africa, mostly in mining, oil and airport management.

The most likely place to find work opportunities is Nigeria. This is the most populous of the African states with some 100 million inhabitants, and it could be the wealthiest with shrewder management of its natural resources. In view of its importance a large number of foreign firms have investments or offices here.

The region has had its share of trouble spots in recent years, including Liberia and Sierra Leone. Others, such as Senegal and Ivory Coast, have proved remarkably stable, and Ghana has changed for the better in recent years. However, political tensions have a tendency to erupt with little warning.

The region has had its share of natural disasters, notably in the Sahel region where the desert is encroaching on the fertile areas. Care has to be taken over one's health, as malaria and other diseases are endemic to the region. The climate by the coast tends to be hot and sticky.

CENTRAL AND EAST AFRICA

Burundi, Central African Republic, Congo (both), Djibouti, Ethiopia, Gabon, Kenya, Rwanda, Somalia, Sudan (southern part), Tanzania, Uganda

This region has had its share of disasters in recent years. Burundi, Congo (Democratic Republic), Rwanda, Somalia and southern Sudan have been rent by political conflict which has greatly impaired development. Natural disasters such as drought and flooding have not made life any easier. Unhappily the best employment prospects lie with relief agencies which are coping with a never-ending refugee problem.

The situation has been looking brighter of late in Ethiopia and newly independent Eritrea, but there is the ever-present possibility that conflict will erupt again between these two countries.

Further south things look a good deal more promising. Kenya still has a substantial expatriate population (European and Indian) and has a number of successful industries, notably tourism. However, away from the main towns time has stood still: communications are poor and agriculture is at subsistence level.

Neighbouring Tanzania is lifting itself out of the economic doldrums of the post-independence era and opportunities will beckon there. Uganda has put the disastrous civil war behind it and is reconstructing fast. Aid and development agencies are very active here. The excellent climate is a further bonus.

SOUTHERN AFRICA

Angola, Botswana, Mozambique, Namibia, Zambia, Zimbabwe,

Zambia has a substantial expatriate workforce in the copper mining sector, though salaries tend to be below the international average for expatriates. Neighbouring Zimbabwe is far less attractive than it used to be. As a result of economic mismanagement and corruption the economy is in a dire state and an upturn is unlikely until the current leadership is replaced.

Botswana with its small population is rich in mineral deposits and has been one of the success stories of Africa, and Namibia seems to be following suit. Both countries have substantial expatriate populations who are engaged in mining and developing the countries' infrastructure.

The former Portuguese colonies of Angola and Mozambique are now rebuilding their economies after years of conflict. Angola is potentially one of the wealthiest countries in Black Africa, and there are already a number of British and other European people involved in its diamond-mining and oil sectors. However, political rivalries continue to simmer below the surface and could break out at any time.

Mozambique is the leading producer of cashew nuts and there is a substantial aid presence there. This is a country which after making good progress and putting its troubled past behind it, was devastated by large-scale flooding in 2000 which has set back economic development by several years.

SOUTH AFRICA

South Africa is the most developed country in Africa with a substantial European minority (mainly Afrikaaner and British) many of whom have lived there for several generations. It was once a popular destination for emigrants – in the same way that Australia and New Zealand were.

However, with the introduction of black majority rule things are changing, and the country is having to strike a careful balance between meeting the aspirations of its black population and retaining the skills of the white minority who, on the whole, enjoy a comfortable standard of living.

International firms no longer have fears that they will be blacklisted because of their involvement in the country and are starting to invest again. However, to improve the country's economic base the government needs to attract people with relevant skills from Europe and elsewhere – at least until it can train enough of the indigenous population to the required standards.

Away from the main centres South Africa is much like the rest of the continent with most of the rural population living at subsistence level or just above. Some of them are now drifting to the towns in search of work, and are blamed for the increase in crime that cities like Johannesburg are suffering.

On the whole, the new South Africa has got off to a good start and there are likely to be good job opportunities there for skilled people for the foreseeable future. However, the jobs are likely to be on contract rather than on a permanent basis.

THE CONTINENT AND ITS PEOPLE

Africa suffers from some of the worst problems of any part of the Third World. Poverty, disease, illiteracy, malnutrition and poor communications characterise many of the countries of the continent, and the situation is not helped by inept leadership, corruption in government and civil wars.

However, that is not the whole story. Since independence a number of countries have made progress on certain fronts (in raising standards of literacy, for example) and a new generation of more pragmatic African leaders is emerging keen to set their economies in order. There are grounds for hope that things will be better in the future.

It would be misleading to present an identikit picture of a typical African since there is considerable variation from country to country and also within countries. A person's outlook and behaviour is conditioned by a number of factors, including the following:

- *Tribal influence*. A person is obliged to help someone from the same tribe before anyone else and in the past tribal allegiance has tended to transcend nationalism.

- *Colonial influences*. The manners and attitudes of the educated élite of former French territories resemble – at least superficially – those of their former colonial masters, and in former British colonies the administration still tends to run along British lines. Some of these influences have tended to hamper rather than promote a country's development. Former British territories, for instance, have in the past produced more arts graduates than people with technical skills.

- *The country's leadership.* The attitudes and political philosophy of the person (or people) in power can have a profound influence on the people of a country. Leaders who exploit their positions to their own advantage or pursue unrealistic policies that cause stagnation, cause feelings of indifference or resignation at the grass roots.

- *The level of education.* Europeans often complain that Africans lack initiative and common sense. The reason for this is that many have received only a rudimentary education, or perhaps no education at all. However, educated Africans are usually able to hold their own with people of other nationalities.

- *Health considerations.* Health care is often developed in urban areas, but in the countryside doctors are scarce, and people can suffer from the most debilitating diseases which produce lethargy. Malaria and Yellow Fever are endemic in most countries and newer diseases, such as AIDS, have reached epidemic proportions in certain countries.

You will also need to come to terms with a differing concept of **time**. There is an absence of rush, and punctuality is not one of Africa's strong points. **Patience** and **resilience** are other characteristic features: Africans seem prepared to wait indefinitely and face up stoically to every eventuality.

African society tends to be **male-dominated**, though women play an important role in commerce and agriculture, particularly in countries like Nigeria. There are significant **minorities** – the Indians in Kenya and South Africa, the Lebanese in parts of West Africa – whose influence in the economy is disproportionate to their numbers.

Foreigners from more sophisticated countries have to learn to take the rough with the smooth. In some countries there may be shortages or a lack of availability of the most basic items. However, people who manage to adjust are usually beguiled by Africa and its peoples.

FURTHER INFORMATION

Major Companies of Africa South of the Sahara (Graham & Whiteside).
Africa and Asia Business Directory, Owen's World Trade, 18 Farndon

Road, Oxford OX2 6RT. Tel: (01865) 514378.

The Africans, D. Lamb (Vintage Books).

Braby's Commercial Directory of Southern Africa (PO Box 1426, Pinetown 3600, Natal, South Africa).

New Africa (IC Publications, London), journal.

Africa Business (IC Publications, London), journal.

New Africa Yearbook (IC Publications, London).

West Africa (West Africa Publishing Co, 43–45 Coldharbour Lane, London SE5 9NR. Tel: (020) 7737 2946).

African Economic Digest (Africa Concord, London).

Job Choices for Graduates in South Africa (Trotman).

South Africa News (Outbound Newspapers).

National Trade Index of South Africa (Intratex). Includes addresses of Chambers of Industries and Mines, Chambers of Commerce, Employers' Trade Associations, etc.

Directory of Scientific and Technical Societies in South Africa (South African Council for Scientific and Industrial Research).

Addresses

The Africa Book Centre, 1st Floor, 38 King Street, Covent Garden, London WC2E 8JT. Tel: (020) 7240 6649. Has a wide range of journals and books devoted to Africa.

School of Oriental & African Studies: see Useful Addresses in the UK.

African Studies Centre, Cambridge University, Free School Lane, Cambridge CB2 2RQ. Tel: (01223) 358381.

Centre for Southern African Studies, University of York, Heslington, York Y01 5DD. Tel: (01904) 459861.

Centre for West African Studies, University of Birmingham, PO Box 363, Birmingham B15 2TT. Tel: (0121) 472 1301.

Contact addresses for individual countries are listed in the Country Directory (Chapter 19).

14

North America

Canada and the USA have attracted settlers since the sixteenth century, and continue to do so. Yet the open door policy no longer applies and you can no longer turn up in either country and start looking for a job. Immigration restrictions mean that before you can enter them to take up employment you need to have an appropriate visa. This regulation applies even if you are only planning to do a vacation job.

Canada accepts around 200,000 permanent immigrants a year and the USA 675,000. Others gain entry to these countries on temporary visas. Most of these will be well-qualified people who will be an asset to the economy. If you lack such skills your chances of being accepted are not high. However, there are also opportunities for investors and entrepreneurs.

Before building up false hopes, you should acquaint yourself with the immigration regulations. This chapter gives a brief survey of them but does not address every eventuality. However, more specialist books and periodicals do, and there are plenty of immigration lawyers and consultants who can assist you for a fee.

CANADA

Canadians enjoy one of the highest standards of living in the world and the country accepts more immigrants per head of population than anywhere else in the world. It is an enormous country, second only to Russia, but the main centres of population are within 100 miles of the border with the USA.

In many respects it is a halfway house between the US and Britain (or France, in the case of Quebec), and although the bulk of Canada's commerce is with its much larger neighbour to the south, Canadians jealously guard their own identity. They tend to be more reserved than Americans.

Over a million UK nationals have emigrated there since the war and found it an easy place to settle in, though some have found the climate rather harsh. The Canadian High Commission in London issues between 9,000 and 10,000 immigration visas annually.

Perhaps as a consequence of the vast area – nearly 10 million square kilometres – the different provinces of Canada have each evolved a character of their own. British Columbia is British in character as well as in name. The province of Quebec – which includes Montreal – is more reminiscent of France and continental Europe. The prairie provinces bear similarities to their US counterparts across the border.

The most cosmopolitan place of all is Toronto with its extensive ethnic mix. People of all nationalities have landed here and it is home to one of the largest Italian communities in the world. Multiculturalism is a cornerstone of government policy and ethnic groups are encouraged to maintain their languages and traditions.

Canada is a country rich in natural resources. However, manufacturing and service industries are playing an increasingly important role in the economy now. The government is therefore keen to attract qualified people who can make a substantial contribution to the economy, particularly entrepreneurs, IT professionals and others with hi-tech skills. Around 60% of immigrants fall into these categories.

Immigration requirements
There are two methods of gaining entry to Canada if you intend to work there:

- Obtain work in advance from a Canadian employer who in turn obtains permission from his local employment centre to offer a post to a foreign national.

- Apply for an immigrant visa. It is not necessary to have secured a job offer before you go.

In order to determine eligibility for a visa, the Canadian Immigration Department assess people according to a points system based on the following criteria:

- education (16)

- knowledge of English/French (15)

- age (10)

- close relatives residing in Canada (5)

- occupational training (18)

- occupational demand (10)

- occupational experience (8)

- arranged employment (10)

- demographic factor (8)

- investor (45)

- personal suitability (10).

The figures in brackets denote the maximum number of points you can score in each category. The required number of points for an independent applicant is currently 70. Certain occupations are regarded as priority occupations and attract a higher number of points. The monthly *Canada News* publishes up-to-date lists.

If you have a relative in Canada, you will receive up to 5 bonus points. Similarly, if you contemplate investing in or setting up your own business in Canada, you will be allotted 45 bonus points towards the 70 you need. Although you will clearly need some cash to get started as an entrepreneur or self-employed person, no minimum amount of capital is required of you. The Entrepreneurial Development Officer of the Immigration Section will be able to supply details of the process.

Quebec assesses people according to slightly different criteria, and you should contact the Quebec Immigration Department for details.

Work opportunities

Toronto tends to attract the lion's share of immigrants followed by Montreal and Vancouver. Indeed, Southern Ontario can be regarded as the country's industrial heartland. However, other provinces are also keen to attract immigrants, including the more sparsely populated ones, such as Manitoba, New Brunswick and Saskatchewan.

To find out the range and type of jobs available it is worth subscribing to a jobs paper such as *Canadian Employment Weekly*. The monthly *Canada News* is also useful since it contains up-to-date news on Canada as well as a job section. Canada House in Trafalgar Square, London has a reading room where you can sit and read a number of leading Canadian newspapers, and so does British Columbia House nearby.

If you feel you need help either in your job search or in completing your visa application form, there are several migration consultants and lawyers who can help you – for a fee. Should you go up this avenue, it is essential to shop around to find the right person for you.

By all means go on holiday to Canada with a view to looking for suitable jobs. But remember that you must get a work visa from a Canadian diplomatic mission abroad before you can undertake paid employment.

Full-time students aged 18–30 wishing to work on a temporary basis in Canada should enquire about special student and youth work visas.

UNITED STATES OF AMERICA

The United States continues to be a magnet for immigrants from all over the world. But like Canada and other countries it limits the number of people entering the country to work and settle. Indeed if you enter the country without a visa and take up employment, you are regarded as an illegal immigrant and face deportation.

To avoid such an ignominious fate it is worth your while finding out about the immigration regulations. These are quite complex, and can only be treated very generally here. Other handbooks, such as *Getting a Job in America* (How To Books), go into much greater detail.

There is one bright spot. Citizens of the European Union and certain other countries no longer need an entry visa for a holiday or business trip lasting less than 90 days (under the Visa Waiver Pilot Programme). But if you plan to live and work in the United States (even just for a vacation job) you will certainly need one. Read on!

There are basically two types of visa:

- non-immigrant or temporary visas – which allow you to reside in the USA for a limited time and may tie you down to a particular job

- immigrant visas – which allow you to take up permanent residence.

Non-immigrant visas

There are a number of different categories, but the most common for a person taking up employment is the H category which is split into five sub-categories:

H-1A – for professional nurses
H-1B – for specialist occupations at graduate level or beyond
H-2A – for agricultural workers
H-2B – for workers in other categories
H-3 – for trainees.

To qualify for any kind of H visa you need to have a pre-arranged job, and in many cases the employer will have to demonstrate that he is unable to recruit suitably qualified people locally.

There are four other visas which are worth mentioning:

- J-1 – The Exchange Visitor Visa for people undertaking educational exchanges, vacation work or au pair work. To obtain your J-1 you need to approach a sponsoring organisation.

- L-1 – Intra Company Transfer Visa. This is for employees transferred by their companies to the US.

- E-1 – Treaty Trader Visa. This applies when you establish a company which trades between the USA and your home country.
- E-2 – Treaty Investor Visa. This is for foreign investors and their key employees.

Immigrant visas

These are for people who wish to live and/or work in the USA permanently or for an indefinite period and result in the issue of the so-called green card.

The number of immigrant visas issued each year in most categories is limited, but certain categories of immigrants are exempt from the numerical limitation (i.e. spouses of American citizens and parents of American citizens over the age of 21).

Full immigrant visas are issued on the basis of:

1. close family relationships

2. your profession or trade

3. other criteria (e.g. refugee status)

4. success in the visa lottery.

Item 4 needs some explanation. In recent years applicants from certain countries have been able to apply for Diversity Immigrant visas which are selected in random order. However, while people born in Ireland and certain other European countries have been eligible, people born in mainland Britain have been excluded. So for the moment English, Scottish and Welsh applicants are best advised to apply for temporary visas which they may be able to change to permanent ones at a later date.

You should note that immigration rules are subject to modification. The above is just a brief overview of the immigration regulations and does not deal with every eventuality.

Finding employment

The easiest way to get over the visa problem is to fix your job up in advance through a recruitment agency which is not based in the USA and is well versed in immigration procedures. There are also a number of consultants who can advise on job opportunities.

Another way is to surf the Internet. American employers and agencies are making considerable use of this facility to recruit staff. The only problem is that you will be competing head on with people who are already resident in the USA and the recruiters may be unsure of recruitment procedures.

Here are a few websites to start you off:

www.monster.com
www.vjf.com
www.espan.com
www.careerpath.com
www.direct-jobs.com
www.ajb.dni.us
www.adamsonline.com
www.jobsamerica.com
www.cweb.com

For names and addresses of specific companies you could visit your local business reference library. Some have US business and telephone directories, while smaller ones may have the more concise *International Fax Directory* (Jaeger & Waldman).

You could also try accessing the websites of states you are interested in working in. These often list local recruitment organisations.

Getting to know the Americans

British people who expect the American way of life to be exactly the same as their own may be in for a shock.

Here are some of the differences:

- *Americans are workaholics.* They are keen to get on and take fewer holidays than Europeans.

- *They express enthusiasm* for what they are doing and for the organisation they work for. Sometimes these enthusiasms are superficial.

- *They are less status conscious.* It is what you have achieved not who you are that is important.

- *Theirs is an acquisitive society* where success is usually measured by how much you earn.

- *They are self-confident* and good at selling themselves.

- *There is a strong conformist element in the USA.* People are expected to act and think American.

- *Americans tend to be restless people*, impatient to get on with things. In discussions they don't like to beat about the bush.

- *They tend to be more spontaneous*, open and optimistic than British people.

- *There is possibly less of a social conscience* in the USA, with little sympathy for the underdog.

The USA is an enormous place, and there are considerable differences between the people on the eastern seaboard and the southern states – who may seem more European in outlook – and those of California and the Mid-West.

In the past there has been a considerable brain drain from Europe to the United States. There are still plenty of opportunities for the well-qualified, but the door is not as open as it was in the past.

FURTHER INFORMATION

Canada

Canada News (Outbound Newspapers Ltd). This contains up-to-date news of interest to prospective immigrants and includes a list of the priority occupations.

How to Emigrate, Roger Jones (How To Books).

Live and Work in Canada, Avril Harper (Grant Dawson).

Finding a Job in Canada, Valerie Gerrard (How To Books).

Getting into Canada, Martin Bjarnason (How To Books).

Culture Shock Canada, Robert Barlas and Pan Guek-Chen (Kuperard/Times Editions).

Canada Employment Weekly (15 Madison Avenue, Toronto M5R 2S2. Tel: 001 416 964 6069. Fax: 001 416 964 3202. www.mediacorp2.com).

The Career Bookstore offers a mail order book service in conjunction with *Canada Employment Weekly* and distributes a number of relevant titles (e.g. *Canadian Directory of Search Firms*, *Who's Hiring*, *The Career Directory*, *Canada's Best Careers Guide*).

USA

Getting a Job in America, Roger Jones (How To Books).

Living & Working in America, Steve Mills (How To Books).

Culture Shock: USA, Esther Wanning (Kuperard/Times Editions).

Going USA (Outbound Newspapers Ltd). Monthly newspaper for migrants and visitors.

For a more extensive bibliography please consult *Getting a Job in America* (How To Books).

Please refer also to the Canada and USA entries in the Country Directory (Chapter 19).

15

Latin America and the Caribbean

A diversity of countries are represented here from small island states to the giant of the South American continent, Brazil. Some remain heavily dependent on aid while others have reasonably successful economies. Though the region is not a big employer of expatriate labour, opportunities do exist for people who are prepared to seek them out.

CENTRAL AND SOUTH AMERICA

Apart from a few enclaves colonised by the British, Dutch and French, the whole of the land mass from Mexico southwards has come under Spanish or Portuguese influence, and the influences are still very much in evidence today in the form of religion (overwhelmingly Roman Catholic), language, institutions and attitudes.

Latin America is often perceived as a troubled region, burdened by debt, overwhelmed by inflation, beset by instability, where poverty and social injustice are the order of the day. This is something of a caricature. Dictatorships are now few and far between, although it has to be admitted that parts of the region face economic problems.

The people of Latin America

Generally speaking, Latin Americans are easy-going people who welcome contact with expatriates. A knowledge of Spanish (Portuguese in the case of Brazil) is, however, vital for every expatriate.

Argentina, Paraguay and Costa Rica are reckoned to be the most European of all the countries of Latin America. Brazil, on the other hand, has a considerable ethnic mix: 55 per cent white, 37 per cent of mixed descent (European/black/Indian), 6 per cent black and 2 per cent native Indians. In the Andean states there is a much higher proportion of Andean Indians in the population.

South Americans take pride in their personal appearance and like to dress smartly, whether or not they can afford it. Family life and personal relationships are very important to them, and take precedence over most other matters.

Punctuality is not a Latin American strong point and you are wise to adopt a more relaxed attitude to time. People relish compliments and praise, but personal criticism should be avoided – especially in public – being regarded as rude and offensive. When speaking to people you should remember to maintain eye contact.

There are certain matters that people find distasteful. In some countries there is a wide chasm between the rich and the poor that people seem to accept rather than endeavour to alter. There is also the Latin American male machismo attitude that women can find trying at first until they learn to live with it.

On the whole, however, Europeans enjoy postings to the region and experience few problems of adaptation.

The opportunities

In the past British expatriates helped develop the infrastructure of the region, building railways and developing the banking system, for example. Nowadays they are more likely to be involved in the aid and education sectors. The multinational companies operating in the region are more likely to recruit their expatriate staff from the USA, while relying for the most part on local expertise.

It is advantageous to have connections with a particular country. Robert Herin of Egon Zehnder cites the case of Brazil: 'Today the far rarer expatriate is likely to be a non-Brazilian who has joined his present employer while overseas and has well-established roots in Brazil.' Fluency in Spanish or Portuguese is also a prerequisite: this region cannot really be regarded as part of the English-speaking world.

One organisation which deserves to be mentioned in connection with employment opportunities is the **International Organisation for Migration** (IOM) in Geneva. One of the Organisation's aims is to facilitate the transfer of suitably qualified people who wish to work or settle in Latin America and who would be able to assist in the development of particular countries in such areas as industry, the economy and education.

The IOM offices in Europe carry out the selection of the professionals and assist them in their transfer in the following ways:

- providing information on the country in question

- obtaining the necessary entry visa

- defraying part of the travel cost from Europe to the country of destination

- providing orientation and special assistance on arrival

- offering a special insurance scheme, if desired.

There is a wide range of jobs on offer with governments and government-funded bodies, e.g. forest engineers, lecturers in international finance, chemical engineers, civil engineers, odontologists, etc.

THE CARIBBEAN

'There are few regions in the world where history has been so critical in shaping the present as in the Caribbean,' writes Tony Thorndike in *The Caribbean Handbook*. The key to understanding Caribbean history is slavery and the forced transportation to the region of multitudes of peoples from Africa, and to a lesser extent from Asia and even Europe. Barely a trace remains of original population: they were either killed off or absorbed. But neither is there much trace of African cultures.

Of the countries that make up the area, 17 are independent, 6 are British colonies, 3 are French dependencies, 2 are Dutch dependencies, and 2 are in association with the USA. The largest is Cuba with a population of 10 million; the smallest is Anguilla with its 7,000 people. The total population of the area is in excess of 30 million.

The largest countries of the region are Cuba and the Dominican Republic (Spanish speaking) and Haiti (French speaking). Cuba's population alone is double that of the islands colonised by Britain. However, the best opportunities for British people undoubtedly lie in the latter.

Many of these countries are slowly diversifying their economies away from primary products (such as bananas, sugar and minerals) into agro-processing, tourism, manufacturing for export, and services. One of the growth sectors for expatriate employment in recent years has been offshore financial services, notably in the Cayman Islands, British Virgin Islands, Turks and Caicos, and Bermuda.

Although they are on the mainland, Belize and Guyana share much of the legacy of the English-speaking islands of the Caribbean.

Many of the expatriates working in the Caribbean have been there for some time – a testimony to the attractions of the area: a good climate, friendly people and a relaxed life-style. However, the picture is not completely rosy, and there are pockets of poverty and deprivation throughout the area.

THE FALKLANDS

This group of islands off the Argentinian coastline sprang to prominence during the Falklands War in the 1980s. But for that conflict, they might have remained forgotten. Because of it the Falklands is beginning to develop its infrastructure. There is still a considerable military presence on the islands, and there are plans to develop the natural resources of the area, notably oil. Watch out for opportunities here.

FINDING JOBS

While you can try visiting some of these countries on spec, the best idea is to try to fix up a job in advance. A few of the organisations mentioned in the Recruitment Directory (Chapter 18) recruit for this part of the world, and you can get tips on how to go about it in Latin America from the library of the Hispano and Luso-Brazilian Council.

FURTHER INFORMATION

Major Companies of Argentina, Brazil, Mexico and Venezuela, S. J. Longrigg (Graham & Whiteside).

Hoover's Masterlist of Major Latin American Companies (Reference Press Inc, Texas).

Travellers' World Guides: South America, Mexico and Central America, The Caribbean Islands (Travel & Trade Publications).

Latin America Weekly Report (Latin America Newsletters, 61 Old Street, London EC1V 9HS. Tel: (020) 7251 0012

Latin America News (Latin America Trade Advisory Group, 2 Belgrave Square, London SW1X 8PJ).

Live and Work in Central America, Avril Harper (Grant Dawson).

The Caribbean Handbook (Financial Times Caribbean, PO Box 1037, St John's, Antigua).

Caribbean Business Directory (Caribbean Publishing Co, Box 1365, Grand Cayman, BWI).

Caribbean Basin Profile (Caribbean Publishing Co).

How to Live in the Caribbean, Sidney Hunt (Macmillan).

Addresses

Hispano & Luso-Brazilian Council, Canning House, 2 Belgrave Square, London SW1X 8PJ. Tel: (020) 7235 2303. Has a library of some 50,000 books on Iberian and Latin American affairs which is open to the public. Although it does not hold newspapers it has a special collection of background economic and trade information of interest to businesspeople and possibly job-seekers.

Latin American Bureau, 1 Amwell Street, London EC1R 1UL. Tel: (020) 7278 2827. An independent, non-profit-making research and publishing organisation founded and supported by church and development agencies. Has an extensive library/resource centre devoted to Latin America and the Caribbean. The library's opening hours are variable so it is advisable to check over the phone before making a visit.

Anglo-Central American Association, 30 Great Bounds Drive, Tunbridge Wells TN4 0GTR. Tel: (01892) 528993.

Centre for Latin American Studies, University of Cambridge, West Road, Cambridge CB3 9EF.

Latin American Centre, University of Essex, Wivenhoe Park, Colchester CO4 3SQ.

Centre for Caribbean Studies, University of Warwick, Coventry CV4 7AL.

West India Committee, 8/9 Northumberland Street, London WC2A 5RA. Tel: (020) 7976 1493.

Contact addresses for individual countries are listed in the Country Directory (Chapter 19).

16

Australasia and the Pacific

Australia and New Zealand have always been popular destinations for British migrants. However, the days of assisted passages, when these countries were crying out for immigrants, are long since past. Nowadays both countries have restricted immigration policies. Foreign nationals are still welcome on a short-term or permanent basis, but only if they have skills the country needs.

What skills are these? It is difficult to generalise, since the situation does not remain static. Currently New Zealand faces a shortage of secondary school teachers, and visas for people in this category are fairly easy to come by. But these countries tend to be self-sufficient in most skills and no longer have to import expertise from abroad.

Like Canada both countries assess potential immigrants using a points test, and you need to achieve a minimum score in order to qualify for a visa. Good qualifications and relevant skills are important, and without them you stand very little chance unless you also happen to be a large investor.

AUSTRALIA

Australia is fast becoming a favourite destination for young people who go off to take up temporary jobs there in much the same way that young Aussies descend on London. For these there is casual work to be had in the catering trade at vacation time and on farms at harvest time – in the middle of the British winter. For permanent employment, however, you will need to possess appropriate skills.

The stereotypical image of an Australian is of a rough, tough, unpretentious, beer-swilling pioneering type. But over the years the image has softened, and although you may still come across such characters in the outback, the majority of Australians are sophisticated urban dwellers.

The country has grown in self-confidence over the past two decades. Australian films and soap operas are shown throughout the world; Australian wines are gaining a considerable reputation; and Australian personalities – from Germaine Greer to Rolf Harris and Barry Humphries – have given the country a high profile.

While New South Wales is the most popular destination for immigrants, increasing numbers of British people are settling in Western Australia also. Prospects look good in South Australia which is actively encouraging immigrants.

When unemployment levels rose a few years ago, the Australian Government reduced immigration quotas and brought in stricter eligibility requirements. Now the economy is buoyant again and employers have been pressing the government to let more skilled people into the country to ensure future economic growth. As a result, professionals whose skills are in greatest demand now benefit from faster processing times and net annual immigration is currently well over the 100,000 mark. To determine your eligibility for either temporary or permanent residence you need to be aware of immigration restrictions and, if neccessary, seek help and advice.

Non-immigrant visas

Visas are now required even for business or recreational trips. If you intend to take up employment you need to be sponsored by an employer in Australia who has to get permission from the authorities. There are various categories:

- Exchange – participants in bi-lateral staff exchange schemes.

- Independent executive – anyone planning to establish a new business under the Business Migration Programme.

- Executive – senior manager.

- Specialist – highly skilled workers offering skills in short supply in Australia.

Working Holidays

Young people aged 18–25 can apply for a Working Holiday visa valid for 13 months which enables them to travel and take up casual work to finance their trip. No sponsorship is needed, the duration of each job should not normally exceed 3 months, and applicants must have sufficient funds to tide them over the first weeks and to purchase a return ticket (if they do not have one on arrival).

Jobs lasting between 4 months and 4 years

- You must be sponsored (preferably by the prospective Australian employer).

- You must offer skills which are in short supply in Australia.

- You cannot be recruited to fill an unskilled, semi-skilled or part-time post.

- You must meet certain character and health requirements.

Permanent migration

If you wish to take up permanent residence in Australia you need to work out which category you qualify for. For most categories you will be assessed according to a points test which will determine your eligibility. The pass mark tends to be adjusted from time to time, but the criteria have tended to be fairly constant. Youth and good qualifications are a definite advantage. Publications, such as *Australian News*, contain up-to-date information on how the points are allotted.

There are three main categories:

1. Preferential Category
If you are sponsored by a spouse, fiancé, dependent relative or parent (provided you are under 18), you do not need to pass the points test.

2. General Skilled Migration

- Independent category. This is for highly skilled people and unless nominated by a state or territory you will need to pass the points test.

- Skill matching category. This is for skilled independent applicants who do not pass the points test but whose skills cannot be supplied by the local labour market. Your details are placed on a skill matching database which is circulated to regional certifying bodies and governments.

- Family sponsored.

3. Business Visas

- Employer sponsored migration.

- Business skills migration. There are three categories under this heading: Business Owner; Senior Executive and Investment Linked. All are subject to a points test and applications must be sent to the Perth Business Skills Processing Centre.

Other information

In order to practise your trade or profession in Australia, you may well have your competence assessed by the Commission on Overseas Professional Qualifications. The Australian High Commission/Embassy should be able to advise on this.

There are a number of recruitment agencies based in London which recruit for Australia and should be able to facilitate the acquisition of a visa. If you need help or advice you could contact some of the consultancies which can assist you in filling out your visa application form and outline the job opportunities Down Under.

If you are on holiday in Australia you could contact a few private recruitment agencies. The government-run Commonwealth Employment Service handles job vacancies at all levels and most cities have Careers Reference Centres, which are careers libraries.

Finally, the monthly newspapers *Australian News* (Outbound) and *Australian Outlook* (Consyl) are essential reading for intending migrants and visitors.

NEW ZEALAND

The climate of New Zealand is similar to that of the UK, but the pace of life is slower and the country is relatively sparsely populated. Some newcomers find the country something of a backwater where nothing ever happens. Others are reminded of Britain as it used to be a few decades back.

However, New Zealand is a relatively prosperous country with a well-developed welfare state. New Zealanders tend to be more 'British' than the Australians and many families still have close connections with the UK.

The government is keen to import expertise from abroad, so there are certainly opportunities here for expatriates with the right kind of skills. They include teachers, academics, doctors, nurses, engineers, scientists and technicians. In recent years the target immigration quota has been 35,000 annually.

While it is possible for a British passport-holder to visit New Zealand for up to six months without the need for a visa for business or vacation purposes, you cannot take up employment – except perhaps on a casual basis, in which case you would need to apply for a work permit when you get to New Zealand.

Immigration formalities

If you have made arrangements to take up a job you must apply for a work visa, which is more than just a formality. New Zealand no longer has an open door policy on immigration.

There are four main immigration categories:

1. General Skills Category

Applicants are assessed according to a points system which takes into account:

- qualifications – up to 15 points for a postgraduate degree

- work experience – maximum of 10 points

- age – the younger the better; the age limit is 55

- settlement factors (funds, sponsorship, investment funds, employment offer).

In recent years around 40% of migrants have been in this category.

2. Business Categories

- Investor – assessed according to a points system.

- Entrepreneur – if you have successfully established a business in New Zealand for a period of two years. (A long-term Business Visa is also available if you do not meet these criteria.)

- Employee of business locating to New Zealand.

3. Family Category

For people with close relatives in New Zealand.

4. Family Quota Category

This involves sponsorship by a relation in New Zealand.

In addition New Zealand grants a limited number of work visas to under-30s with no dependants to enable them to undertake working holidays in the country.

For further details you should contact the New Zealand Immigration Service which in London is based at New Zealand House. The Service publishes a number of leaflets on life in New Zealand and can provide an up-to-date occupational priority list.

Finding work

The Saturday editions of New Zealand newspapers are a particularly good source of job vacancies. The leading paper in the country is the *New Zealand Herald* represented in London by New Zealand Associated Press, 107 Fleet Street, London EC4A 2AN. Or you could take out a subscription to *News New Zealand*.

The Employment Service of the Department of Labour provides a comprehensive job placement service and has branches at 50 locations throughout the country. However, it is unable to assist applicants from overseas.

Relatively few agencies based in London recruit for New Zealand, one exception being Ranfurly Johnston Mackey. However, there are several migration consultants in Britain and elsewhere who can assist you in your search and advise on immigration matters.

THE PACIFIC

The Pacific covers a vast area but is sparsely populated. Many of the island countries in this region are small and dependent on aid. The opportunities tend to be in government service (recruited by Crown Agents or DFID) or with voluntary organisations. There are mining interests on a few of the islands.

The Pacific Islanders have the reputation of being easy-going, friendly people. English – or rather Pidgin English – is the lingua franca on a number of the islands which can often boast a profusion of languages and dialects. On the Solomon Islands, for instance, there are no fewer than 60 languages and dialects amongst a population of 25,000.

On some of the smaller islands facilities tend to be somewhat restricted, and residents have to rely very much on their own resources. The native population is Melanesian or Polynesian, but in some of the larger centres there is a substantial Indian, European and Chinese presence.

Australia has close ties with Papua New Guinea and should be a good place to explore job prospects from. Meanwhile New Zealand could be a good starting-off point for the Polynesian islands.

FURTHER INFORMATION

Australia

Job Guide for . . . (State) (Department of Employment and Industrial Relations/Australian Government Publishing Service).

Australian Graduate Opportunities (Trotman).

Jobson's Year Book of Public Companies (Dun & Bradstreet International).

Directory of Australian Associations (Information Australia Group, 45 Flinders House, Melbourne, Victoria 3000).

Oz Weekly Newsletter (Oz-Link UK, Higher Elstone Cottage, Chumleigh, Devon EX18 7DB. Tel: 01769 581225. Fax: 01769 580318). Jobs, business and investment opportunities.

How To Emigrate, Roger Jones (How To Books).

Living & Working in Australia, Laura Veltman (How To Books).

New Zealand

The New Zealand Business Who's Who (Fourth Estate Holdings Ltd).

The Public Service Official Circular advertises details of all public service jobs.

The Education Gazette publishes details of all teaching jobs.

Other jobs are advertised in the newspapers particularly on Wednesdays and Saturdays.

New Zealand News UK (Commonwealth Publishing).

New Zealand Outlook (Consyl Publishing).

Destination New Zealand (Outbound Newspapers). Contains jobs vacancies.

News New Zealand (PO Box 247, Tauranga, NZ. Tel. 0064 757 64147; Fax: 0064 757 63050; E-mail: margord@voyager.co.nz). Subscription newpaper containing employment pages of NZ newspapers.

Pacific

Pacific Island Business & Trade Directory (Universal Business Directories Ltd, New Zealand News Centre, 360 Dominion Road, Auckland 3, New Zealand).

Pacific Islands Monthly (Fiji Times, 20 Gordon Street, Suva – UK distributor: F. A. Smyth & Associates, 23 Aylmer Parade, London N2).

Addresses (Pacific)

Pacific Islands Chamber of Commerce, 12 Bulstrode Street, London W1M 5FR. Tel: (020) 7487 5794.

Pacific Island Society, 2 Elm Walk, Raynes Park, London SW20 9ED. Tel: (020) 8544 1370.

Contact addresses for individual countries are listed in the Country Directory (Chapter 19).

PART SIX: REFERENCE

17

Job Opportunities by Profession

The information on the following pages serves a dual purpose:

- To give an overview of the opportunities to practise your chosen vocation abroad.
- To provide contacts (periodicals, recruitment organisations, employers, etc) which deal with your particular specialism. Where no address is given you will find full details of individual recruitment organisations in the Recruitment Directory following this chapter.

ACCOUNTANCY

Qualified accountants are in demand in virtually every sector of commerce and industry and in the public sector, too. International accountancy firms, such as Ernst & Whinney, PricewaterhouseCooper and KPMG have offices in most major capitals of the world.

The Institute of Chartered Accountants operates an appointments service exclusively for its members (Chartac Recruitment Services), and some of the appointments are overseas ones. Opportunities for newly qualified Chartered Accountants are primarily from the public practice sector, principal locations being Europe, Australasia, Africa, the Caribbean and Bermuda and the Middle East.

For more experienced members seeking commercial positions, occasional instructions are received from a variety of sources, including multinationals needing staff for their overseas operations.

Recruitment:
ACORD, AIESEC, Chartac, Financial Recruitment International, Grafton, Medecins sans Frontieres, NPA, Offshore Specialist Appointments, OPU, Robert Walters, TMP.

Reference:
Accountancy, ICA Journal.
Accounting Jobs Worldwide (Vacation Work).

AGRICULTURE & RURAL DEVELOPMENT

The main opportunities these days tend to be in the Third World, as the governments of these countries seek to become self-sufficient in food production. This means that most of the jobs are on contract terms – often with organisations such as the Department for International Development, Crown Agents, the volunteer agencies, international aid organisations and FAO (See UN entry).

For young agriculturalists and horticulturalists in search of work experience overseas there are exchange schemes based at the National Agricultural Centre, Kenilworth, Warwickshire CV8 2LG.

Recruitment:
Agriventure AIEA, ATD, DFID, Gap Challenge, Gorkha, ICD, IVS, Oxfam, VSO.

Reference:
Opportunities in Agriculture and Development (Agraria Press, Yew Tree House, Horne, Horley, Surrey RG6 9JP. Telephone: (01342) 843173.)

AU PAIRS, NANNIES, GOVERNESSES

Nannies/governesses have usually received some kind of training and are usually expected to have Nursery Nurse Examination Board (NNEB) certificate or equivalent. They usually live in and can expect a full salary. For further information contact the Professional Association of Nursery Nurses, St James' Court, 99 Friar Gate, Derby DE1 1EZ or the National Association of Certified Nursery Nurses, 162 Langdale Road, Thornton Heath, Surrey CR4 7PR.

Au pairs are in a different category. While usually qualified to A Level, they are not professionally qualified. Normally they are required to look after children and perform light household tasks. They are treated as a member of the family and receive pocket money rather than a salary.

Au pairing is perceived as an educational experience rather than as a job, and as such it is relatively easy to obtain a work permit, if this is required. There are au pair agencies throughout the country, and your search might start in your local *Yellow Pages*.

Recruitment:
Au Pair in America, Edgware Au Pair Agency, Norfolk Care Search Agency, Solihull Au Pair Agency. See Chapter 18.
Others include:
Academy Au Pair Agency, 42 Cedarhurst Drive, Eltham, London SE9 5LP.
Helping Hands Au Pair & Domestic Agency, 39 Rutland Avenue, Thorpe Bay, Southend on Sea, Essex.
Imperial Nannies, 222 Old Brompton Road, London SW5 0BZ.
Jolaine Au Pair & Domestic Agency, 18 Escot Way, Barnet, Herts EN5 3AN.

Reference:
The Au Pair and Nanny's Guide, S. Griffith & S. Legg (Vacation Work Publications).

AVIATION

Engineers and technicians are needed not only for the manufacture of aeroplanes but also for their maintenance at airports and other extablishments around the world. Experts are also needed to run airports and other aircraft installations. Boeing and other US aircraft manufacturers advertise vacancies on a regular basis.

Recruitment:
British Aerospace, Butler, CDI-Anders, Lineup Aviation Personnel, Modis, Morson, Nestor, OPU, ORS, TMP, Top Choice.

BANKING

A number of High Street banks have operations abroad, such as Barclays in Spain. But the best plan might be to gain experience of banking in this country and then approach a bank – or division of a bank – the majority of whose branches are overseas, such as:

Standard Chartered Bank, 1 Aldermanbury Square, London EC2V 7SB.
HSBC Bank Middle East, 29 Hill Street, London W1X 7FD.

There are also opportunities with foreign banks and with merchant (or investment) banks, and – in the aid sector – to offer specialist advice and services to national banks. Opportunities have also been created with the establishment of the European Central Bank in Frankfurt.

Recruitment:
AIESEC, Crown Agents, Financial Recruitment International, Grafton, Nestor, Offshore Specialist Appointwents, OPU, TMP, Robert Walters.

Reference:
International Bankers' Directory (Financial Publishing Group, 43 Hamilton Street, Chester CH2 3JQ. Tel: (0244) 316879).
The Bankers Almanac and Yearbook (Reed Publishing Group).

Addresses:
Foreign Banks and Securities Houses Association, 6 Laurence Pountney Lane, London EC4R 0EE.

COMMUNICATIONS

The communications business – telecommunications, radio communications, satellite communications – is buoyant these days, particularly with the rapid development of cellular phones networks, and if you join one of the large mobile phone firms, such as Vodaphone Airtouch, there may well be opportunitiess to travel. There are also a number of firms in the field that specialise in the installation and maintenance of these systems.

Expatriate expertise is needed especially for projects in Third World countries that are often developing nationwide communications systems for the first time. (See Construction).

Recruitment:
Beechwood, Butler, CDI-Anders, Daulton, Dexton, Executive Recruitment Services, Forsyth, Hays IT, Modis, OPU, Prima, Professional Management Resources, TMP.

COMPUTERS/INFORMATION TECHNOLOGY

The IT industry has expanded at an unprecedented rate over the past two decades, and the number of competent professionals in this field has not kept pace with demand. So if you are a qualified and experienced computer programmer, systems analyst, systems designer or computer engineer you have some eminently marketable skills and can be quite choosy as to where you work.

To get an idea of where the opportunities lie, look through the vacancy columns of specialist journals such as *Computer Weekly, Computing, Computer Talk, Electronics Express, Freelance Informer.*

For a long-term career in computing with plenty of opportunities for assignments or postings abroad you could approach one of the leading computer firms which advertise regularly in the trade papers and nationals. For IT jobs in Asia and Australasia there are a number of useful websites, eg www.jobnet.com.au.

Recruitment:
ABB-Lutech, AIESEC, Anglo-Arabian, Arabian Careers, James Baker Associates, BDS, Beechwood, Butler, CDI-Anders, Compuware, Computing Resource Centre, Daulton, Delton, FM Recruitment, Forsyth, Grafton, Jenrick, Hays IT, Modis, MRK, Nestor, Network Overseas, OCC, OPU, Prima, Just Engineers, Randall Massey, Track International, TRC, Robert Walters, Woodland.

Reference:
Computer Weekly, Computing, Computer Talk, Electronics Express, Freelance Informer.

CONSERVATION

There is a growing number of conservation projects in different parts of the world, and the main recruiters tend to be voluntary agencies. Some of the projects are short and would appeal to people wishing to spend their vacations usefully and also Gap Year students.

BCTV, Concern, Concordia, Coral Cay, DFID, Earthwatch, Frontier, Gap Activities, Gap Challenge, Gorkha, ICD, i to i, IVS, Project Trust, Student Partnership Worldwide, Teaching & Projects Abroad, VSO.

CONSTRUCTION

A large construction project requires people with a variety of skills: site managers, site engineers, plant engineers, electricians, quantity surveyors, structural engineers, store managers, finance personnel, personnel managers, catering staff, procurement officers, and so on.

According to Expats International, many of whose members get jobs in the construction industry, staff turnover on construction projects is high – as much as 100% over a period of 15 months. There are several reasons for this:

- Recruits are ill-prepared for the environment in which they will be operating, which could be a camp miles from anywhere.

- The jobs tend to be bachelor status posts. Construction camps do not have facilities for many dependents – and some people dislike prolonged separation from their partners.

● Some camps suffer from poor facilities, bad management and poor working relationships. 'A lot depends on the personality of the site/project manager,' comments Keith Edmonds of Expats International. In *The Expat's Cartoon Book* (Expats International) the site manager is depicted as halfway between a prison governor and Attila the Hun, but perhaps he has to be.

Working in construction means leading an itinerant life, but many grow accustomed to it moving on to another project when the one they are working on comes to an end. Some projects are short-term; others can last for years – the construction of a port or an oil refinery, for instance.

It is an industry which is sensitive to economic change. In the seventies and early eighties the Arabian peninsula was an an El Dorado for construction companies. But these countries have been hit by a decline in the oil price and as a consequence there are fewer construction projects. Profit margins for construction companies have grown tighter and companies are tending to recruit supervisory staff and skilled workers from Asia who are cheaper to employ.

However opportunities have opened up elsewhere, notably in Central Asia where countries are keen to build up their infrastructures. Opportunities also exist for craftsmen throughout Europe, notably Germany and Eastern Europe which is experiencing a construction boom. In Asia the gloomy economic prospects have brought construction projects to a halt.

Recruitment:
Anders Glaser Wills, Anglo-Arabian, BDS, Beechwood, Beresford, Brunel Energy, CDI-Anders, Daulton, Delton, Dexton, G & T, Peter Glaser, Grafton, Grove Personnel, Harrison Jones, Heston, Hill McGlynn, International Staffing Europe, Just Engineers, KMS, LA, Malla, Morgan Bryant, Morson, NES, Network Overseas, OPU, Premier Personnel, Prima, Professional Management Resources, Rosta, RSL, RW, Sherry Sherratt, Sherwood, Stepp. TA Group, Taylor Recruitment, Top Choice, TTI, Woodland.

Alternatively you could approach a construction firm direct specifying your interest in working abroad. Among the leading British construction firms that operate abroad are:

Balfour Beatty, 7 Mayday Road, Thornton Heath, CR7 7XA.
Kier, Tempsford Hall, Sandy, Beds SG19 2BD.
Taylor Woodrow International, 345 Ruislip Rd, Southall, Middlesex UB1 2QX.

John Laing Construction, Page Street, Mill Hill, London NW7 2ER.
Mowlem International, Foundation House, Eastern Road, Bracknell, Berks RG12 2UZ.
Carillion International, Construction House, Birch Street, Wolverhampton WV1 4HY.
Costain Group, 111 Westminster Bridge Road, London SE1 7UE.
ARC Construction Ltd, Sutton Courtenay, Abingdon, Oxon OX14 4PD.
George Wimpey International, 3 Shortlands Grove, London W6 7EN.

CONSULTANCY

There is a continuing demand for consultants in a variety of areas such as agriculture, architecture, economics, engineering, finance, health, leisure, management, planning, rural development, transport, etc. Opportunities exist in both the private and public sector, with international organisations and governments. In recent years there have been several interesting opportunities in Eastern Europe and Central Asia as well as in the Third World. *The Economist* usually has a number of consultancy vacancies in each issue and if you have considerable experience in this field it is worthwhile making your name known to the Department for International Development, Scottish Development Overseas and various development agencies.

Some of the best known consultancy firms are those of consulting engineers, such as:

The Ove Arup Partnership, 8 Fitzroy Street, London W1P 6BQ.
Halcrow, Burderop Park, Swindon SN4 0QD.
Sir Owen Williams International, Hagley Road, Birmingham B16 8NH.

Management consultancy is an expanding sector at present with a number of multi-national groups – often the offshoots of accountancy firms – catering for a range of multi-national clients. However, some consultants work on a self-employed basis, or find jobs as advisers to governments or government organisations – often in the Third World.

Addresses:
The British Consultants Bureau, 1 Westminster Palace Gardens, 1-7 Artillery Row, London SW1P 1RJ publishes an extensive handbook of around 500 UK based consultancy firms that operate internationally. Website: www. brbforum.demon.co.uk.
Association of Consulting Engineers, Alliance House, Caxton Street, London SW1H 0QL.
Management Consultancies Association, 11 West Halkin Street, London SW1 8JZ.

DIPLOMACY

Diplomatic Service

The role of British Diplomatic Service is to promote the national interests of the United Kingdom and to contribute to a strong world community. To achieve this the UK has 224 diplomatic posts in 184 countries. Its personnel spend between one half and two thirds of their careers posted abroad at:

● embasssies (called high commissions in Commonwealth countries)

● consulates

● missions to international organisations.

Embassies/high commissions are headed by an ambassador (high commissioner) supported by the deputy head of mission. Posts are divided into sections:

● Consular section: This processes and issues passports, visas, and is involved in helping and advising UK nationals abroad.

● Chancery section: This monitors the political, economic and social developments in the host country, liaising between London and the host government. In some places this would also include the policy and administration of British aid.

● Commercial section: This promotes British commercial interests abroad, advises British exporters and investors and encourages direct investment in Britain.

● Information section: This section promotes and explains British policy abroad presenting a positive image of Britain.

● Administration section: This section looks after the day to day running of the post, its budgets and facilities as well as the welfare of its staff.

The work of the diplomatic service is varied and challenging, but deeply rewarding. The opportunities to travel and experience other cultures are fascinating and life-enriching. But it can be tough. Diplomats may be posted to Rome, Paris and Washington, but they also have to serve in Rwanda, Sierra Leone and Angola, which are not always easy places to live. But to compensate for these difficulties the FCO looks after its employees well. Although staff are subjected to UK income tax, they sometimes receive overseas allowances, particularly in the more difficult posts, and also free accommodation during their posting abroad.

Staff need to regard their duties as a way of life rather than just a job, since they may be required to attend functions at any hour of the day.

There are a three entry levels into the Diplomatic Service.

- Policy entry: Officers in the policy grade help to formulate policy on political, commercial and economic matters. Applicants must be graduates with a second class honours degree or higher.

- Operational entry: Officers at this level are involved in a wider range of tasks including trade promotion, consular, immigration and information word. Academic qualifications to apply for this grade are 5 GCSEs (or equivalent) and 5 years' work experience OR 2 A Levels and 3 years' work experience OR a degree plus relevant life experiences.

- Executive assistance branch: Executive assistants essentially support the work of other officers, providing administrative back-up. They are also responsible for the registry and communications systems at post and may also help in immigration work and accounts. There are no academic qualification requirements, but applicants must have 2 years' work experience in an office environment and a minimum typing speed of 30 wpm.

Promotion at all levels is based on merit.

Further information and application forms are available from the Recruitment Section, 1 Palace Street, London London SW1H 5HE. Tel: (020) 7238 4265.
Website: www.fco.gov.uk.
E-mail: pmd.fco@gtnet.gov.uk.

The British Council
The British Council might well be seen as the cultural wing of the Foreign and Commonwealth Office, although it prides itself on its independence. Originally set up in the 1930s the Council is involved in 'promoting a wider knowledge of our United Kingdom and the English Language abroad and developing closer cultural relations with other countries'. It achieves this though its network of libraries, its scholarship programme, the promotion of cultural events, its language institutes and its educational advisory services. It also assists ODA administer the Government's aid programme.

In addition to recruiting contract staff the Council has a permanent cadre of overseas career service personnel who spend some two thirds of their working lives overseas as science officers, librarians, accountants, English language specialists and as generalists. Around 300 of the Council's overseas careers service officers are at a foreign posting at any one moment.

For further details contact Staff Recruitment Department, British

Council, 10 Spring Gardens, London SW1A 2BN. Tel: (020) 7930 8466. Website: www.britcoun.org.

EDUCATION AND TRAINING

There are opportunities for teachers, lecturers and training personnel all over the world, and though there are some posts that offer security of tenure, most of the jobs are on contract. There are four main categories:

- EFL teachers (teachers of English as a foreign language). There are opportunities in virtually every country of the world (including Eastern Europe) in both the public and private sectors and at all levels from primary to post-graduate level. Positions are advertised mainly in the *Times Educational Supplement*, the *Education Guardian*, *EL Gazette*, *Opportunities Abroad* (WSE) and on the website www.tefl.net.

- Teachers of other subjects. Opportunities occur particularly in the international school sector, mission schools, in bi-lingual schools in the Middle East and elsewhere, and in service schools. Positions are advertised in the *Times Educational Supplement,* the *Education Guardian*, in teaching union journals and sometimes in church news-papers and magazines (e.g. *Church Times*).

- University and college lecturers. Positions are advertised in the *Times Higher Education Supplement*, the *Education Guardian* and in specialist journals. The Association of Commonwealth Universities (36 Gordon Square, London WC1H 0PF) assists its members with the recruitment of staff by advertising positions and circulating details of them to universities, but is not equipped to deal with speculative applications. Some embassies and high commissions recruit teaching staff on behalf of their governments.

- Training staff. Positions are advertised mainly in the relevant professional and trade journals. Among the organisations recruiting personnel of this nature are the volunteer and missionary organisations, petroleum, construction and hospital operating firms in the Middle East.

Recruitment:
APSO, Arabian Careers, British Aerospace, British Council, BUNAC, Central Bureau, Christians Abroad, Crown Agents, Council Exchanges, ECIS, Gabbitas, Gap Challenge, GAP Activities, Gorkha, Inlingua, International House, i to i, League for the Exchange of Commonwealth

Teachers, Hays IT, Network Overseas, Outreach, OPU, Project Trust, Search Associates, Skillshare Africa, Students Partnership Worldwide, Teaching & Projects Abroad, Travellers Worldwide, UNAIS, VSO.

ELECTRONICS

(See also Computers, Communication entries.)
Demand for specialists in electronics and associated hi-tech manufacturing applications continues to be buoyant, with opportunities all around the world, particularly in Europe and North America.

Recruitment:
BDS, Beechwood, Ingineur, OPU, Randall Massey, TMP, TTI,

Reference:
Electronics Times, Electronics Weekly.

ENGINEERING

See under Communications, Computers, Construction, Consultancy, Electronics, Mining, Oil and Gas.

EUROPEAN UNION INSTITUTIONS

British people tend to be overrepresented in most international organisations, so it is a surprise to find any body where they are actually underrepresented. However such is the case in the institutions of the European Union. These are:

The European Commission, 200 rue de la Loi, B-1049 Brussels. Telephone: 00 32 2 299 1111.
The Council of the European Union, 175 rue de la Loi, B-1048 Brussels. Telephone: 00 32 2 285 6111.
The European Parliament, Bâtiment Robert Schuman, Plateau du Kirchberg, L-2920 Luxembourg. Telephone: 00 352 43001.
The European Court of Auditors, 12 rue Alcide de Gasperi, L-1615 Luxembourg. Telephone: 00 352 4398 45410.
The European Court of Justice, Boulevard Konrad Adenauer, Kirchberg, L-2925 Luxembourg. Telephone: 00 352 43031.
The Economic and Social Committee, rue Ravenstein 2, B-1000 Brussels. Telephone: 00 32 2 546 9011.

Committee of the Regions, rue Belliard 79, B-1040 Brussels. Telephone: 00 32 2 282 2211.

There are also a number of specialist agencies of the European Union such as:

- European Environmental Agency, Copenhagen.
- European Central Bank, Frankfurt.
- European Centre for the Development of Vocational Training, Thessaloniki.

The European Commission is the largest of the Community's institutions with around 20,000 staff including:

- administrators
- support staff (eg secretarial)
- linguists
- technical and scientific staff.

Most of them work in Brussels or Luxembourg but the majority of technical and scientific staff work in the Community's joint research centres at Ispra (Italy), Karlsruhe (Germany), Petten (Netherlands), Geel (Belgium) and Seville (Spain). Most of these staff are employed on temporary contracts.

There are five grades:

Category A: Graduates engaged in policy formation and administration and also advisory duties, often of a political nature.
Category LA: Graduates who work as translators or interpreters.
Category B: Executive officers with 'A' Levels or equivalent.
Category C: Clerical and secretarial staff with GCSEs of equivalent.
Category D: Manual and service staff.

Career opportunities are good and employees receive good pay and allowances. There are opportunities for training and transfers between departments, and career development of this nature is positively encouraged.

The main problem is getting into the EU institutions since the entry procedures are rigorous and highly competitive. Candidates for all grades of permanent staff are usually required to take a written examination and later, if successful, an oral test. A sound knowledge of at least one other European language in addition to one's own is a prerequisite – more in the case of interpreters and translators.

The different institutions of the European Union are responsible for their own recruitment and do indeed recruit separately. But the number of inter-institutional competitions is increasing, and successful candidates are placed on a reserve list open to all the institutions involved.

Notices of competitions are published in the 'C' series of the Official Journal of the European Union which are distributed by the Stationery Office in the UK and the Government Supplies Agency in Ireland. Such competitions are also advertised widely in the newspapers of the member states.

Information about career opportunities in the European Commission is obtainable from either the Commission's representation offices. These offices also have details of forthcoming competitions. In the UK and Ireland there are such offices in London, Belfast, Cardiff, Edinburgh and Dublin. (See Useful Addresses).

Alternatively you can apply direct to the institutions of the European Union for information. In the case of the European Commission (address given above) you should address your enquiry to:

- Info-Recruitment for information about competitions and temporary posts.

- Joint Interpreting & Conference Service for information about a career as an interpreter.

- Translation Service for information about a career as a translator.

- The Research & Development Directorate-General for information about research posts.

- The Traineeships Office (*Bureau des Stages*) for information about trainee positions. Recruitment for the graduate trainee scheme takes place twice a year in March and October.

UK nationals can obtain help and advice as well as information on vacancies through a website operated by the Cabinet Office: www.eu-careers-gateway.gov.uk.

You could also try two websites which offer general information on the European Union's institutions:

http:/europa.eu.int
http://www.cec.org.uk.

FINANCE

Financial services are a growing sector, and most major financial institutions have branches throughout the world. While some of these branches are manned by locally recruited staff, the more important centres which have a corporate clientele often have at least one expatriate among their senior staff. However, in most cases prior experience at home is required before an employee is sent abroad.

Opportunities on the sales side may be easier to come by – not least, selling insurance and financial services to well-heeled expatriates in Southern Spain, the Gulf States, etc. You might also look into the possibilities of off-shore financial services in places such as the Cayman Islands.

Finally, many financial and securities firms have offices in important financial centres with staff who trade shares, financial futures, bonds, etc on the local exchanges and provide analysis for head offices.

Recruitment:
AIESEC, Anglo-Arabian, Arabian Careers, Crown Agents, Executive Recruitment Services, Financial Recruitment International, FM Recruitment, Grafton, International Staffing Consultants, IPS, OPU, Offshore Specialist Appointments, Robert Walters, TMP.

Reference:
Financial Times World Insurance Yearbook (Cartermill Publishing).

HOTELS AND CATERING

At one end of the spectrum there are casual jobs to be found in hotels and restaurants in Europe, Australasia or the Americas, particularly during the holiday season – at both ski resorts and summer resorts. Such jobs are not hard to find but you could face long working hours during the height of the season for low remuneration.

The speculative approach is as good a way as any of landing such jobs, but it makes sense to fix up your employment prior to your arrival. Certain agencies, such as Jobs in the Alps and Job Centres, recruit for the hospitality sector, and job advertisements in this sector occur from time to time in British newpapers and *Overseas Jobs Express.*

At the other end of the spectrum there are management posts in top rated international hotels throughout the world. Many of these belong to major hotel chains, such as Hilton, Inter-Continental, Sheraton, Hyatt, but these are definitely only for qualified professionals.

There are also good opportunities world wide in institutional catering. Opportunities exist with the major hospital groups operating in the Middle East, with oil and gas companies abroad, in construction camps, on merchant ships and cruise liners.

Jobs abroad are advertised regularly in *Caterer & Hotelkeeper* and other specialist publications. Alternatively you might shoot off speculative applications to one of the large international chains, such as Holiday Inn or Hilton International.

National tourist offices can often supply lists of hotels in specified resorts for you to contact, while tourist information bureaux at resorts may be able to put you in touch with hotels that require staff.

Recruitment:
DH, FM, Gap Challenge, Jobs in the Alps, OPU, Profile, VIP.

Reference:
OAG Official Hotel Guide (0AG, Church Street, Dunstable, Beds LU5 4HB) would be of particular relevance to experienced personnel.
Financial Times World Hotel Directory (Cartermill Publishing).
Caterer & Hotelkeeper.

LAW

There are opportunities for lawyers throughout the world – in international companies and organisations, with international law firms, and with foreign govenments. However, you will encounter differences in the practice of law in different parts of the world. For example, in most other countries there is no distinction between barristers and solicitors.

You may also find there are restrictions placed on foreign lawyers designed to protect members of the local bar. The Legal Practice Directorate (International) of the Law Society can provide up-to date information on conditions within a member state of the European Community. The Directorate also publishes notes for the guidance of solicitors applying for admission to a bar or law society outside England and Wales. The Directorate's address is: The Law Society, 50 Chancery Lane, London WC2A 1SX.

A useful reference work is *Regulation of Foreign Lawyers* (American Bar Association – 1984). This deals with the jurisdictions in 11 American states, Australia, Belgium, Brazil, Canada, China, France, West Germany, Hong Kong, Israel, Italy, Japan, Mexico, the Netherlands, Nigeria and Singapore.

Multinational companies often employ their own in-house lawyers, and a number of commercial law practices have opened offices in overseas locations in order to serve their multinational clients more effectively. The Department for Overseas Development sometimes recruits for legal posts with Third World governments.

Recruitment:
Executive Recruitment Services, HW Group, Offshore Specialist Appointments, TMP.

MANUFACTURING

This sector covers a wide field from aerospace to petrochemicals. Opportunities arise in multinational companies which have set up subsidiary plants abroad and need their own managers and technical staff to develop production. Foreign governments often need technical advisers to help set up new factories and workshops. There are an increasing number of opportunities in Eastern Europe, Central Asia and China, as these countries seek to modernise.

Recruitment:
ABB Lutech, Anglo Arabian, BDS, Beechwood, Butler, Carlcrest, CDI-Anders, Delton, Dexton, G & T, Heston, Morson, NES Overseas, OPU, Rosta, RSL, RW, Sherry Sherratt, Sherwood, TMP, Premier Personnel, Top Choice, TTI, WEL Technical, Wickland Westcott, Woodland.

MARKETING & SALES

Opportunities arise in import/export companies, marketing and PR organisations and distribution organisations for people with experience in marketing, sales and customer service.

Recruitment:
AIESEC, Anglo-Arabian, Beechwood, DM Management Consultants, Eurocell, Grafton, International Staffing Consultants, Merrow, MRK, OPU, RW, TMP, Top Choice.

MEDICINE & HEALTHCARE

Doctors, nurses and other healthcare practitioners (mainstream and alternative) are much in demand all over the world, though some countries (notably the USA) require you to take an examination before you are allowed to practise.

Some of the best paid jobs are in hospitals in the countries of the Arabian Peninsula, many of which are managed by British or American companies. Nurses, physiotherapists and other similarly qualified staff are also sought after in North America, Canada and on the European continent. In the Third World missionary organisations run clinics and hospitals and are always on the lookout for suitably qualified staff.

Medical staff are needed too in industrial and construction projects, for emergency relief operations, and in mission hospitals around the world. In countries where there is a large expatriate community there may be opportunities in clinics and medical practices that cater for expatriates.

Overseas positions are advertised in the relevant professional journals. Some of the relevant professional organisations may be able to help with overseas jobs either by operating a placement service or by putting you in touch with sister bodies abroad. Most of them are able to offer advice to their members.

Recruitment:
Action Health, Arabian Careers, British Red Cross, Christians Abroad, Earthwatch, Fellowship Foundation, GAP Activities, Gorkha, Grafton, Health Projects Abroad, International Health Exchange, Médecins sans Frontières, Medical Missionary Association (see Missionary Organisations), MERLIN, OPU, Save the Children, Skillshare Africa, Teaching & Projects Abroad, VSO, Worldwide Healthcare Exchange. See also Missionary Organisations section in this Chapter.

Reference:
Notes and Contracts for Appointments Overseas (British Medical Association).
Health Professionals Abroad (Vacation Work).
The Lancet, British Medical Journal, British Dental Journal, *Nursing Times*, *The Gazette* (Institute of Medical Laboratory Sciences), *Saving Health* (Medical Missionary Association), etc.

MILITARY

The services usually place great emphasis in their recruitment literature on the opportunities they offer for foreign travel. Sometimes, of course, this can be too much of a good thing, and considerable strain can be placed on family relationships by frequent changes of residence (in the case of army personnel) and prolonged periods of separation (as happens in the case of Royal Navy personnel).

Nevertheless, for those who can accept the rigours of military life, the forces offer a good deal in terms of travel opportunities, though they are not as extensive as they were two or three decades ago. Most British service people will spend part of their service life in Germany, and there is a possibility of being based in Belize, the Falklands, Gibraltar or Cyprus for a while.

There are also opportunities to serve with NATO forces in Europe, to be seconded to a UN peace-keeping force, or to train forces in selected countries of the Third World. And for naval personnel there is shore leave in various exotic climes.

If you plan to become an officer, it is best to start young. The cut-off age for graduates applying for commissions tends to be around 25, and for nongraduates a year or so earlier. An exception may be made if you have specialist skills or only plan to apply for a short service commission.

The cut-off age for NCOs, privates and RN ratings is 33, while the RAF will accept people aged up to $38\frac{1}{2}$ in the case of air traffic control officers and fighter control officers. The nearest armed forces careers office will be able to offer more precise details of what qualifications and attributes are required or you could contact the different websites: www.army.mod.uk; www.royal-navy.mod.uk; www.raf.mod.uk.

Opportunities also arise for ex-service people to train the armed forces of other countries through specialist armed forces resettlement organisations.

MINING

In recent years opportunities for expatriates in the mining sector overseas have diminished considerably, and opportunities for skilled craftsmen have virtually dried up altogether. Employees at this level tend to be recruited either locally or from other parts of the world – notably the Far East.

Where there is a demand, it is for graduate geologists and engineers with four years' experience behind them. The only exception is perhaps South Africa which still seems prepared to take on inexperienced graduates. There are a few opportunities in Australia, Canada and elsewhere in Africa – on the Copper Belt in Zambia, for instance.There are opportunities in countries such as Namibia and Angola as they start to exploit their resources.

Half of the 5,000 or so members of the Institution of Mining and Metallurgy work overseas, many in mining camps or settlements in remote locations. But the pattern of employment seems to be changing. While many mining engineers and geologists will continue to be employed by prospecting companies and producing mines, others will work for companies undertaking the development and management of mines for others, notably foreign governments.

A career in mining brings with it plenty of responsibility. 'There is no room in a prospecting team, a mine, a mill or a smelter for those who depend on routine, nor for the nine to five watcher,' observes the Mineral Industry Manpower and Careers Unit. 'Mining is full of surprises, sometimes pleasant, usually not. You will be expected to cope with changing conditions, occasionally with emergencies. You will be expected both to think and to act.'

Recruitment:
Thomas Mining, OPU. Individual mining companies are listed in the *FT Mining International Year Book.*
Reference:
International Mining: A Career for Professional Engineers (Mineral Industry Manpower & Careers Unit, Prince Consort Road, London SW7 2BP).
Financial Times Mining International Year Book (Cartermill Publishing).

MISSIONARY WORK

Mention the word 'missionary', and most people picture a priestly figure striding forth into the jungle, Bible in hand, ready to face up to innumerable hazards in his quest to convert the heathen. The modern reality, however, is somewhat different. Indeed, a missionary today is just as likely to be a community worker, nurse, engineer or teacher as someone with a qualification in Divinity.

While some missionary posts offer contract posts, missionary work is normally seen as an open-ended commitment. A number of societies invest a good deal of time and effort in preparing their recruits – offering them language tuition as well as professional induction at an institution such as Kingsmead College, Selly Oak, Birmingham.

Potential missionaries have to be adaptable and willing to learn. 'We go to serve and look for opportunities to serve. We don't go to dictate,' insists Beryl Hulbert of the Methodist Church Overseas Division. 'Nowadays we only go to places by invitation. Once we are there, we're told what to do. We're not given an option. We work alongside our colleagues from the country concerned and we're not usually expected to take the lead.'

Although people tend to join the society which is most closely linked with their own denomination, mission work these days is becoming increasingly ecumenical with close collaboration between the different churches. Some missionary societies specialise in a particular region of the world, such as the South American Missionary Society. Others recruit people for virtually everywhere.

One way into a missionary career is to approach your chaplain or parish priest who will put you in touch with the appropriate authorities. For an idea of the enormous range of skills that missionaries are called upon to deploy, you should peruse the monthly vacancies list *Opportunities Abroad* published by Christians Abroad. WSE.

Alternatively, you could approach a society direct. There are some 200 missionary organisations in the UK, and a few of them are listed below.

Africa Evangelical Fellowship, 4 Station Court, Station Approach, Borough Green, Sevenoaks TN15 8AD. Telephone: (01732) 885590.

African Inland Mission, 2 Vorley Road, Archway, London N19 5HE. Telephone: (020) 7281 1184.

Baptist Missionary Society, PO Box 49, 129 Broadway, Didcot OX11 8XA. Telephone: (01235) 512077.

Crosslinks, 251 Lewisham Way, London SE4 1XF. Telephone: (020) 8691 6111.

Christian Outreach, 1 New Street, Leamington Spa, Warwickshire CV31 1HP. Telephone: (01926) 315301.

Church Missionary Society, 157 Waterloo Road, London SE1 8UU. Telephone: (020) 7928 8691.

Church of Scotland, 121 George Street, Edinburgh EH2 4YN. Telephone: (0131) 225 5722.

Interserve, 325 Kennington Road, London SE11 4QH. Telephone: (020) 7735 8227.

The Leprosy Mission, 80 Windmill Roads, Brentford, Middlesex TW8 0QH. Telephone: (020) 8569 7292.

Medical Missionary Association, 244 Camden Road, London NW1 9HE. Telephone: (020) 7267 1411. Acts as a clearing house for Protestant missionary societies which require medical personnel.

Methodist Church, World Church Office, 25 Marylebone Road, London NW1 5JR. Telephone: (020) 7486 5502.

The Missions to Seamen, St Michael Peternoster Royal, College Hill, London EC4 2RL. Telephone: (020) 7248 5202.

Overseas Missionary Fellowship, Station Approach, Borough Green, Sevenoaks, Kent TN15 8BG. Telephone: (01732) 887224.

Quaker Peace and Service, Friends House, Euston Road, London NW1 2BJ. Telephone: (020) 7387 3601. Can also supply information on Quaker work camps.

The Red Sea Mission, 33/35 The Grove, Finchley, London N3 1QU. Telephone: (020) 8346 1222.

Salvation Army, 101 Queen Victoria Street, London EC4P 4EP. Telephone: (020) 7332 0101.

SIM International, Joint Mission Centre, Ullswater Cresent, Coulsdon, Surrey CR5 2HR. Telephone: (020) 8660 7778.

South American Missionary Society, Unit 1, Prospect Business Park, Langston Road, Loughton, Essex IG10 3TZ. Telephone: (020) 8502 3504.

The SUM Fellowship, 302 Pickhurst Lane, West Wickham, Kent BR4 0HT. Telephone: (020) 8313 3246.

The Tear Fund, 100 Church Road, Teddington, Middlesex TW11 8QE.

Telephone: (020) 8977 9144.

United Reformed Church, 86 Tavistock Place, London WC1H 9RT. Telephone: (020) 7916 2020.

United Society for the Propagation of the Gospel, 157 Waterloo Road, London SE1 8XA. Telephone: (020) 7928 8681.

Voluntary Missionary Movement, University Chaplaincy Building, Mount Pleasant, Liverpool L3 5TQ. Telephone: (0151) 709 7676. www.iol.ie/~vmmeurgo. E-mail: alice@vmmuk.freeserve.co.uk. Dublin HQ, Telephone: 00 353 1 837 6565.

WEC International, Bulstrode, Oxford Road, Gerrards Cross, Bucks SL9 8SZ. Telephone: (01753) 884631.

OIL AND GAS

The oil and gas industry is a wide-ranging sector comprising such activities as exploration, drilling, production, refining and distribution. In addition to the famous oil companies that are household names, there are hundreds of contractors involved in support activities: transport, maintenance, catering, shipping, pipeline construction, fire and safety, and so on.

A wide range of skills are employed in the industry. In virtually every location there is a need for engineers, geologists, computer personnel, accountants, administrators, medical staff and training personnel. Oil companies operating in the Third World are usually expected to employ as many local staff in their operations as possible, and there is a tendency for only senior and specialist positions to be held by expatriates from the West.

There are still opportunities for tradesmen in certain countries, but increasingly such positions are held by local staff or – in the case of the Arabian Peninsula – by Asians. However, there are usually contract jobs available at most levels on offshore oil rigs where staff turnover is high and the work is demanding. Such jobs usually pay well and offer generous and frequent leave.

The best employment prospects continue to be in Algeria, Libya, the Arabian Peninsula, West Africa, Venezuela, Indonesia, the Gulf of Thailand and Central Asia.

Recruitment:
ABB Lutech, AMA, Anglo-Arabian, Brunel Energy, Carlcrest, CDI-Anders, Delton, Dexton, G & T, Hunterskil, International Staffing Consultants, LA, Modis, NES Overseas, Nestor, Network Overseas, OPU, Professional Management Resources, RSL, Sherry Sherratt, TA Group, Taylor Recruitment, Top Choice, Umm Al Jawaby, WEL Technical Services, Woodhead, Hill McGlynn, Just Engineers, Premier Personnel.

If you want to make a direct approach to leading oil companies here are a few addresses:

BP Exploration, Britannic House, 1 Finsbury Circus, London EC2Y 9BU.
Esso Exploration and Production, Esso House, Victoria Street, London
SW1H 9BE.
Phillips Petroleum, 35 Guildford Road, Woking GU22 7QT.
Shell International PLC, Shell Centre, London SE1 7NA.

Reference:
Oil and Gas International Yearbook (Financial Times).

POLICE

Most countries rely on their own nationals to staff their police forces these days, but opportunities exist for experienced police officers to train local staff either on secondment or through recruitment by an agency such as Crown Agents.

There are three main ways of getting a job abroad:

● secondment from your own force to a force in another – usually Commonwealth – country

● through an advertisement in the *Police Review*

● applying direct to police forces in other countries.

PUBLISHING AND THE MEDIA

Book publishing

Limited opportunities exist for breaking into the publishing world abroad, but they seldom occur on the editorial or production side. Given that marketing employs more people than these two departments combined and that over one third of the books published in Britain are exported, the main openings are for publishers' representatives, many of whom reside abroad.

Since educational books are big business these days in most countries, you are more likely to be promoting these than the latest state of the art novel. In such cases, someone who has worked in education abroad – particularly Teaching English as a Second Language – is ideal for the job. There may be opportunities to move into other branches of publishing at a later date since a number of publishers have overseas branches which publish their own books.

The main advertising medium for these jobs is the *Media Guardian* on Mondays. Vacancies also appear in *The Times, The Independent, The Daily*

Telegraph and specialised publications such as *Publishing News.*
Among the firms that employ staff abroad are:

Addison Wesley Longman Group, Burnt Mill, Harlow, Essex CM20 2JE.
Macmillan Education Ltd, Brunel Road, Houndmills, Basingstoke, Hants RG21 2XS.
Oxford University Press, Walton Street, Oxford OX2 6DP.
Cassell's *Directory of Publishing, The Writer's Handbook* (Macmillan) or *The Writers'* and *Artists' Yearbook'* (A & C Black) can provide further addresses.

Newspapers and journalism

If you work for a newspaper or journal that is part of an international group, (e.g. News International, Reed Elsevier),you should enquire about the possibility of secondment to a sister publication abroad. Otherwise the best idea might be to get hold of *Benn's International Media Directory* or *Willings Press Guide* and apply direct to a selection of periodical publishing firms. The *UK Press Gazette* is the main recruitment medium.

The likelihood of your landing a foreign reporter's position with a national newspaper is very slim indeed. Such posts are few and far between. A better idea might be to join an agency such as Reuters or UPI which maintains a network of correspondents throughout the world.

Reuters Ltd, 7 Thomas More Street, London EC4P 4AJ.
United Press International (UK) Ltd, 4 Ingate Place, London SW8.

Opportunities arise on English language journals and newspapers abroad. In recent years a number of newspapers have been established in Eastern Europe and the Middle East to cater for the international community in these countries.

Another possibility is to become a freelance or – in newspaper parlance – a 'stringer'. This is a particularly attractive idea for an accompanying spouse who is not allowed to take up gainful employment in the country to which the family is posted or as a part-time occupation. However given dedication and plenty of contacts there is no reason why a freelance in the right place should not eventually gain enough commissions to survive.

Broadcasting

You would need to be a seasoned reporter to be offered the chance of a resident post abroad with the BBC, BSkyB or ITN since these opportunities are very few indeed, and they normally have a chosen few who are sent off on short-term assignments. In fact, you may have more opportunity for foreign travel if you are an executive in the marketing section of BBC Worldwide or work for the BBC External Services at Bush House.

If you want to live abroad, a better bet might be to look for radio stations in countries outside the English speaking world, such as the countries of the Arabian Peninsula. Some of these are state-run, while others are commercial or supported by religious foundations. Many of these have an English language service for both internal and external consumption and use British people to produce and broadcast their programmes. *The World Radio and TV Handbook* can provide details.

Writers and translators

Technical authorship is a growing field and leading hi-tech companies throughout Europe recruit British staff either on a freelance or contract basis. Such companies also recruit translators, who are also in demand at international organisations everywhere. Watch out for advertisements in the media and technology sections of journals. The Translators' Guild, 26-27 Boswell Street, London WC1N 3JZ or the Institute of Scientific and Technical Communicators, 17 Bluebridge Avenue, Brookmans Park, Hatfield, Herts AL9 7RY may be able to advise, as may the Institute of Linguists (Address in Chapter 20).

SECRETARIAL, CLERICAL, ADMINISTRATIVE

There appears to be an expanding market for well qualified secretaries and administrative staff with foreign language skills, in Europe and countries where well qualified PAs and administrators are at a premium. Employers tend to be either multinational companies or international organisations. International vacancies are advertised in the columns of *The Times* and *The Guardian*.

Recruitment:
ACORD, Sheila Burgess, Grafton, Merrow, Multilingual Services, MERLIN, Offshore Specialist Appointments, OPU, Rosta, Robert Walters.

SPORT AND ENTERTAINMENT

If you are a tennis star you probably enjoy an international career anyway, but you do not have to be one of the top names to work abroad. On the Arabian Peninsula, for instance, there are several expatriate football coaches and managers, and on the Continent you may find UK and Irish golf and tennis professionals at sports clubs and leisure complexes.

One area where there is considerable scope is in the field of ski instruction, though this work tends to be seasonal. However, as for most jobs, qualifications are vital, and you would be wise to take an instructor course with an organisation such as the British Association of Ski Instructors if you intend to pursue this option. You could then move on to work either for a holiday firm or on a freelance basis in a ski resort.

The best source of information on coaching jobs and other opportunities is the professional magazine devoted to your particular sport. The relevant sports association or its sister association in your target country may be able to suggest openings.

Opportunities also occur for English speaking entertainers and disc jockeys in ski resorts and summer resorts, at international hotels, on cruise ships, etc. Most professionals in the entertainment business rely on the services of an agent who will usually have foreign contacts, but you can always make a direct approach to the companies themselves. They include:

- cruise ship companies (eg P & O Cruises)

- international hotel chains (eg Hilton, Sheraton)

- tour companies (eg Thomson)

- international leisure companies (eg Club Méditerranée).

Reference:
The White Book (Inside Communications, Telephone: (01203) 559658). Directory dealing with the entertainment and leisure industries which has an international section which lists agents in other countries.

The Stage
Record Mirror. Carries advertisements mainly for disc jockeys.

TECHNICAL CO-OPERATION

Most countries of the developed world are in the business of giving aid to the Third World either channelling it through international aid agencies or running their own bi-lateral programmes. Some of this aid takes the form of professional and skilled personnel who advise and assist governments and governmental organisations within these countries – and who are salaried or employed on volunteer terms. Virtually all these posts are contract posts.

Organisations that recruit in this field include:

- Department for International Development

- Crown Agents

- British Council

- The UN and its various agencies

- Voluntary organisations.

Chapters 7 and 8 deal with this sector in greater detail.

Reference:
British Overseas Development, Information Department, DFID, 94
    Victoria Street, London SW1E 5JW. Telephone: (020) 7917 7000.
Third World Directory (Directory of Social Change).

TOURISM AND TRAVEL

Many of the jobs in the tourist industry are seasonal. The work can involve
acting as a resort representative or courier for a package holiday firm based
in Britain. Some knowledge of foreign languages is useful for sorting out
problems with the local populace, though many of the people you will be
dealing with (including the tourists in your charge) will speak English.

There are permanent jobs, too, but most are British based with off-sea-
son visits to resorts to negotiate terms with hotels and local travel agencies.
One of the best ways to land such a job is to approach a package holiday
firm direct. Here is a selection of those you might try:

Thomson Holidays, Greater London House, Hampstead Road, London
    NW1 7SD.
Club Méditerranée, 115 Hamersmith Road, London W14.
Ski Total, 10 Hill Street, Richmond, Surrey TW9.
Club Cantabrica Holidays Ltd, 146-148 London Road, St Albans AL1 1PQ.
Eurocamp Travel, Summer Jobs, PO Box 170, Liverpool L70 1ES.
Mark Warner Ltd, 20 Kensington Church Street, London W8 4EP.
Simply Ski, 598-608 Chiswick High Road, London W4 5RT.
Canvas Holidays, 12 Abbey Park Place, Dunfermline, KY12 7PD.
First Choice Ski, 18 Marine Parade, Brighton BN2 1TL.

However virtually every travel organisation takes on extra staff during the
holiday season, and for addresses you have only to look at travel advertisements in newspapers and magazines.

The Association of British Travel Agents, 68 Newman Street, London
W1P 3PG or The Association of Independent Tour Operators, The Knoll
House, Purser's Lane, Peaslake, Guildford, Surrey GU5 9SJ, should be able
to provide a list of their members.

A few travel companies advertise in *The Guardian* on Mondays and in *Overseas Jobs Express*. Vacancies are also notified to Job Centres through the Overseas Placing Unit.

Children's holiday camps represent a growing sector in tourism, and require supervisors, instructors, medical and support staff. Organisations, such as Camp America, Camp Counselors USA and BUNAC recruit for such camps in the USA. But there are also opportunities in Europe with such organisations as:

Village Camps, 1260 Nyon, Switzerland. www.villagecamps.com.
PGL Ltd, Alton Court, Penyard Lane, Ross on Wye HR9 5GL, Herefordshire. www.pgl.com.

If you are in search of adventure as well as work, you could join an overland tour operator as a driver/guide. In many cases you will need to have an HGV or PSV licence, and since you could find yourself in remote areas the ability to communicate in foreign languages and do mechanical repairs is generally demanded. Among the companies currently operating in this field are:

Encounter Overland Ltd, 267 Old Brompton Road, London SW5.
Exodus Expeditions, 9 Weir Road, London SW12 0LT.
Top Deck Travel, 133 Earls Court Road, London SW5 9RH.

Finally, if you are fond of the sea there are opportunities aboard passenger cruise liners, ferries, cargo ships and tankers. A list of shipping lines appears in *The Traveller's Handbook* or you could contact The Marine Society, 202 Lambeth Road, London SE1 7JW for further information.

Reference:
Travel Trade Directory, Morgan Grampian Books, 30 Calderwood Street, London SE18 4QH.
Working in Ski Resorts – Europe, V. Pybus and C. James (Vacation Work Publications).
Careers in the Travel Industry, C. Chester (Kogan Page).
Working on Cruise Ships, Steve Marks (How To Books).
Getting a a Job in Travel & Tourism (How To Books).

THE UNITED NATIONS & OTHER INTERNATIONAL INSTITUTIONS

The United Nations and its agencies have offices throughout the world, and employ over 25,000 people. There are two kinds of permanent positions available:

● Professional posts: specialists in economics, science, data processing, statistics, social affairs, finance, etc. Translators, précis writers, interpreters. Technical assistance experts (mainly high level personnel).

● General Service posts: secretarial, administrative, information, clerical, accounting. (Much of the promotion is done internally). In addition there are contract positions which are advertised in international publications (e.g. *The Economist*).

The UN and its agencies recruit from all UN member states and endeavour to maintain a geographical balance in their staffing. To this end priority in recruitment is given to nationals of countries that are underrepresented on the staff. Unfortunately for British applicants, the UK is heavily overrepresented, so the selection process may be weighted against you. However, applicants for the secretarial and linguistic branches are not affected by this proviso.

United Nations Secretariat
Headquarters (New York)
UN Geneva Office
UN Vienna Office
UNCTAD – United Nations Conference on Trade and Development (Geneva)
UNDRO – United Nations Disaster Relief Co-ordinator (Geneva)
HABITAT – United Nations Centre for Human Settlements (Nairobi)
ECE – Economic Commission for Europe (Geneva)
ESCAP – Economic Commission for Asia and the Pacific (Bangkok)
ECA – Economic Commission for Africa (Addis Ababa)
ECLAC – Economic Commission for Latin America and the Caribbean (Santiago)
ESCWA – Economic and Social Commission for Western Asia (Amman)

Applications for posts in any of these departments of the UN Secretariat should be sent to: Professional Recruitment Service, Room 2465, UN

Secretariat, New York, NY 10017, USA. Website: www.un.org. The Recruitment Programmes Section at the same address can evaluate a candidate's credentials and hold a person's details on file.

Other departments of the UN Secretariat
Some departments are responsible for their own recruitment, notably:
ICJ – International Court of Justice, Peace Palace, 2517 KJ The Hague, Netherlands.
UNICEF – United Nations Children's Fund, 866 UN Plaza, 6th Floor, New York, NY 10017. Website: www.unicef.org.
UNDP – United Nations Development Programme, 1 UN Plaza, New York, NY 10017. Website: www.undp.org.
UNPFA – United Nations Population Fund, 801 UN Plaza, New York, NY 10017. Website: www.unfpa.org.
UNEP – United Nations Environment Programme, P O Box 30552, Nairobi, Kenya.
UNRWA – United Nations Relief and Works Agency for Palestinian refugees, Vienna International Centre, P O Box 700, A-1400, Vienna, Austria.
UNHCR – United Nations High Commissioner for Refugees, Palais de Nations, CH-1211 Geneva 10, Switzerland.
UNITAR – United Nations Institute for Training and Research, 801 UN Plaza, New York, NY 10017. Website: www.uniar.org.
UNU – United Nations University, Toho Seimei Building, 29th Floor, 15-1 Shibuya 2-chome, Shibuya-ku, Tokyo 150, Japan.

Specialised UN agencies and other international organisations
FAO – Food and Agricultural Organisation, Via delle Terme di Caracalla, 00100 Rome, Italy.
ILO – International Labour Organisation, 4 route des Morillons, CH-1211 Geneva 22, Switzerland.
UNESCO – United Nations Educational, Scientific and Cultural Organisation, 7 Place de Fontenoy, 75700 Paris, France.
ICAO – International Civil Aviation Organisation, 1000 Sherbrooke Street West, Suite 400, Montreal, Quebec, Canada H3A 2R2.
WHO – World Health Organisation, 20 avenue Appia, CH-1211 Geneva 27, Switzerland.
IMF – International Monetary Fund, 700 19th Street NW, Washington, DC 20006, USA. Website: www.imf.org/recruitment.
UPU – Universal Postal Union, Casa postale, CH-300 Berne 15, Switzerland.

ITU – International Telecommunication Union, Palais de Nations, CH-1211 Geneva 10, Switzerland.

WMO – World Meteorological Organisation, Case postale No. 5, CH-1211 Geneva 20, Switzerland.

WIPO – World Intellectual Property Organisation, 34 Chemin des Colombettes, CH-1211 Geneva 20, Switzerland.

IFAD – International Fund for Agricultural Development, Via del Serafico 107, 00142 Rome, Italy.

UNIDO – United Nations Industrial Development Organisation, Vienna International Centre, P O Box 300, A-1400, Vienna, Austria.

IAEA – International Atomic Energy Agency, Vienna International Centre, P O Box 100, A-1400 Vienna, Austria.

GATT – General Agreement on Tariffs and Trade, Centre William Rappard, 154 Rue de Lausanne, CH-1211 Geneva 21, Switzerland.

World Bank (including International Bank for Reconstruction and Development, International Development Association, International Finance Corporation), 1818 H Street, NW, Washington, DC 20433, USA. Website: www.worldbank.org.

Council of Europe, Recruitment Office, Human Resources Development Department, 67075 Strasbourg Cedex, France, Website: www.coe.fr/jobs.

Organisation for Security and Co-operation in Europe, Kärntner Ring 5–7, A-1010 Vienna, Austria. Website: www.osce.org.

International Organisation for Migration, PO Box 71, CH121 Geneva 19, Switzerland. Website: www.iom.int.

Further information on opportunities with the UN and its agencies is available from United Nations Information Centres, including the one in London at Millbank Tower, Millbank, London SW1P 4GT. Telephone: (020) 7630 1981. *The Europa Year Book* has a comprehensive list of international organisations.

UTILITIES

Power stations, desalination plants, water treatment plants, ports – all need to be managed and maintained. In the developing world this work is sometimes contracted out to foreign firms or foreign experts are recruited to oversee these operations – at least, until sufficient well-qualified people are available locally.

Recruitment:
Brunel Energy, Carlcrest, CDI-Anders, Morgan Bryant, Peter Glaser, Hill McGlynn, NES Overseas, Prima, Professional Management Resources, OPU, Rosta, RSL, Taylor Recruitment, Woodland.

18

Recruitment Directory

The following section lists in alphabetical order recruitment agencies, governmental organisations, voluntary and non-profitmaking organisations which recruit for abroad. Please note that organisations which specialise in work experience placements may charge fees.

A typical entry includes the following information:

- *Type of Organisation*:
- *Address*
- *Telephone* – usually a UK telephone number or a number which can be dialled direct from UK.
- *Fax* number
- *Website* – which would normally have further information on the organisation and vacancies it is handling.
- *E-mail* – which can be used for instant communication.
- *Job sectors* – type of job and what kind or organisation you will be working for.
- *Countries or regions* – the places the organisation recruits for.
- *Candidate profile* – what qualifications and experience you need to have for the post.
- *Additional information* – overseas offices, length of contracts, etc.

ABB Lutech Resources Ltd

Type of Organisation: Private recruitment agency.
Address: Knowles House, Cromwell Road, Redhill RH1 1RT.
Telephone: (01293) 442110.
Fax: (01293) 414225.
E-mail: lutech@gb.abb.com.
Job sectors: Engineering contracting for oil, gas, petrochemical and energy industries and information technology.
Countries or regions: Europe, Middle East, Far East, West Africa.
Candidate profile: Technically qualified staff with relevant work experience.

ACORD (Agency for Co-operation and Research in Development)
Type of Organisation: Voluntary organisation.
Address: Dean Bradley House, 52 Horseferry Road, London SW1P 2AF.
Telephone: (020) 7227 8600.
Fax: (020) 7799 1868.
Website: www.acord.org.uk.
E-mail: info@acord.org.uk.
Job sectors: Aid administration: programme co-ordinators, regional programme officers, financial officers, etc.
Countries or regions: Africa.
Candidate profile: Graduate with 3-5 years' experience with NGOs.
Additional information: An international consortium of aid agencies.

Action Health
Type of Organisation: Development organisation.
Address: The Gate House, 25 Gwydir Street, Cambridge CB1 2LG.
Telephone: (01223) 460853.
Fax: (01223) 461787.
E-mail: actionhealth@compuserve.com
Job sectors: Health.
Countries or regions: East Africa, India.
Candidate profile: Midwives, health visitors, occupational therapists, speech therapists, physiotherapists, doctors with a minimum of 2 years' post-qualification experience and supervision and training skills.
Additional information: Contracts are 12-24 months. Stipend, accommodation, flights, medical insurance, and other benefits. Advertises in professional journals and through other organisations (e.g. VSO Return Volunteer Jobs List).

Adler Recruitment
Type of Organisation: Private recruitment agency.
Address: 71 Friar Street, Droitwich, Worcs WR9 8EQ.
Telephone: (01905) 795388.
Fax: (01905) 795009.
E-mail: info@adler-recruitment.co.uk.
Job sectors: Civil engineers, structural engineers, design engineers, quantity surveyors and estimators.
Countries or regions: Europe, Africa, Far East and Middle East.
Candidate profile: Graduates with several years' experience.

AgriVenture/IAEA
Type of Organisation: Non-profit organisation.

Address: YFC Centre, National Agricultural Centre, Stoneleigh Park, Kenilworth, Warwickshire CV8 2LG.

Telephone: (024) 7669 6578 and 0800 783 2186.

Fax: (024) 7669 6684.

Website: www.agriventure.com.

E-mail: uk@agriventure.com.

Job sectors: Agricultural and horticultural exchanges.

Countries or regions: Australia, Canada, Europe, Japan, New Zealand, USA.

Candidate profile: UK and Irish passport holders (and certain other EU nationals) aged 18-30 with approximately one years' experience in their chosen category of agriculture or horticulture. Other requirements are a full driving licence and no dependants.

Additional information: Current costs are all-inclusive and start at around £1,800 and programmes last 5 to 9 months.

AIESEC (Association Internationale des Etudiants en Sciences Economiques.

Type of Organisation: International voluntary organisation specialising in professional exchanges.

Address: 2nd Floor, 29-31 Cowper Street, London EC2A 4AT.

Tel: (020) 7549 1800.

Fax: (020) 7336 7971.

Website: www.uk.aiesec.org.

E-mail: workabroad@uk.aiesec.org.

Job sectors: Accountancy, finance, marketing, computing and other branches of business.

Countries or regions: Worldwide.

Candidate profile: Business students.

Additional information: The world's largest student run educational charity. Offers paid work placements lasting from 8 weeks to 78 weeks.

AMA (Anthony Moss Associates)

Type of Organisation: Private recruitment agency.

Address: Suite 350, Princess House, 50–60 Entwhistle Street, London W1W 8EW.

Telephone: (020) 7388 0918.

Fax: (020) 7387 4973.

Website: www.amoss.com.

Job sectors: Oil and gas.

Countries or regions: Europe, Middle East, Central Asia, South East Asia.

Candidate profile: Qualified personnel at all levels from technician to project manager.

CDI-Anders Elite Ltd (formerly Anders Glaser Wills)
Type of Organisation: Private recruitment agency.
Address: Capital House, 10th Floor, Houndwell Place, East Street, Southampton SO14 5HU.
Telephone: (023) 8022 3511.
Fax: (023) 8022 7911.
Website: www.anderselite.com.
E-mail: resource@anderselite.com.
Job sectors: Automotive, aerospace, construction, IT, petrochemical, power generation, and marine engineering sectors.
Countries or regions: USA, Africa, Europe, Middle East and Far East.
Candidate profile: Minimum qualification HND, but most of the jobs are for graduates. Five years' experience desirable.
Additional information: Now part of the CDI Corporation, the largest suppliers of temporary technical staff in the USA. Member of REC.

Anglo Arabian Recruitment Services
Type of Organisation: Private recruitment agency.
Address: 53/54 Haymarket, London SW1Y 4RP.
Telephone: (020) 7925 0177.
Fax: (020) 7930 4261.
Job sectors: Construction, oil and gas, manufacturing, trading, etc.
Countries or regions: Middle East, especially Saudi Arabia, Dubai, Abu Dhabi and Oman.
Candidate profile: Management, technical, IT, finance, marketing, sales with at least 5 years' post-qualification experience.
Additional information: Dubai associate. Contact name in London: John Steeds.

APSO (Agency for Personal Service Overseas)
Type of Organisation: Voluntary organisation.
Address: Bishops Square, Redmonds Hill, Dublin 2.
Telephone: 00 353 1 478 9400.
Fax: 00 353 1 475 1006
Website: www.apso.ie.
E-mail: recept@apso.ie.
Job sectors: Administration, healthcare, social work, engineering, agriculture/environment.
Countries or regions: Africa, Central America, Asia (Cambodia).
Candidate profile: Graduate with two years' work experience.
Additional information: Ireland's national voluntary organisation.

Arabian Careers
Type of Organisation: Private recruitment agency
Address: 7th Floor, Berkeley House, Berkeley Square, London W1X 5LB.
Telephone: (020) 7495 3285.
Fax: (020) 7355 2562.
Website: www.arabiancareers.com.
E-mail: recruiter@arabiancareers.com.
Job sectors: Medical, financial, computer and education sectors.
Countries or regions: Saudi Arabia.
Candidate profile: Graduate or equivalent.

ATD Fourth World
Type of Organisation: International voluntary organisation
Address: 48 Addington Square, London SE5 7LB.
Telephone: (020) 7703 3231.
Fax: (020) 7252 4276.
Website: www.atd-uk.org.
E-mail: atd.uk@ukonline.co.uk.
Job sectors: Eradication of poverty by training people in new skills, etc.
Countries or regions: Europe (for shorter assignments); Africa, Asia, South
America, USA for longer ones (more than 2 years).
Additional information: Offers short voluntary work programmes of 2
weeks and 3 months as well as long term engagements. Has around 400
core workers active in 25 countries. Founded in Paris in 1957 by Joseph
Wresinski. ATD stands for Aide à Toute Détresse.

Au Pair in America
Type of Organisation: Private recruitment agency.
Address: 37 Queen's Gate, London SW7 5HR.
Telephone: (020) 7581 7322; 0800 413116.
Fax: (020) 7581 7355.
Website: www.aupairamerica.co.uk
E-mail: info@aupairamerica.co.uk.
Job sectors: Au pair exchanges.
Countries or regions: USA.
Candidate profile: Aged 18-26.
Additional information: One year engagements as well as vacation oppor-
tunities. Refundable deposit payable.

James Baker Associates
Type of Organisation: International personnel consultants.
Address: 105 Queens Road, Reading, Berks RG1 4DA.
Telephone: (0118) 950 5022.

Fax: (0118) 950 5056.
E-mail: info@jba.clara.net.
Job sectors: IT from technical specialists to senior managers for contract and permanent positions.
Countries or regions: Europe, USA, and Middle East.
Candidate profile: Graduates with 2-3 years' experience.

BCTV (formerly) British Trust for Conservation Volunteers
Type of Organisation: Voluntary organisation.
Address: 36 St Mary's Street, Wallingford OX10 0EU.
Telephone: (01491) 821600
Fax: (01491) 839646.
Website: www.bctv.org.
E-mail: information@bctv.org.uk.
Job sectors: Conservation.
Countries or regions: Europe, North America, Australia, Asia, Africa.
Candidate profile: Conservation skills are not normally required, just energy and enthusiasm. Candidates must be over 18 years of age for projects outside UK.
Additional information: The working holidays last around two weeks and cost from £150 to £1,000. Recent assignments have included turtle monitoring in Turkey, restoring terraced paddy fields in Japan and heritage trail building in USA.

BDS Challenge International
Type of Organisation: Private recruitment agency.
Address: 240 Bay Street, North Brighton, VIC 3186, Australia.
Telephone: 00 613 9596 8699.
Fax: 00 613 9596 0968.
Website: www.bdsglobal.com.
E-mail: aallebone@bdschall.com.au.
Job sectors: Construction, general engineering, petrochemicals, IT, electronic engineering.
Countries or regions: Australia, China, Indonesia, Malaysia, New Zealand, Qatar, Singapore, Thailand, UAE, Vietnam and other countries.
Candidate profile: HND, BSc, MSc, PhD, etc.
Additional information: Four offices in Australia and networking offices in UK, USA, India, Korea, New Zealand, Singapore and UAE.

Beechwood Recruitment Ltd
Type of Organisation: Private recruitment agency.
Address: 219 High Street, London W3 9BY.

Telephone: (020) 8992 8647.
Fax: (020) 8992 5658.
Website: www.beechwoodrecruit.com.
E-mail: mail@beechwoodrecruit.com.
Job sectors: IT, construction, electronics, manufacturing, mechanical engineering, telecommunications, etc including engineers, scientists, technologists, sales, marketing and computer professionals.
Countries or regions: USA, European Union, Scandinavia and the Far East.
Candidate profile: Graduate or professional candidate profile plus experience.
Additional information: Operates a candidate databank. Advertises in specialist publications. Member of REC.

Beresford, Blake & Thomas Ltd
Type of Organisation: Private recruitment consultancy.
Address: 14 Buckingham Palace Road, London SW1 0QP.
Tel: (020) 7233 8999.
Fax: (020) 7233 8004.
Website: www.bbt.co.uk.
E-mail: recruit@bbt.co.uk.
Job sectors: Civil engineering, construction, health and social care.
Countries or regions: Middle East, Australasia and Africa.
Candidate profile: Various for permanent, temporary, freelance and locum vacancies.
Additional information: Part of Select Appointment (Holdings) Group of Companies, the second largest staffing services organisation in the world. Branches in Birmingham, Bristol, Leeds, Liverpool, Glasgow, Johannesburg, Melbourne. Advertises in trade journals and also recruits through referrals.

British Aerospace
Type of Organisation: Public company.
Address: Saudi Arabian Support Department, Warton Aerodrome, Preston, Lancs PR4 1LA.
Telephone: (01772) 634317.
Fax: (01772) 852096.
Website: www.baesystems.com.
Job sectors: Military aviation support and training.
Country: Saudi Arabia.
Candidate profile: Professionally qualified teachers, trainers and engineers.

British Council
Type of Organisation: Government supported organisation.
Address: Central Management of Direct Teaching, 10 Spring Gardens, London SW1A 2BN.
Telephone: (020) 7389 4914.
Fax: (020) 7389 6347.
Website: www.britcoun.org.
E-mail: calice.miller@britcoun.org
Job sectors: English language teaching (TEFL).
Countries or regions: Worldwide.
Candidate profile: Diploma or PGCE in TEFL plus 2 years' experience usually required; MA or MBA for managerial posts.
Additional information: Recruits for its own language teaching centres normally on contract terms. Permanent positions are also available which involve foreign postings.

British Council
Type of Organisation: Government supported organisation.
Address: Overseas Appointments Services, Bridgewater House, 58 Whitworth Street, Manchester M1 6BB.
Telephone: (0161) 957 7383.
Fax: (0161) 957 7397.
Website: www.britcoun.org.
E-mail: mark-hepworth@britcoun.org.
Job sectors: Mainly education (including TEFL)
Countries or regions: Worldwide.
Candidate profile: Qualified specialists in ELT and other disciplines mainly for public sector posts and projects which often form part of Britain's aid programme.

British Executive Service Overseas (BESO)
Type of Organisation: Voluntary organisation.
Address: 164 Vauxhall Bridge Road, London SW1V 2RB.
Telephone: (020) 7630 0644.
Fax: (020) 7630 0624.
Website: www.beso.org.
E-mail: reception@beso.org.
Job sectors: Advises private, public and voluntary sector organisations.
Countries or regions: Africa, Latin America and Caribbean, Asia and Pacific, Central and Eastern Europe.
Candidate profile: Skilled and experienced professionals.
Additional information: Funded by DFID, business and industry, European

Union, international aid agencies, charitable trusts and individuals, All expenses are paid for the volunteer. Assignments last from 2 weeks to 6 months.

British Red Cross
Type of Organisation: Voluntary organisation.
Address: International Aid Department, 9 Grosvenor Crescent, London SW1X 7EJ.
Telephone: (020) 7235 5454.
Fax: (020) 7245 6315.
Website: www.redcross.org.uk.
Job sectors: Aid and disaster emergencies.
Countries or regions: Worldwide.
Candidate profile: Surgeons, anaesthetists, nurses, accountants, relief administrators, logistics experts, water and sanitation engineers, warehouse and workshop managers, development specialists, information officers, programme managers, tracing officers and telecommunications specialists who are either British nationals or UK residents and with at leat 3-5 years' experience depending on the occupation.
Additional information: Part of the largest aid agency in the world. Maintains a candidate register. Recruits for its own bilateral projects and for the International Red Cross and Red Crescent Movement. See also Chapter 8.

Brunel Energy (formerly Alasdair Graham Associates)
Type of Organisation: Private recruitment agency.
Address: Epic House, 28-32 Cadogan Street, Glasgow G2 7LP.
Telephone: (0141) 302 3000.
Fax: (0141) 302 3001.
Website: www.brunelenergy.net.
E-mail: energy@brunel-uk.com.
Job sectors: Oil & gas, water, power and construction.
Countries or regions: Worldwide.
Candidate profile: Professional engineers.
Additional information: Recruits for multinational companies. Associate office in Houston.

BUNAC (British Universities North American Club)
Type of Organisation: Non-profit educational organisation.
Address: 16 Bowling Green Lane, London EC1R 0BD.
Telephone: (020) 7251 3472.
Fax: (020) 7251 0215.

Website: www.bunac.org.

E-mail: enquiries@bunac.org.uk.

Job sectors: Student exchanges in a wide range of occupations.

Countries or regions: Australia, Argentina, Canada, Ghana, Jamaica, New Zealand. South Africa, USA.

Candidate profile: Full-time undergraduates or graduates. Some programmes accept school leavers.

Additional information: Arranges vacation jobs, one year work experience and also Gap Year placements. Has branches on many university campuses and works in conjunction with USIT (the Union of Students in Ireland), 19 Aston Quay, Dublin 2.

Sheila Burgess International

Type of Organisation: Private recruitment consultancy.

Address: 62 rue St Lazare, 75009 Paris, France.

Telephone: (UK): (020) 7584 6446; (France): (00331) 4463 0257.

Fax: (00 33 1) 4463 0259.

Job sectors: Multi-lingual secretaries and administrative personnel.

Countries or regions: Mostly France, and occasionally Germany and Switzerland.

Candidate profile: Graduates with secretarial training and post A level language qualifications or confirmed bilingual secretaries.

Additional information: Correspondence should be sent to Paris office.

Butler International

Type of Organisation: Private recruitment agency.

Address: Kings Mill, Kings Mill Lane, South Nutfield, Redhill, Surrey RH1 5NE.

Telephone: (01737) 822000.

Fax: (01737) 823031.

Website: www.butlerinternational.co.uk.

E-mail: info@butlerinternational.co.uk.

Job sectors: Aerospace, automotive, telecommunications, chemicals, pharmaceuticals, IT, general manufacturing.

Countries or regions: Europe, Middle East, USA.

Candidate profile: Engineers and IT specialists with HNC or BSc and a minimum of 3 years' experience.

Additional information: Salary range is £18,000 – £80,000. Contract rates are £12 – £35+ per hour. One of the largest specialist technical recruitment companies in the USA with 50 offices there. Over 6,000 contractors employed at any one time. *Website:* www.butler.com.

Camp America
Type of Organisation: Exchange organisation.
Address: 37 Queen's Gate, London SW7 5HR.
Telephone: (020) 7581 7373.
Fax: (020) 7581 7377.
Website: www.campamerica.co.uk.
Job sectors: Summer children's camps.
Countries or regions: USA.
Candidate profile: Full-time students and other suitable people aged 18-35.
Additional information: See Chapter 7.

Camp Counselors USA
Type of Organisation: Exchange organisation.
Address: Green Dragon House, Unit 4CC, 64–70 High Street, Croydon, Surrey CR0 9XN.
Telephone: (020) 8688 9051.
Fax: (020) 8680 4539.
Website: www.campcounselors.com.
E-mail: unitedkingdom@ccusa.com.
Job sectors: Summer children's camps.
Countries or regions: USA.
Candidate profile: Full-time students and qualified teachers and nurses up to age 30.
Additional information: Office in Scotland: 27 Woodside Gardens, Musselburgh, Edinburgh EH21 7LJ. Tel: (0131) 665 5843.

Carlcrest
Type of Organisation: Private recruitment agency.
Address: Oakridge, West End, Woking, Surrey GU27 9PJ.
Tel: (01483) 485485.
Fax: (01483) 485499.
Website: www.tps.co.uk.
E-mail: carlcrest@sgsgroup.com.
Job sectors: Oil, gas, utilities, petrochemical, scientific.
Countries or regions: Worldwide.
Candidate profile: Site engineers and technicians, normally with degrees.
Additional information: Has an Internet jobsite. Member of REC.

CDI-Anders Elite Ltd (formerly Anders Glaser Wills)
Type of Organisation: Private recruitment agency.
Address: Capital House, 10th Floor, Houndwell Place, East Street, Southampton SO14 5HU.
Telephone: (023) 8022 3511.

Fax: (023) 8022 7911.

Website: www.anderselite.com.

E-mail: resource@anderselite.com.

Job sectors: Automotive, aerospace, construction, IT, petrochemical, power generation, and marine engineering sectors.

Countries or regions: USA, Africa, Europe, Middle East and Far East.

Candidate profile: Minimum qualification HND, but most of the jobs are for graduates. Five years' experience desirable.

Additional information: Now part of the CDI Corporation, the largest suppliers of temporary technical staff in the USA. Member of REC.

Central Bureau for International Education and Training

Type of Organisation: Government agency.

Address: The British Council, 10 Spring Gardens, London SW1A 2BN.

Telephone: (020) 7389 4004.

Fax: (020) 7389 4426.

Website: www.centralbureau.org.uk.

E-mail: centralbureau@britishcouncil.org.

Job sectors: Education.

Countries or regions: Worldwide, except Commonwealth countries.

Candidate profile: Undergraduates or graduates aged 20-30 for teaching assistantships. Also qualified and experienced teachers for exchange placements in Europe and the USA.

Christians Abroad

Type of Organisation: Agency of Churches Together in Britain.

Address: 233 Bon Marche Centre, 241–251 Ferndale Road, London SW9 8BJ.

Telephone: (0870) 770 7990.

Fax: (0870) 770 7991.

Website: www.cabroad.org.uk.

E-mail: admin@cabroad.org.uk.

Job sectors: Teaching, medical, development.

Countries or regions: Africa, Asia. Mainly, but not exclusively, Third World countries.

Candidate profile: Normally qualified and experienced. Some vacancies for volunteers.

Commonwealth Secretariat

Type of Organisation: International governmental organisation.

Address: Marlborough House, Pall Mall, London SW1Y 5HX.

Telephone: (020) 7747 6185.
Fax: (020) 7747 6520.
Website: www.thecommonwealth.org.
E-mail: info@commonwealth.int.
Job sectors: Mainly public sector: all disciplines.
Countries or regions: All Commonwealth countries, especially the developing ones.
Candidate profile: Academic/professional qualifications, preferably advanced ones; at least ten years' practical experience.
Additional information: Maintains a candidate database and advertises vacancies in the *Economist* and the *Guardian*. Technical assistance assignments range from a few weeks to two or more years. For the Commonwealth Service Abroad Programme which supplements the former volunteers are contracted for up to three months on a no fee basis but with a daily living allowance, air tickets as well as personal and medical insurance cover.

Compuware Ltd (formerly Computec)
Type of Organisation: Private recruitment agency
Address: 34 Francis Grove, Wimbledon, London SW19 4DY.
Telephone: (020) 8288 4880.
Fax: (020) 8288 4882.
Website: www.compuware.com.
E-mail: cir@compuware.com.
Job sectors: IT.
Countries or regions: Australia, Canada, New Zealand and USA.
Candidate profile: IT skills such as SAP, Oracle Financials, GSM, Hogan, Adabas Natural, Smalltalk, Baan/Triton.

Computing Resource Centre
Type of Organisation: Private recruitment agency.
Address: West Lodge, 407 Uxbridge Road, London W3 9SH.
Telephone: (020) 8896 3110.
Fax: (020) 8896 2912.
Website: www.itjobs.net.
E-mail: it@itjobs.net.
Job sectors: IT.
Countries or regions: USA and Europe.
Candidate profile: Hands-on SAP integrated software experience either in computer implementation or business.

Concern

Type of Organisation: Voluntary relief and development agency.
Address: 248-250 Lavender Hill, London SW11 1LJ.
Telephone: (020) 7738 1033.
Fax: (020) 7738 1032.
Website: www.concern.ie.
E-mail: infolondon@london.concernworldwide.org.
Job sectors: Education, emergency relief, long-term development.
Countries or regions: Africa, Asia, Caribbean.
Candidate profile: Well qualified teachers and other specialists for pro-
gramme design, curriculum development, administration and programme
implementation.
Additional information: Has around 150 volunteers in the field at one time.

Concordia Ltd

Type of Organisation: Voluntary organisation.
Address: Heversham House, 20/22 Boundary Road, Hove BN3 4ET.
Telephone: (01273) 422218.
Fax: (01273) 422218.
Website: www.concordia-iye.org.uk.
Job sectors: Conservation, social work, teaching, arts and cultural projects.
Countries or regions: Europe (including Eastern Europe and Turkey),
North Africa, North America, Japan.
Candidate profile: Aged 18-30. No experience normally required.
Additional information: Projects normally last up to one month. Food,
accommodation and insurance are provided. Volunteers have to pay travel
costs and a registration fee.

Coral Cay Conservation

Type of Organisation: Non-profit organisation.
Address: 154 Clapham Park Road, London SW4 7DE.
Telephone: (020) 7498 6248.
Fax: (020) 7498 8447.
Website: www.coralcay.org.
*E-mail:*ccc@coralcay.org.
Job sectors: Surveying coral reefs.
Countries or regions: Caribbean (Belize), South East Asia (Philippines,
Indonesia).
Candidate profile: Minimum age is 16. No previous experience required as
full training is provided on site.
Additional information: An expedition fee is payable plus air fares.
Expeditions last from 2 weeks to 12 weeks. Opportunities on site for expe-
dition leaders and instructors for periods of 4-6 months.

Council on International Educational Exchange (Council Exchanges)
Type of Organisation: Non profit organisation promoting work abroad and study programmes.
Address: 52 Poland Street, London W1V 4JQ.
Telephone: (020) 7478 2000/2010.
Fax: (020) 7734 7322.
Website: www.councilexchanges.org.
E-mail: infouk@councilexchanges.org.
Job sectors: Work experience and exchanges, teaching English.
Countries and regions: Japan, China, USA, Australia, Canada, Europe.
Candidate profile: For work experience programmes normally a full-time student. For teaching programmes a Bachelor degree. Also has some programmes for Gap Year and non-degree holding students.
Additional information: A sponsoring organisation for vacation work in the USA.

Crown Agents
Type of Organisation: Government corporation.
Address: International Recruitment Division, St Nicholas House, St Nicholas Road, Sutton, Surrey SM1 1EL.
Telephone: (020) 8643 3311.
Fax: (020) 8643 9331.
Website: www.crownagents.co.uk
E-mail: enquiries@crownagents.co.uk.
Job sectors: Supply, financial and technical support services to governments and public sector bodies mainly in the Third World.
Countries and regions: Worldwide.
Candidate profile: Suitably qualified people including police, port operators, bankers, utilities engineers, broadcasting experts, teachers and lecturers.
Additional information: Maintains a candidate database.

Daulton Personnel
Type of Organisation: Private recruitment agency.
Address: 2 Greycoat Place, London SW1P 1SB.
Telephone: (020) 7222 0817.
Fax: (020) 7233 0734.
Website: www.daultonpersonnel.co.uk.
E-mail: info@daultonpersonnel.co.uk.
Job sectors: Construction and building industries. Opportunities for architects, builders, building service engineers, civil engineers, construction

plant managers, cost engineers, estimators, HVAC engineers, planning engineers, project managers, quantity surveyors, telecommunications engineers.
Countries or regions: Worldwide, particularly Germany and Eastern Europe.
Candidate profile: Appropriate candidate profile. Knowledge of a European language is a bonus.

Delton Group
Type of Organisation: Private recruitment agency.
Address: Ribblesdale House, Ribblesdale Place, Preston, Lancs PR1 3NA.
Telephone: 01772 884545.
Fax: 01772 885005.
E-mail: delton@provider.co.uk/
Job sectors: Petrochemical, oil & gas, power, construction industries.
Countries or regions: Worldwide.
Candidate profile: Qualified engineers, technicians and instructors.
Additional information: Offices in Singapore and Thailand. Associate company in Belgium.

Department for International Development (DFID)
Type of Organisation: Government department.
Address: Abercrombie House, Eaglesham Road, East Kilbride, Glasgow G75 8EA. (Resource Development Group, Procurement, Appointments and NGO Department.)
Telephone:(0845) 300 4100 and (01355) 843132.
Fax: (01355) 843632.
Website: www.dfid.gov.uk.
E-mail: enquiry@dfid.gov.uk.
Job sectors: Agriculture, forestry, fisheries, surveying, engineering, architecture, social development, finance, management, health and population, education, legal.
Candidate profile: Relevant qualifications and normally extensive experience.
Countries and regions: Developing countries, Eastern and Central Europe.
Additional information: Contract posts are advertised on the DFID website and in the national press. DFID also publishes a free guide *Working in Development*. There are also opportunities for permanent staff members to work at DFID's overseas offices in New Delhi, Bangkok, Nairobi, Harare, Pretoria, Dhaka, Bridgetown and Kathmandu.

Dexton Ltd
Type of Organisation: Private recruitment agency.
Address: Eastwards, Birchy Way, Sway, Hants SO14 6BJ.
Telephone: (01590) 681110.
Fax: (01590) 681110.
Website: www.eningeerssite.com.
E-mail: richard@dexton.demon.co.uk.
Job sectors: Oil and gas, civil engineering, building, power, telecom, utilities.
Countries and regions: Far East, Middle East, Europe.
Candidate profile: Professional and managerial.
Additional information: Related offices in Singapore and Hong Kong. Recruitment through advertisements in *Nexus*, website and candidate database.

DH Associates
Type of Organisation: Private recruitment agency.
Address: 29 Woodside Road, Amersham on the Hill, Bucks HP6 6AA.
Telephone: (01494) 434898.
Fax: (01494) 434899.
E-mail: recruit@d-ha.fsworld.co.uk.
Job sectors: Industrial catering (e.g. mining projects, hospitals, construction camps, accommodation compounds, offshore rigs, etc).
Countries or regions: Worldwide.
Candidate profile: Camp managers, chefs, facilities managers, logistics experts, recreation managers, general managers with a degree or professional qualification. For operations in war zones ex-service people are preferred.
Additional information: Market leaders in this specialised field.

DM Management Consultants Ltd
Type of Organisation: Private recruitment consultant.
Address: 19 Clarges Street, London W1Y 7PG.
Telephone: (020) 7499 8030.
Fax: (020) 8948 6306.
Website: www.dmmc.co.uk
E-mail: enquiries@dmmc.co.uk.
Job sectors: Direct marketing and mail order.
Countries or regions: Worldwide.
Candidate profile: Normally graduate senior marketing and general managers in their 30s or 40s.

Earthwatch Europe

Type of Organisation: Voluntary organisation.
Address: 37 Woodstock Road, Oxford OX2 6HJ.
Telephone: (01865) 318838.
Fax: (01865) 311383.
Website: www.earthwatch.org.
E-mail: info@uk.earthwatch.org.
Job sectors: Archaeology, conservation, environment, endangered species, world health.
Countries or regions: Worldwide.
Candidate profile: 17 upwards. No experience required.
Additional information: Affiliated organisation in Australia, Japan and USA. Paying volunteers are wanted on scientific projects lasting from 2 days to 4 weeks. Average length is 2 weeks with training, where needed, given on site. In 2000 the organisation had 130 propects in 50 countries.

Edgware Au Pair Agency

Type of Organisation: Private recruitment agency.
Address: 19 Manor Park Crescent, Edgware, Middlesex HA8 7NH.
Telephone: (020) 8952 5522.
Website: www.100s-aupair.co.uk.
E-mail: edgware@100s-aupair.co.uk.
Job sectors: Au pairs, nannies.
Countries and regions: Europe, North America.
Candidate profile: No qualifications needed for au pair vacancies. Nannies should have NNEB qualification or equivalent.
Additional information: Associated with Solihull Au Pair & Nanny Agency.

Eurocell Associates

Type of Organisation: Private training and sales consultancy which also undertakes placements.
Address: Beechknowe, Townsend Lane, Marsh Gibbon, Oxon OX6 0EY.
Telephone: (01869) 277292.
Fax: (01869) 277292.
E-mail: eurocell@barclays.net.
Job sectors: Car and truck dealerships.
Countries or regions: Saudi Arabia, Kuwait, UAE and Bahrain.
Candidate profile: Professionally qualified managers, sales and marketing executives for the motor industry, vehicle rental and finance and insurance.

European Council of International Schools (ECIS)

Type of Organisation: Schools association.
Address: 21 Lavant Street, Petersfield, Hants GU32 3EL.
Telephone: 01730 268244.
Fax: 01730 267914.
Website: www.ecis.org.
E-mail: ecis@ecis.org.
Job sectors: Education.
Countries and regions: Worldwide.
Candidate profile: Qualified teachers of all subjects and with at least two years' experience teaching in their home country. Also senior school administrators.
Additional information: Publishes the annual ECIS Directory, organises twice yearly recruitment fairs and operates candidate register.

Executive Recruitment Services

Type of Organisation: Private recruitment agency.
Address: Ambassador House, 575-599 Maxted Road, Hemel Hempstead. Hertfordshire HP2 7DX.
Telephone: (01442) 231691.
Fax: (01442) 230063.
Website: www.ers.co.uk/ers.
E-mail: ers_plc@ers.co.uk.
Job sectors: Business, technology, financial, communication, environmental, legal, technical, defence.
Countries and regions: Mainly USA and Europe.
Candidate profile: Varies according to job.
Additional information: Office in Texas.

Financial Recruitment International

Type of Organisation: Private recruitment agency.
Address: Southmead, Long Hey Road, Caldy, Wirral L48 1LY.
Telephone: (0151) 625 0565
Fax: (0151) 625 0058.
Job sectors: Banking, insurance, fund management, public accountancy practice.
Countries or regions: Caribbean, Europe, Middle East, Far East, USA.
Candidate profile: Accountants with ACA or equivalent qualification.

Fircroft Group

Type of Organisation: Private recruitment agency.

Address: Trinity House, 114 Northenden Rd, Sale, Cheshire M33 3HD.
Telephone: (0161) 905 2020.
Fax: (0161) 969 1743.
Website: www.fircroft.co.uk.
E-mail: recruitment@fircroft.co.uk.
Job sectors: Engineering (all branches, especially oil & gas).
Countries or regions: Worldwide.
Candidate profile: Graduate engineers with at least 5 years' experience.
Additional information: Member of REC.

F M Recruitment,

Type of Organisation: Private recruitment agency.
Address: Hedges House, 153-155 Regent Street, London W1R 7FD.
Telephone: (020) 7287 5400.
Fax: (020) 7287 5411.
E-mail: fm@fmrecruitment.co.uk.
Job sectors: Financial and systems managers for the hotel and leisure industry.
Countries or regions: Particularly Europe (including Eastern Europe), Middle East, Asia and the Pacific.
Candidate profile: Graduate or equivalent.
Additional information: Short-term and permanent appointments available. Member of REC.

Forsyth Group

Type of Organisation: Private recruitment consultant.
Address: 4 Thorne Passage, Barnes, London SW13 0PA.
Telephone: (020) 8878 9189.
Fax: (020) 8878 8586.
Website: www.forsythgroup.co.uk
E-mail: enquiries@forsythgroup.com.
Job sectors: IT: hardware and software companies involved in the Internet, Intranet, e-commerce, wireless and telecommunication sectors.
Countries or regions: USA and Europe.
Candidate profile: Graduates with a highly technical background and with Internet programming skills.
Additional information: Associate company based in Boston, New York and San Francisco.

Frontier

Type of Organisation: International non-governmental organisation.
Address: 50–52 Rivington Street, London EC2A 3QP.
Telephone: (020) 7613 2422.

Fax: (020) 7613 2992.
Website: www.frontierprojects.ac.uk.
E-mail: enquiries@frontierprojects.ac.uk.
Job sectors: Conservation (surveying vulnerable habitats such as tropical rain forests, coral reefs, savannahs).
Countries or regions: East Africa, S E Asia.
Candidate profile: People aged 17+. No scientific background required. Many of the volunteers tend to be Gap Year students and recent graduates.
Additional information: Ten week or 20 week expeditions in January. April. July and October. Cost to participant: approx £2,500 plus air fare and visa. Current projects are in Madagascar, Tanzania and Vietnam.

Gabbitas Educational Consultants

Type of Organisation: Teacher recruitment agency.
Address: Carrington House, 126-130 Regent Street, London W1R 6EE.
Telephone: (020) 7439 2071.
Fax: (020) 7437 1764.
Websites: www.teacher-recruitment.co.uk and www.gabbitas.co.uk.
E-mail: reccon@gabbitas.co.uk.
Job sectors: Education.
Countries or regions: Worldwide.
Candidate profile: Teachers of all GCSE, A Level and IB subjects for British schools overseas which follow a British style curriculum.
Additional information: Maintains a register of candidates.

G & T Associates

Type of Organisation: Private recruitment agency.
Address: Suite B, William Knox House, Britannic Way, Llandarcy, Neath, West Glamorgan SA10 6EL.
Telephone: (01792) 321202.
Fax: (01792) 321295.
Website: www.gtassociates.co.uk.
E-mail: info@gt-associates.co.uk.
Job sectors: Mainly steel industry, but also oil, gas, construction, etc. Wide range of disciplines at the management and supervisory level.
Countries or regions: Eastern Europe, India, Middle East, Far East, North and South America, etc.
Candidate profile: Managerial or supervisory experience.
Additional information: Recruits for permanent positions and long or short-term contracts.

GAP Activity Projects

Type of Organisation: Organisation which co-ordinates volunteering for 18 & 19 year olds.
Address: 44 Queens Road, Reading, Berks RG1 4BB.
Telephone: (0118) 959 4914.
Fax: (0118) 957 6634.
Website: www.gap.org.uk.
E-mail: volunteer@gap.org.uk
Job sectors: Various: education, conservation, caring, medical, social work, outdoor activities.
Countries or regions: Worldwide.
Candidate profile: School and college leavers aged 18/19.
Additional information: Specialists in Gap Year placements.

Gap Challenge

Type of Organisation: Educational expeditions company.
Address: Black Arrow House, 2 Chandos Road, London NW10 6NF.
Telephone: (020) 8728 7274 & 7200.
Fax: (020) 8961 1551.
Website: www.gap-challenge.co.uk.
E-mail: welcome@world-challenge.co.uk.
Job sectors: Carework, conservation, eco-tourism, trekking, teaching, agriculture, youth work, hotel work.
Countries or regions: Australia, Belize, Borneo, Canada, Costa Rica, Ecuador, India, Nepal, Peru, South Africa, Tanzania.
Candidate profile: Students aged 18-25 who want to do something worthwhile in their Gap Year and are cool-headed, able to think for themselves, comfortable working as part of a team and prepared for a challenge.
Additional information: Run by World Challenge Expeditions who have pioneered educational expedition programmes since 1987. Offer 24 hour back-up and support while students are on their placement as well as the opportunity to travel and work.

Peter Glaser & Associates

Type of Organisation: International human resource consultants and advisers.
Address: PO Box 55, Bodmin PL30 4YH.
Telephone: (07071) 221155.
Fax: (07071) 221166.
Website: www.pga.co.uk.
E-mail: pglaser@pga.co.uk.

Job sectors: Engineers, scientists and technicians for the construction, power, water and environmental sectors (private and public).
Countries or regions: Middle East, Far East, Africa and South America.
Candidate profile: Age 25 to 60, HND to PhD.
Additional information: Salary range: £15,000 to £100,000. Openings in design, site supervision, general management, and at executive director level. Member of REC.

Gorkha District Health and Educational Development Scheme
Type of Organisation: Voluntary organisation.
Address: Witches Ride, Whiteshill, Stock, Ingatestone, Essex CM4 9QD.
Telephone: (01277) 840406.
Fax: (01277) 841224.
Website: www.nepal.co.uk.
E-mail: info@leighton.org.
Job sectors: Agriculture, construction, education, engineering, environmental health, handicrafts, medical, music, social welfare.
Countries or regions: Nepal.
Candidate profile: Volunteers aged 18 and over, ideally with experience and qualifications. Suitable for Gap Year students.
Additional information: The charity was founded in 1988 to provide development assistance to a region 70 miles west of Kathmandu.

Grafton International
Type of Organisation: Private recruitment agency.
Address: 35-37 Queen's Square, Belfast BT1 3FG.
Telephone: (028) 9024 2824.
Fax: (028) 9024 6429.
Website: www.grafton-group.com
E-mail: info@grafton-group.ie
Job sectors: Sales, marketing, engineering, construction, finance, nursing, medical.
Countries or regions: Worldwide.
Candidate profile: Relevant qualifications and experience.
Additional information: Candidates should contact the appropriate branch of the agency: healthcare; industrial; or technical, IT and engineering. Works in conjunction with its offices in Budapest, Prague, Santiago, Kuala Lumpur, Auckland and Johannesburg.

Grove Personnnel
Type of Organisation: Private employment agency.
Address: 46/48 Southbourne Grove, Bournemouth BH6 3RB.

Telephone: (01202) 417533.
Fax: (01202) 421746.
Website: www.grovepersonnel.co.uk.
E-mail: jobs@grovepersonnel.co.uk.
Job sectors: Construction.
Countries or regions: Middle East, Far East, Europe and Africa.
Candidate profile: Degree, HNC or City & Guilds and aged 23-55.

Harrison Jones Associates
Type of Organisation: Private recruitment agency.
Address: Buckingham House East, The Broadway, Stanmore, Middlesex HA7 4EB.
Telephone: (020) 8385 7881.
Fax: (020) 8385 7882.
Website: www.hja.co.uk.
E-mail: international@hja.co.uk.
Job sectors: Various sectors including air base support services, construction, retailing.
Countries or regions: Middle East.
Candidate profile: Qualified graduates and professionals.

Hays IT
Type of Organisation: Private recruitment agency.
Address: The Tythe Barn, High Street, Edlesborough, Dunstable   LU6 2HS.
Telephone: (01525) 222222.
Fax: (01525) 222466.
Website: www.hays-it.com.
E-mail: perm@hays-it.com (permanent appointments) and contract@hays-it.com (contract appointments).
Job sectors: IT.
Countries or regions: Australia, Europe, South Africa, USA.
Candidate profile: Qualified and experienced IT professionals.

HB Associates
Type of Organisation: Private recruitment agency.
Address: 101 High Street, Evesham, Worcs WR11 4DN.
Telephone: (01386) 49856.
Fax: (01386) 41925.
E-Mail: hbassociates.co.uk.
Job sectors: IT.
Countries and regions: USA, France, Germany.

Candidate profile: Graduate software engineers aged 25-35.

Additional information: Advertises in IS Opportunities, maintains a candidate register, and undertakes executive search. Associate office in Boston, USA.

Health Projects Abroad (HPA)

Type of Organisation: Voluntary organisation.

Address: PO Box 24, Bakewell, Derbyshire DE45 1ZW.

Telephone: (01629) 640051.

Fax: (01629) 640054.

Website: www.volunteerinafrica.org.

E-mail: info@hpauk.org.

Job sectors: General, medical, engineering.

Countries or regions: East Africa.

Candidate profile: Professional volunteers (medics and engineers) over 25 with at least 2 years' relevant experience; volunteers aged 18-30 need no special skills but need to show motivation, enthusiasm and commitment.

Additional information: Volunteers have to raise funds towards the cost of their programme. Full training and support are provided.

Heston (Middle East) Ltd

Type of Organisation: Manpower contractors.

Address: Norton House, Farrants Way, Castleton, Isle of Man IM9 1NR.

Telephone: (01624) 824595.

Fax: (01624) 825657.

Website: www.heston.net

E-mail: iom@heston.net.

Job sectors: Oil & gas, petrochemicals, construction, civil engineering.

Countries or regions: Middle East.

Candidate profile: Suitably qualified people in all disciplines from supervisors upwards.

Additional information: Branch offices in Kuwait, Bahrain, Qatar, etc. Do not respond to CVs due to the number of speculative applications received.

Hill McGlynn International Appointments

Type of Organisation: Private recruitment agency.

Address: Prospect House, Meridiens Cross, Ocean Village, Southampton SO14 3TJ.

Telephone: (02380) 221122.

Fax: (02380) 220011.

Website: www.hillmcglynn.com.

E-mail: international@hillmcglynn.com
Job sectors: Civil engineering, construction, rail, oil and gas, facilities management.
Countries or regions: Worldwide.
Candidate profile: People with sector experience from engineer to director level.
Additional information: Established in 1976. Network of offices across the UK. Office in Melbourne, Australia.

HW Group Accountancy and HW Group Legal (See TMP Worldwide)

IAESTE (International Association for the Exchange of Students for Technical Experience)
Type of Organisation: Non-profit organisation.
Address: Central Bureau, British Council, 10 Spring Gardens, London SW1A 2BN.
Telephone: (020) 7389 4774.
Fax: (020) 7389 4426.
Website: www.iaeste.org.uk
E-mail: iaeste@centralbureau.org.uk
Job sectors: Scientific, technical and professional work experience.
Countries or regions: Worldwide.
Candidate profile: Full-time students aged 19-30.
Additional information: Normally students are nominated by their educational institution or sponsored by a company.

Ingineur Ltd
Type of Organisation: Private recruitment agency.
Address: Draycote, Rugby CV23 9RB.
Telephone: (01926) 633006.
Fax: (01926) 633003.
Website: www.ingineur.co.uk.
E-mail: cvs@ingineur.co.uk.
Job sectors: Electronics.
Countries or regions: European Union countries.
Candidate profile: Qualified electronics engineers with least 2 years' industrial experience in R & D.

Inlingua Teacher Training & Recruitment
Type of Organisation: Recruitment division of an international language training company.
Address: Rodney Lodge, Rodney Road, Cheltenham GL50 1JF.
Telephone: (01242) 253171.

Fax: (01242) 253181.
Website: www.inlingua-cheltenham.co.uk.
E-mail: training@inlingua-cheltenham.co.uk.
Job sectors: Teaching English as a foreign language.
Countries or regions: Germany, Italy, Indonesia, Poland, Russia, Spain, Singapore, Venezuela and elsewhere.
Candidate profile: TEFL certificate minimum.
Additional information: Preference given to Inlingua-trained teachers.

International Co-operation for Development (ICD)

Type of Organisation: Voluntary organisation
Address: Unit 3, Canonbury Yard, 190a New North Road, London N1 7BJ.
Telephone: (020) 7354 0883.
Fax: (020) 7359 0017.
Website: www.ciir.org.
E-mail: jobs@ciir.org.
Job sectors: Development projects in agriculture, agricultural economics, small business and community development, gender and organisational training, primary health care, health education, environmental education, popular education and media, appropriate technology, vocational training.
Countries or regions: Africa, Middle East, Latin America and the Caribbean.
Candidate profile: Qualified professionals with a minimum of 2 years' experience who are willing to spend 2 years working for a modest but adequate local salary.
Additional information: A department of the Catholic Institute for International Relations.

International Health Exchange (IHE)

Type of Organisation: Non-profit charitable organisation.
Address: 134 Lower Marsh, London SE1 7AE.
Telephone: (020) 7620 3333.
Fax: (020) 7620 2277.
Website: www.ihe.org.uk.
E-mail: info@ihe.org.uk.
Job sectors: Medical.
Countries or regions: Worldwide.
Candidate profile: Qualified doctors, nurses and other health workers (including anaesthetists and occupational therapists) at all levels.
Additional information: Maintains a candidate register and acts as a clearing house for international aid and relief agencies that need medical personnel. Its publications *The Health Exchange* and *Job Supplement* list job vacancies.

International House

Type of Organisation: Private language training company.
Address: Human Resources, 106 Piccadilly, London W1V 9FL.
Telephone: (020) 7518 6970.
Fax: (020) 7518 6971.
Website: www.ihworld.com.
E-mail: br@ihlondon.co.uk.
Job sectors: Teaching English as a foreign language (TEFL).
Countries and regions: Argentina, Armenia, Australia, Belarus, Brazil, Czech Republic, Egypt, Estonia, Finland, France, Georgia, Germany, Hungary, Italy, Lithuania, Macedonia, Malaysia, Mexico, Mongolia, New Zealand, Poland, Portugal, Romania, Russia, Singapore, South Africa, Spain, Switzerland, Turkey, Ukraine, Uruguay, USA.
Candidate profile: Minimum requirement: Cambridge CELTA or Trinity TESOL certificate.
Additional information: Recruits teachers and more senior academic staff for International House affiliated schools worldwide on a year-round basis, though the majority of posts start in September/October.

International Rescue Corps

Type of Organisation: Voluntary organisation.
Address: 8 Kings Road, Grangemouth FK3 9BB.
Telephone: (01324) 665011.
Job sectors: Emergency rescue teams for natural disasters.
Countries or regions: Worldwide.
Candidate profile: Experience in rescues.
Additional information: Maintains candidate database.

International Staffing Consultants, Europe

Type of Organisation: Private recruitment agency.
Address: PO Box 124, Eastleigh. Hants SO50 8ZE.
Telephone: (023) 8065 1281.
Fax: (023) 8062 0877.
Website: www.iscworld.com.
E-mail: isceurope@iscworld.com.
Job sectors: Sales and marketing, finance, management, construction, oil and gas.
Countries or regions: USA, Canada, Middle East, worldwide.
Candidate profile: Qualified managers, engineers in middle management and above.
Additional information: Members of the world's largest and oldest place-ment network. Affiliates in USA, Canada, Australia, Singapore, Taiwan, Europe (including Eastern Europe).

International Voluntary Service (IVS)
Type of Organisation: Voluntary organisation.
Address: 21 Otley Road, Headingley, Leeds LS6 3AA.
Telephone: (0113) 230 4600.
Fax: (0113) 230 4610.
Website: www.ivsgbn.demon.co.uk.
E-mail: ivsgbn@ivsgbn.demon.co.uk.
Job sectors: International work camps/projects including conservation, working with the disadvantaged, construction, renovation, education.
Countries or regions: Europe, North America, Japan, North Africa, Middle East.
Candidate profile: Aged 18 or over. No prior experience needed except for projects of longer duration (3-12 months).
Additional information: The UK branch of Service Civil International with partner organisations in over 30 countries. Sends around 350 volunteers abroad each year. Most camps are for 3-4 weeks with a few opportunities for longer assignments. Participants pay travel and registration fee.
Other offices at
Old Hall, East Bergholt, Colchester C07 6TQ. *Telephone:* (01206) 298215. *Fax:* (01206) 299043. *Website:* www.ivsgbsouth.demon.co.uk. *E-mail:* ivs@ivsgbsouth.demon.co.uk.
7 Upper Bow, Edinburgh EH1 2JN. *Telephone:* (0131) 226 6722. *Fax:* (0131) 226 6723. *Website:* www.ivsgbscot.demon.co.uk. *E-mail:* ivs@ivsgbscot.demon.co.uk

IPS Group
Type of Organisation: Private recruitment agency.
Address: Lloyd's Avenue House, 6 Lloyd's Avenue, London EC3N 3ES.
Telephone: (020) 7481 8111.
Fax: (020) 7481 0994.
Website: ipsgroup.co.uk.
E-mail: enquiries@ipsgroup.co.uk.
Job sectors: Insurance – all branches.
Countries or regions: Worldwide.
Candidate profile: Qualified to ACII level.

i to i International Projects Ltd
Type of Organisation: Charity.
Address: 9 Blenheim Terrace, Leeds LS2 9HZ
Telephone: (0870) 333 2332.
Fax: (0113) 242 2171.

Website: www.i-to-i.com.
E-mail: info@i-to-i.com.
Job sectors: Teaching English, conservation, business, IT, medical, media, film and journalism.
Countries or regions: Australia, Bolivia, Costa Rica, Georgia, Ghana, India, Russia, Sri Lanka, Taiwan, Thailand, Uganda.
Candidate profile: Ranges form Gap Year students to more experienced people.
Additional information: Typical contract is for three months, but longer and shorter placements are possible. A fee is payable. Publishes a quarterly newsletter *Inspired.*

Jenrick-CPI Ltd
Type of Organisation: Private recruitment agency.
Address: The Clock Tower, Bridge Street, Walton on Thames KT12 1AY.
Telephone: (01932) 245500.
Fax: (01932) 245900.
Website: jenrick-cpi.co.uk.
E-mail: info@jenrick-cpi.co.uk.
Job sectors: IT.
Countries or regions: Mainly Holland, Germany, France, Belgium, Germany. Also other European countries.
Candidate profile: Qualified and experienced computer consultants at all levels. Knowledge of Dutch and German is useful but most requirements are for English speakers.

Jobs in the Alps
Type of Organisation: Private recruitment agency.
Address: 17 High Street, Gretton, Northants NN17 3DE.
Telephone: (01536) 771150.
Fax: (01536) 771914.
Website: www.jobs-in-the-alps.com.
E-mail: enquiries@jobs-in-the-alps.com.
Job sectors: Hotels and restaurants.
Countries or regions: France, Germany, Switzerland.
Candidate profile: Vacation jobs for German and/or French speakers, winter and summer. Waiters, waitresses, porters, housekeepers, kitchen staff, reception or crêche personnel.
Additional information: Please send SAE with enquiries.

Just Engineers.Net PLC

Address: Pembroke House, Carrington Business Park, Manchester M31 4DD.
Telephone: (0845) 050 2000.
Fax: (0845) 050 2001.
Websites: www.justengineers.net and www.justgraduates.net.
Job sectors: Engineering, IT, construction.
Countries and regions: Middle East, France, Worldwide.
Candidate profile: Relevant qualifications and experience.
Additional information: Check websites.

Kibbutz Representatives

Type of Organisation: Voluntary organisation.
Address: 1a Accommodation Road, London NW11 8ED.
Telephone: (020) 8458 9235
E-mail: enquiries@kibbitz.org.uk
Job sectors: Various on kibbitzim in Israel.
Countries or regions: Israel.
Candidate profile: Aged 18-32 and willing to work hard for a minimum of two months in return for bed and board.

KMS Ltd

Network House, Bradfield Close, Woking, Surrey GU22 7RE.
Telephone: (01483) 756856.
Fax: (01483) 756864.
Website: www.kmsltd.com
E-mail: kms@kingsfieldgroup.com.
Job sectors: General construction.
Countries or regions: Middle East, Europe (esp. Germany, Holland, France).
Candidate profile: Various.
Additional information: Offices in Singapore and Dubai. Advertises in *Nexus* and *Construction News*. Operates candidate database.

LA Recruitment & Management Services

Type of Organisation: Private recruitment agency.
173 Union Street, Aberdeen AB11 6BB.
Telephone: (01224) 212929,
Fax: (01224) 573845.
Website: www.larecruitment.co.uk.
E-mail: info@larecruitment.co.uk.
Job sectors: Oil & gas, construction, engineering.
Countries or regions: Qatar, UAE, Saudi Arabia, Kuwait, Oman,

Myanmar, Nigeria.

Candidate profile: Degree or HNC with five years' experience in chosen field.

Additional information: Recruits mainly for senior engineering positions. Advertises in *Nexus* and *Daily Telegraph*.

League for the Exchange of Commonwealth Teachers

Type of Organisation: Exchange association.

Address: Commonwealth House, 7 Lion Yard, Tremadoc Road, London SW4 7NQ.

Telephone: (020) 7819 3933.

Fax: (020) 7720 5403.

Website: www.lect.org.uk.

Job sectors: Education.

Countries and regions: Canada, Australia, New Zealand and other Commonwealth countries in Africa, Asia and the Caribbean.

Candidate profile: Teachers with at least 3 years' experience.

Line Up Aviation Personnel

Type of Organisation: Private recruitment agency.

Address: 7 City Business Centre, Brighton Road, Horsham, Sussex RH13 5BA.

Telephone: (01403) 217688.

Fax: (01403) 217922.

Website: www.luap.com.

E-mail: info@luap.com.

Job sectors: Aircraft maintenance personnel.

Countries or regions: Europe, Middle East.

Candidate profile: Suitably qualified aircraft maintenance engineers.

Additional information: Also operate specialised project airline support services and second tier airline support.

Malla Overseas Recruitment

Type of Organisation: Private recruitment agency.

Address: 77 Cornhill, London EC3V 3QQ.

Telephone: (020) 7556 1122.

Fax: (020) 7387 8312.

Website: www.malla.com.

E-mail: recruit@malla.com.

Job sectors: Construction, telecommunications, railways.

Countries or regions: Europe, Central Asia, Middle East, Africa, Far East.

Candidate profile: Professionals of all disciplines connected with construction, telecommunications and railways to senior management level.

Médecins sans Frontières
Type of Organisation: International voluntary organisation providing medical emergency relief.
Address: 67–74 Saffron Hill, London EC1 8QX.
Telephone: (020) 7404 6600.
Fax: (020) 7404 4466.
Website: www.msf.org.
E-mail: office@london.msf.org.
Job sectors: Medical.
Countries or regions: Over 80 countries worldwide.
Candidate profile: Fully qualified medical doctors and nurses, logisticians, water and sanitation experts. Two years' post-qualification experience in their field of work. Doctors and nurses need a degree/certificate in tropical medicine.
Additional information: Recruits through tropical medicine schools, word of mouth and media exposure. UK office handles UK and Irish based applicants only.

Medical Emergency Relief International (MERLIN)
Type of Organisation: Humanitarian aid organisation.
Address: 5-13 Trinity Street, Borough, London SE1 1DB.
Telephone: (020) 7378 4888.
Fax: (020) 7378 4899.
Website: www.merlin.org.uk.
E-mail: hq@merlin.org.uk.
Job sectors: Emergency medical relief.
Countries or regions: Worldwide.
Candidate profile: Qualified doctors, nurses, administrators with financial experience and logisticians preferably with overseas experience. All staff should have at least 2 years' post-qualification experience.
Additional information: Maintains a register of qualified people who can be called upon for postings of up to 12 months. Package includes accommodation, travel, insurance and allowance of £450-£1,100 per month.

Merrow
Type of Organisation: Private recruitment agency.
Address: 23 Bentinck Street, London W1Y 2EZ.
Telephone: (020) 7935 5050.

Fax: (020) 7935 5454.
Website: www.merrow.co.uk.
E-mail: recruit@merrow.co.uk.
Job sectors: Secretarial, administrative, customer service personnel.
Countries or regions: France, Germany, Belgium.
Candidate profile: Experienced secretaries and PAs fluent in languages.
Additional information: Recruits through advertisements and from candidate database.

Modis International

Type of Organisation: Private recruitment agency.
Address: 3rd Floor, 16–18 New Bridge Street, London EC4V 6HU.
Telephone: (020) 7832 3888.
Fax: (020) 7832 3801.
Website: www.modisintl.com.
E-mail: info@modisintl.com.
Job sectors: IT and communications (tele and data) in the oil and aerospace sectors and also with governmental bodies.
Countries or regions: Worldwide.
Candidate profile: Graduates with at least three years' experience.
Additional information: Jobs are with multinationals. Contracts vary from three months to three years. Member of REC.

Morgan Bryant

Type of Organisation: Private recruitment agency.
Address: 3A Walpole Gardens, Twickenham, Middlesex TW2 5SL.
Telephone: (020) 8255 6246.
Fax: (020) 8255 6248.
E-mail: mbperson@aol.com.
Job sectors: Construction industry and other sectors including dredging.
Countries or regions: Arabian Gulf.
Candidate profile: HNC/graduate engineers, quantity surveyors and other disciplines at the management and senior supervisory level.
Additional information: Contracts are normally for one year renewable. CV should state availability, present/last salary, whether a single or married status post is required, and be accompanied by two passport photos.

Morson International

Type of Organisation: Private recruitment agency.
Address: Stableford Hall, Monton, Eccles, Manchester M30 8AP.
Telephone: (0161) 707 1516.

Fax: (0161) 788 8372.
Website: www.morson.com.
E-mail: recruit@morson.com.
Job sectors: Oil and gas, construction, petrochemical and aerospace industries.
Countries or regions: Worldwide.
Candidate profile: At least a first degree or HND. Multidisciplinary experience desirable.
Additional information: Office throughout UK and in Canada. *Telephone:* 001 905 820 0697.

MRK Consulting Ltd

Type of Organisation: Recruitment agency.
Address: 3a The Deans, Bridge Road, Bagshot GU19 5AT.
Telephone: (01276) 476866.
Fax: (01276) 479666.
Website: www.mrk-consulting.co.uk.
E-mail: recruit@mrk-consulting.demon.uk.
Job sectors: IT
Countries or regions: Europe, Middle East, New Zealand and elsewhere.
Candidate profile: Graduate.
Additional information: Recruits directors and executives, business managers, technical managers, sales and marketing executives, engineers and support specialists, project managers, programmers, developers, computer operators, logistics personnel, e-commerce professionals. Member of REC.

Multilingual Services

Type of Organisation: Private recruitment agency.
Address: 59 Charlotte Street, London W1T 4PE.
Telephone: (020) 7307 8870.
Fax: (020) 7436 4046.
Website: www.multilingual.co.uk.
Job sectors: Administrative, secretarial.
Countries or regions: Europe (especially France and Germany).
Candidate profile: Professional candidate profile and language skills.
Additional information: Recruits clerical and secretarial staff, PAs, receptionists, sales staff, executives, customer relations personnel.

NES Overseas Ltd

Type of Organisation: Private recruitment agency.
Address: Station House, Stanford New Road, Altrincham, Chesire WA14 1EP.

Telephone: (0161) 942 4000.
Fax: (0161) 941 4873.
Website: www.nes.co.uk
E-mail: manchester@nes.co.uk.
Job sectors: Oil, gas, petrochemical, chemical, power, water, construction and infrastructure sectors (engineers, managers and supervisors).
Countries or regions: Europe, Far East, Middle East, North Africa, North and South America.
Candidate profile: From C&G to degree level.
Additional information: Part of the NES Group, one of the largest technical agencies in Europe with branches in Aberdeen, Glasgow, London, Newcastle, Abu Dhabi, Hong Kong, Tunis and Orlando (Florida).

Nestor International Ltd
Type of Organisation: Private recruitment consultancy.
Address: Pembroke House, Llanfarnam Way, Cwmbran NP44 3AU.
Telephone: (01633) 421302.
Fax: (01633) 421302.
Website: www.nestorint.com
E-mail: info@nestorint.com
Job sectors: Banking, oil & gas, computing, airlines.
Countries or regions: Arabian Gulf.
Candidate profile: IT professionals with at least 3 years' experience.
Additional information: Recruits through advertisements and candidate database.

Network Overseas
Type of Organisation: Private recruitment agency.
Address: 34 Mortimer Street, London W1N 8JR.
Telephone: (020) 7580 5151
Fax: (020) 7580 6242.
Website: www.networkoverseas.cc.
E-mail: overseas@networkoverseas.cc.
Job sectors: Engineering, construction, oil and gas, operations and maintenance, nursing and medical (for private, military and government hospitals), IT (mainly in oil and gas industry), education and training (including science, engineering and TEFL).
Countries or regions: Middle East (notably Saudi Arabia, Qatar, Kuwait and the UAE).
Additional information: Recruits for contract and permanent positions.

Norfolk Care Search Agency
Type of Organisation: Private recruitment agency.
Address: 19 London Road, Downham Market, Norfolk PE38 9BJ.
Telephone: (01366) 384448.
Fax: (01366) 385226.
Job sectors: Au pairs, nannies, mother's helps.
Countries or regions: South of France (Nice), Germany, Italy.
Candidate profile: Au pairs: female or male EU citizens aged 18-27 who like children and are prepared to do light housework. Nannies and mother's helps (Italy only): EU citizens aged over 18.
Additional information: Placement charge of £45 for au pairs. No charge for other categories. Minimum stay for au pairs: 3 months (6 weeks summer only). Minimum stay for other categories: 6 months.

OCC Computer Personnel
Type of Organisation: Private recruitment agency.
Address: 108 Welsh Row, Nantwich, Cheshire CW5 5EY.
Telephone: (01270) 627206.
Fax: (01270) 629168.
Website: www.occ-computing.co.uk.
E-mail: consulting@occ-computing.co.uk.
Job sectors: IT for financial institutions, multinationals, software houses and the space/satellite industry .
Countries or regions: Western and Central Europe.
Candidate profile: Graduates with a minimum of two years' experience (preferably single).

ODG Recruitment International
Type of Organisation: Private recruitment agency.
Address: 5 Manfred Road, London SW15 2RS.
Telephone: (020) 8874 2844.
Fax: (020) 8874 1178.
Website: www.migrationbureau.com.
E-mail: info@migrationbureau.com.
Job sectors: All sectors, but for prospective permanent migrants only.
Countries or regions: Australia, New Zealand, Canada.
Candidate profile: Graduate, professional or trade qualifications.
Additional information: Offices in Sydney, Auckland and Toronto. Affiliated to the longest established migration consulting group for Australia, New Zealand and Canada which provides professional assistance with residence visa processing, job search and resettlement.

Offshore Specialist Appointments
Type of Organisation: Private recruitment agency.
Address: Suite C2, Hirzel Court, St Peter Port, Guernsey GY1 2NH.
Telephone: (01481) 712891.
Fax: (01481) 713205.
Website: www.osagroup.com.
E-mail: admin@osa.guernsey.net.
Job sectors: Accountancy, banking, company/trust administration.
Countries or regions: Luxembourg, Monaco, Bermuda, Bahamas, Cayman Islands, Channel Islands, Isle of Man.
Candidate profile: Professionally qualified individuals in offshore finance (ACIB, ACCA, ICSA or STEP).

Outreach International Ltd
Type of Organisation: Non-profit organisation.
Address: Bartletts Farm, Hayes Road, Compton Dundon, Somerset TA11 6PF.
Telephone: (01458) 274957.
Fax: (01458) 274957.
Website: www.outreachinternational.co.uk
E-mail: projects@outreachinternational.co.uk
Job sectors: Working in orphanages, with street children and the disabled; teaching English, sports, computer skills, art, dance; conservation work including coral reefs, dolphins, whales; humanitarian aid work.
Countries or regions: Cambodia, Mexico.
Candidate profile: Typically aged 18–25 but for some projects older volunteers are preferred. No qualifications are necessary. Enthusiasm, energy and an open mind are essential.
Additional information: Places committed volunteers in interesting overseas projects with in-country back up. Minimum period of three months. An ideal Gap Year activity or for those wishing to take a career break.

Overseas Placing Unit (OPU), Employment Service
Type of Organisation: Government agency.
Address: Level 1, Rockingham House, 123 West Street, Sheffield S1 4ER.
Telephone: (0114) 259 6051/6052.
Fax: (0114) 259 6040.
Websites: www.jobcentreplus.gov.uk and www.euresjobs.com
Job sectors: All sectors.
Countries or regions: Worldwide.
Candidate profile: Varies according to job specification.
Additional information: A specialist branch of the Employment Service

(DWP) which advertises jobs and also operates a database. Contact a Job Centre for further details.

Oxfam

Type of Organisation: International relief and development agency.
Address: 274 Banbury Road, Oxford OX2 7DZ.
Telephone: (01865) 311311.
Website: www.oxfam.org.uk.
Job sectors: Emergency relief, community health, engineering, social development in the Third World.
Countries and regions: Worldwide.
Candidate profile: Qualified and experienced.
Additional information: Contracts usually last for 3-6 months.

Premier Personnel Ltd

Address: 25/29 High Street, Leatherhead, Surrey KT22 8AB.
Telephone: (01372) 379183.
Fax: (01372) 372301.
Website: www.premierpersonnel.co.uk.
E-mail: candidate@prem-per.demon.co.uk.
Job sectors: Engineering (civil, mechanical, electrical), construction, oil and gas, electronics, manufacturing, business administration, quantity surveying.
Countries and regions: Worldwide.
Candidate profile: A cross section of qualifications from City and Guilds to degree with varying levels of experience as indicated in advertisments.
Additional information: Recruits through candidate register, executive search, advertising in *Overseas Jobs Express, Expats International, Nexus* and on websites.

Professional Management Resources Ltd

Type of Organisation: Private recruitment agency.
Address: PO Box 23, Wadhurst, East Sussex TN5 6XL.
Telephone: (01892) 748226.
Fax: (01892) 784228.
Website: www.pmr-worldjobs.co.uk
E-mail: info@pmr-worldjobs.co.uk
Job sectors: Petrochemical, oil and gas, hydrocarbon, power utilities, civil construction, telecommunications.
Countries or regions: Middle East, Far East, North & West Africa, Europe.
Candidate profile: Suitably qualified engineers for line management and lead discipline.

Profile Management & Specialist Recruitment
Type of Organisation: Private recruitment agency.
Address: 201 Haverstock Hill, Belsize Park, London NW3 4QG.
Tel: (020) 7692 3000.
Fax: (020) 7794 4229.
Website: www. profile-int.co.uk.
E-mail: office@profile-int.co.uk.
Job sectors: Hotels, restaurants, leisure.
Countries and regions: Worldwide.
Candidate profile: Experienced senior managers.

The Project Trust
Type of Organisation: Non-profit organisation.
Address: The Hebridean Centre, Ballyhaugh, Isle of Coll, Argyll PA78 6TE.
Telephone: (01879) 230444.
Fax: (01879) 230357.
Website: www.projecttrust.org.uk.
E-mail: info@projecttrust.org.uk.
Job sectors: Work experience for Gap Year students.
Countries or regions: 26 countries in Latin America, Africa and the Middle East.
Candidate profile: 17-20 year old school leavers taking a Gap Year.

QD Group (See TMP Worldwide)

Randall Massey
Type of Organisation: Private recruitment agency.
Address: Ambrose House, 30-33 Milton Road, Swindon SN1 5JA.
Telephone: (01793) 614700.
Fax: (01793) 619243.
Website: www.randallmassey.com
E-mail: bill@randallmassey.com.
Job sectors: Electronics, IT.
Countries or regions: USA, Europe, Far East.
Candidate profile: Qualified electronics and IT specialists.

Recruitment Services Ltd
Type of Organisation: Private recruitment agency.
Address: Penthouse Suite, 2-6 South Street, Worthing, West Sussex BN11 3AE.
Telephone: (01903) 820303.

Fax: (01903) 821414.
Website: www.recruitmentservicesltd.com.
E-mail: rsl@recruitmentservicesltd.com.
Job sectors: Oil & gas, petrochemical, civil industries, railways.
Countries or regions: Worldwide.
Candidate profile: Senior managers through to inspectors for design, construction and maintenance with appropriate experience and qualifications.
Additional information: Recruits through candidate database and national advertising – *Nexus, Daily Telegraph.*

RedR (Engineers for Disaster Relief)
Type of Organisation: Relief agency.
Address: 1 Great George Street, London SW1P 3AE.
Telephone: (020) 7233 3116.
Fax: (020) 7222 0564.
Website: www.redr.org.
E-mail: info@redr.org.
Job sectors: Emergency personnel support for relief agencies.
Countries or regions: Worldwide.
Candidate profile: Qualified personnel, engineers, managers, logisticians.
Additional information: Maintains a register of experienced personnel (non-medical) at all levels who can be called on a short notice. Contracts 2 weeks to 6 months.

RIBA Appointments Bureau
Type of Organisation: Official recruitment service of Royal Institute of British Architects.
Address: 66 Portland Place, London W1N 4AD.
Telephone: (020) 7580 9588.
Fax: (020) 7636 4108.
Website: www.riba-appointments.com.
Job sectors: Architecture.
Countries or regions: Africa, Asia, Middle East, Europe.
Candidate profile: Qualified architects.

Rosta Engineering Co Ltd
Type of Organisation: Technical recruitment specialists.
Address: 144 Castle Street, Edgeley, Stockport SK3 9JH.
Telephone: (0161) 429 5333.
Fax: (0161) 429 5322.
Website: www.rosta.com.
E-mail: mail@rosta.com.

Job sectors: Auto, construction, petrochemical, pharmaceutical, utilities.
Countries or regions: Australia, Korea, Middle East, Malaysia, Nigeria, Poland and the USA.
Candidate profile: Suitably qualified technical and engineering personnel, design personnel, project managers, administrators, managers and construction supervisors.

RW Recruitment International Ltd
Type of Organisation: Private recruitment agency.
Address: 22 Grafton Street, London W1S 4EX.
Telephone: (020) 7499 9669; 01444 243224.
Fax: (020) 7724 4046; 01444 239168.
Website: www.recruitment.com.
E-mail: rwrecruitment@ic24.net
Job sectors: Retail, trading, manufacturing, motor retailing, construction and energy related.
Countries or regions: Middle East, Mediterranean, North Africa.
Candidate profile: Appropriate skills, a positive attitude, family circumstances and the right motivation to live and work in the Middle East.

Save the Children Fund
Type of Organisation: International charity.
Address: Mary Datchelor House, 17 Grove Lane, London SE5 8RD.
Telephone: (020) 7703 5400.
Fax: (020) 7703 2278
Website: www.scfuk.org.uk.
Job sectors: Child-centred relief work mainly in Third World.
Countries or regions: Worldwide.
Candidate profile: Mainly qualified doctors and nurses.

Search Associates,
Type of Organisation: Private teacher recruitment agency.
Address: PO Box 168, Chieng Mai 5000, Thailand.
Telephone: 00 66 53 244322.
Fax: 00 66 53 260118.
Website: www.search-associates.com
E-mail: deelman@loxinfo.co.th
Job sectors: Education: international schools, including pre-school, nursery, primary and secondary.
Countries or regions: Worldwide.
Candidate profile: Qualified teachers in all subjects with at least two years' experience. Also experienced school administrators.

Additional information: Associate offices in Canada and the USA. Interviews are conducted in the UK, Australia and other countries.

Sherry Sherratt Technical Recruitment Ltd
Type of Organisation: Private recruitment agency.
Address: PO Box 4529, London SW18 3XD.
Telephone: (020) 8875 1895 (civil engineering, building); (020) 8875 1849 (oil & gas, petrochemicals).
Fax: (020) 8875 1894.
E-mail: sstr.ltd@pobox.com.
Job sectors: Civil engineering, construction, oil and gas, petrochemicals.
Countries or regions: Worldwide.
Candidate profile: Qualified engineers and quantity surveyors aged 30 plus with overseas experience.
Additional information: Recruits for consulting engineers and contractors. Offers salaried staff appointments, not contract work. British or EU passport holders only.

Sherwood Engineering Recruitment
Type of Organisation: Private recruitment agency.
Address: Sherwood House, 200 Sheffield Road, Tinsley, Sheffield S9 1UP.
Telephone: (0114) 244 6600.
Fax: (0114) 244 7800.
Website: www.sherwoodrecruitment.com.
E-mail: robert@sherwoodrec.f9.co.uk.
Job sectors: Construction and process industries.
Countries or regions: Worldwide.
Candidate profile: Experienced and suitably qualified for positions ranging from foreman supervisor to project director level.

Skillshare Africa
Type of Organisation: Voluntary organisation.
Address: 126 New Walk, Leicester LE1 7JA.
Telephone: (0116) 254 1862.
Fax: (0116) 254 2614.
Website: www.skillshare.org.
E-mail: info@skillshare.org
Job sectors: Agriculture, education (specifically vocational training and EFL), health, community development, business, technical (engineering).
Countries or regions: Botswana, Lesotho, Mozambique, Namibia, South Africa, Swaziland.
Candidate profile: Qualified professionals with a minimum of 2 years' rel-

evant post qualification experience.

Additional information: Placements are usually for 2 years; paid travel to and from the countries; pre and post placement grants; medical insurance cover; National Insurance payments; free accommodation.

Solihull Au Pair & Nanny Agency

Type of Organisation: Private employment agency.
Address: 1565 Stratford Road, Hall Green, Birmingham B28 9JA.
Telephone: (0121) 733 6444.
Fax: (0121) 733 6555.
Website: www.100s-aupairs.co.uk.
E-mail: solihull@100s-aupairs.co.uk.
Job sectors: Au pairs and nannies.
Countries or regions: Europe and USA.
Candidate profile: Au pairs must be 18-27, single and have childcare experience. Nannies must have experience, NNEB or similar candidate profile with two written references, certificates of achievement (e.g. first aid).
Additional information: Has associate agency (Edgware Au Pair Agency) and network of agents.

Stepp Recruitment

Address: 156 Hagley Road, Oldswinford, Stourbridge, West Midlands DY8 2JL.
Telephone: (01384) 443773.
Fax: (01384) 443883.
Website: www.appointments.uk.com.
E-mail: maggie@appointments.uk.com.
Job sectors: Construction: curtain walling, building facades, aluminium windows, roofing/cladding.
Countries or regions: Europe, Middle East, Far East.
Candidate profile: Experience in the building facade industry.
Additional information: The only specialist recruiter to the building facade industry. Advertises in *Construction News, Building, Contract Journal.* Also undertakes executive search and recruits through referral.

Students Partnership Worldwide

Type of Organisation: Non-profit organisation.
Address: 17 Dean's Yard, London SW1P 3PB.
Telephone: (020) 7222 0138.
Fax: (020) 7233 0008.
E-mail: spwuk@gn.apc.org
Job sectors: Educational, environmental and social development in rural

communities in Asia and Africa.
Countries or regions: Tanzania, Uganda, Zimbabwe, Nepal, India.
Candidate profile: Young people aged 18-28.
Additional information: Programmes last up to 10 months. Participants work with local volunteers and are required to cover their placement cost.

TA Group Ltd
Type of Organisation: Private recruitment agency.
Address: 266 South Town Road, Great Yarmouth NR31 0JJ.
Telephone: (01493) 416890.
Fax: (01493) 603377.
E-mail: philip.caton@gtyarm.freeserve.co.uk.
Job sectors: Construction, oil and gas.
Countries or regions: Azerbaijan, Libya, Saudi Arabia, Kazakhstan, Kuwait, Qatar, Tunisia, Equatorial Guinea.
Candidate profile: Relevant technical candidate profile and experience.
Additional information: Part of Fluor Daniel International, the largest construction and engineering company in the world. Associate office: Badentoy Avenue, Porthlethen, Aberdeen AB1 4YB. *Telephone:* 01224 780790. *Fax:* 01224 783078.

Taylor Recruitment
Type of Organisation: Private recruitment agency.
Address: 1 St John's Court, Farncombe Street, Godalming, Surrey GU7 3BA.
Telephone: (01483) 418383.
Fax: (01483) 418989.
Website: www.taylorrecruitment.com
E-mail: jobs@taylorrecruitment.com
Job sectors: Oil & gas, construction, maintenance and civil engineering (supervisors to senior management).
Countries or regions: Middle East.
Candidate profile: HNC to degree level.
Additional information: Contact Edward Bradley, Senior Consultant.

Teaching & Projects Abroad Ltd
Type of Organisation: Voluntary organisation.
Address: Gerrard House, Rustington, West Sussex BN16 1AW.
Telephone: (01903) 859911.
Fax: (01903) 785779.
Website: www.teaching-abroad.co.uk.
E-mail: info@teaching-abroad.co.uk.

Job sectors: Teaching, mainly English as a foreign language, journalism, conservation and business, medical work.

Countries or regions: China, Ghana, India, Mexico, Nepal, Russia, Ukraine, Thailand, Togo.

Candidate profile: At least university entrance qualifications. Age range: 17 to 70.

Additional information: Contract arrangements are flexible ranging from one month to one year. In 2000 there were 600 participants on the teaching scheme and 400 in other categories. Support is provided by a network of 50 local organisers.

Thomas Mining Associates

Type of Organisation: Mining recruitment specialists.

Address: PO Box 2010, Lancing, W Sussex BN15 8HZ.

Telephone: (01903) 753511.

Fax: (01903) 753510.

Website: www.thomasmining.com.

E-mail: dennis@thomasmining.prestel.co.uk.

Job sectors: Mining, quarrying, exploration.

Countries or regions: World-wide, expecially Russia, Central Asia, South America, Middle East and Pacific Rim.

Candidate Profile: Mostly management and technical staff with degrees or higher for organisations of all types. Some artisan/face level staff also recruited.

Additional information: Operates candidate database. Offices in Australia, New Zealand, South America.

TMP Worldwide

Type of Organisation: Private recruitment agency.

Address: Chancery House, 53–64 Chancery Lane, London WC1A 1QS.

Telephone: (020) 7406 5000.

Fax: (020) 7406 5001.

Website: www.eresourcing.tmp.com.

Job sectors: Most sectors including hi-tech industry electronics, aerospace, semiconductors, telecommunications, software within multinationals, major corporations, R & D facilities. Also legal and accountancy.

Countries or regions: North America, Europe, Middle East, Far East, Australasia.

Candidate profile: At least a degree plus 3-4 years' experience in the relevant disciplines.

Additional information: Part of TMP Worldwide, the largest recruitment advertising group in the world. Offices throughout Europe. Largest search and selection company in Australia (TMP Morgan & Banks). In recent years TMP has acquired the HW Group and the QD Group which specialised in legal and financial recruitment. Owners of websites monster.com and monster.co.uk. Advertises in *Daily Telegraph, Sunday Times. Electronics Weekly, Electronics Times, Computing.*

Top Choice Recruitment Ltd
Type of Organisation: Private recruitment agency.
Address: 81 Fulwell Park Avenue, Twickenham, Middlesex TW2 5HG.
Telephone: (020) 8893 3030.
Fax: (020) 8893 3091.
Website: www.top-choice.co.uk.
E-mail: recruitment@topchoice.co.uk.
Job sectors: Engineering and technical (including avionics, power, oil & gas, petrochemicals, IT), research, development and manufacture, sales, planning, design and construction.
Countries or regions: Europe and worldwide.
Candidate profile: Specialist engineers. Degree is essential in most cases.
Additional information: Advertises in national and international press and in expatriate journals. Prospective candidates should apply by sending a CV. Relevant CVs will be added to a database.

Track International
Type of Organisation: Private recruitment agency.
Address: PO Box 1, Perranporth, Cornwall TR6 0YG.
Telephone: (01872) 573937.
Fax: (01872) 571282.
Website: www.trackint.com.
E-mail: work@trackint.com.
Job sectors: IT (all levels),
Countries or regions: USA, Austria, Germany, Switzerland and other European countries.
Candidate profile: Graduates in the relevant discipline.
Additional information: Recruits for permanent positions and long-term contracts.

Travellers Worldwide
Type of Organisation: Non profit organisation.
Address: 7 Mulberry Close, Ferring, West Sussex BN12 5HY.
Telephone: (01903) 502595.
Fax: (01903) 502595.
Website: www.travellersworldwide.com.

E-mail: info@travellersworldwide.com.

Job sectors: Voluntary work in teaching, conservation. Work experience in journalism, law, medicine, veterinary, tourism, hospitality and catering.

Countries or regions: Argentina, Brazil, China, Cuba, Ghana, India, Malaysia, Nepal, Russia, South Africa, Sri Lanka, Ukraine.

Candidate profile: 17 years upwards. No qualifications or experience are necessary.

Additional information: Founder member of the Year Out Group.

TTI Personaldienstleistung

Type of Organisation: Private recruitment agency.

Address: Ziegelweg 2, A-4481 Asten, Austria.

Telephone: 00 43 7224 675510.

Fax: 00 43 7224 675511.

Website: www.tti.at.

E-mail: office@tti.at.

Job sectors: Mechanical engineering, steel, construction, industrial plants.

Countries or regions: Africa, Middle East, Far East.

Candidate profile: Technicians, engineers, manufacturing supervisors, erection supervisors, admin personnel, quality controllers, claims managers with a minimum of 10-15 years' experience, technical qualifications and a degree, if required.

Additional information: Partner companies world-wide. Does not recruit for blue collar positions. Recruitment is via web-page, the Internet, advertisements in *Nexus*, etc. Cannot handle speculative applications.

Umm Al-Jawwaby Oil Service Co Ltd

Type of Organisation: Private recruitment agency,

Address: 15-17 Lodge Road, London NW8 7JA.

Telephone: (020) 7314 6000.

Fax: (020) 7314 6001/2/3.

Website: www.jawaby.co.uk.

E-mail: info@jawaby.co.uk.

Job sectors: Oil and gas industry.

Countries or regions: Libya.

Candidate profile: Qualified engineers, technicians and instructors.

United Nations Association International Service (UNAIS)

Type of Organisation: Voluntary organisation.

Address: Hunter House, 57 Goodramgate, York YO1 7FX.

Telephone: (01904) 647799.

Fax: (01904) 652353.

Website: www.internationalservice.org.uk.
E-mail: unais-uk@geo2.poptel.org.uk
Countries or regions: West Africa, Latin America, West Bank & Gaza.
Job sectors: Health education, community education and skills training.
Candidate profile: Suitably qualified people with experience.

V I P International

Type of Organisation: Private recruitment agency.
Address: 17 Charing Cross Road, London WC2H 0EP.
Telephone: (020) 7930 0541.
Fax: (020) 7930 2860.
Website: www.vipinternational.co.uk.
E-mail: vip@vipinternational.co.uk.
Job sectors: Tourism and hospitality industry (including catering, hotels, cruise ships).
Countries or regions: Worldwide.
Candidate profile: Qualified catering personnel, 4 years' experience (minimum).

Voluntary Service Overseas (VSO)

Type of Organisation: Voluntary organisation.
Address: 317 Putney Bridge Road, London SW15 2PN.
Telephone: (020) 8780 7500.
Fax: (020) 8780 7300.
Website: www.vso.org.uk.
E-mail: enquiry@vso.org.uk.
Job sectors: Education, business, health, social and community work, technical and natural resources.
Countries or regions: Eastern Europe, Africa, Asia, the Pacific, Belize and Guyana.
Candidate profile: Wide range of disciplines. Qualifications and experience essential.
Additional information: Now administers the former East European Partnership programmes. Also runs two programmes for less experienced people under 25: the Youth for Development Programme offering one-year placement to 18–25-year-olds to gain practical experience; and the World Youth Millennium Awards (formerly the International Volunteer Exchange) where young people work in community projects in the UK and then in Africa or Asia for six months.

Robert Walters Associates
Type of Organisation: Private recruitment agency
Address: 10 Bedford Street, London WC2E 9HE.
Telephone: (020) 7379 3333.
Fax: (020) 7915 8714.
Website: www.robertwalters.com.
E-mail: info@robertwalters.com.
Job sectors: Banking and finance, accountancy, IT, commerce, secretarial and support staff.
Countries or regions: Australia and New Zealand.
Candidate profile: Professionally qualified, though there may be opportunities for the partly qualified.
Additional information: Offices in Auckland, Amsterdam, Brussels, Hong Kong, Melbourne, New York, Sydney and Wellington (NZ). Associated with Options Consulting, an office staff agency in Sydney.

WEL Technical Services Ltd
Type of Organisation: Private recruitment agency and structural engineers.
Address: Weltec House, Romney Place, Maidstone, Kent ME15 6LG.
Telephone: (01622) 678031.
Fax: (01622) 683813.
Website: www.weltec.co.uk.
E-mail: admin@weltec.co.uk.
Job sectors: Designers, engineers and supervisors for the oil and petrochemical industries.
Countries or regions: Europe, Middle East and Far East.
Candidate profile: Relevant qualifications and experience.
Additional information: Has a Malaysian office whose e-mail is: weladin@po.jaring.my.

Wickland Westcott & Partners
Type of Organisation: Private recruitment agency.
Address: Walker House, 1 Walker Street, Macclesfield, Cheshire SK10 1BH.
Telephone: (01625) 508100.
Fax: (01625) 508101.
Website: www.wickland-westcott.co.uk.
E-mail: ww@wickland-westcott.co.uk.
Job sectors: Manufacturing and service industries.
Countries or regions: Europe.
Candidate profile: Experienced senior managers and directors.

Woodland Consultancy Services
Type of Organisation: Private recruitment agency.
Address: 4 Fairway, Petts Wood, Kent BR5 1EG.
Telephone: (01689) 828999.
Fax: (01689) 898980.
Website: woodland.co.uk.
E-mail: wcs-jobs@woodland.co.uk.
Job sectors: Engineering consultants and contractors, petrochemical oil/gas companies, and utilities.
Countries or regions: Locations include Europe, Middle East and Far East.
Candidate profile: Professional and technical engineers for design, site and project management, IT specialists and computing personnel.
Additional information: Recruits for UK companies requiring permanent and temporary personnel to work abroad. Member of REC.

Worldwide Health Care Exchange
Type of Organisation: Private recruitment agency.
Address: The Colonnades, Beaconsfield Close, Hatfield, Herts AL10 8YD.
Telephone: (01707) 259233.
Fax: (01707) 259223.
Website: www.bnauk.com
E-mail: bna@dial.pipex.com
Job sectors: Healthcare (doctors, nurses, RGNs, etc).
Countries or regions: Worldwide.
Candidate profile: Appropriate qualifications and experience.
Additional information: Offices throughout UK, Australia, New Zealand, South Africa, Germany, Netherlands, etc. Permanent and temporary vacancies in hospitals, clinics and homes.

Notes:
REC denotes that the agency is a member of the Recruitment and Employment Confederation. ASSC denotes that the agency is a member of the Association of Search and Selection Consultants. (See Useful addresses in the UK).

19

Country Directory

This part of the book offers a list of contact addresses specific to particular countries which can provide you with further information about the country in question and perhaps indicate what kind of opportunities are available.
A typical entry will include:

- *Embassy, High Commission or Consulate in UK or Europe:* This can provide details about immigration requirements, though a number of representations now charge a premium rate for this service. Some embassies also have reading rooms or publish information leaflets for intending residents.

- *Cultural Centre:* Some European countries have these and they are a useful source of information. They may have a library or reading room and arrange language courses.

- *Societies and Associations:* Another source of information about the country. Some of these will have business leanings while others are designed to promote friendship between Britain and the country concerned.

- *British Embassy or High Commission in country itself.* This can provide you with information about living conditions and business opportunities.

- *Chambers of Commerce:* These will have information about business conditions within the country and may be able to assist anyone planning to set up a business. In rare cases they may be able to suggest member organisations which are recruiting staff.

- *Employment Agencies and Publications:* In the case of several European countries the national employment agency is included as well as newspapers and periodicals which contain job advertisements.

AFGHANISTAN

Pop: 25 m.   *Area:* 652,225 sq km.
Afghanistan Embassy: 31 Prince's Gate, London SW7 1QQ. Tel: (020) 7589 8891
British Embassy: Karte Parwan, Kabul.
SAFE (UK), Denver Cottage, Vernham Dean, Andover, Hants SP11 0JY. Tel: (01264) 737233. Afghan educational and development charity.

ALBANIA

Pop: 3.5 m.   *Area* 27,398 sq km.
Albanian Embassy: 2nd Floor, 24 Buckingham Gate, London SW1E. Tel: (020) 7828 8897.
British Embassy: Rruga Skenderbeg 12, Tirana. (For British Council see Yugoslavia)
Anglo-Albanian Association: Flat 6, 38 Holland Park, London W11 3RP. Tel: (020) 7727 0287.

ALGERIA

Pop: 32 m.   *Area:* 2.4 m sq km.
Algerian Embassy: 54 Holland Pk, London W11 3RS. Tel: (020) 7221 7800.
Algerian Consulate: 6 Hyde Park Gate, London SW7. Tel: (020) 7589 6885.
British Embassy, Résidence Cassiopée, Bâtiment B, Chemin des Glycines, Algiers.
British Council: 7 chemin des Glycines, BP 43, Alger-Gare, Algiers.

ANDORRA

Pop: 80,000.   *Area:* 468 sq km.
Andorran Delegation: 63 Westover Road, London London SW18 2RF. Tel: (020) 8874 4806.
Honorary British Consulate: Prat de la Creu 22, Bloc D, Alt 2, PO Box 1041, Andorra La Vella.

ANGOLA

Pop: 13 m.   *Area:* 1.25 m sq km.
Angolan Embassy: 98 Park Lane, London W1. Tel: (020) 7495 1752.
British Embassy: 4 Rua Diogo Cao, CP 1244, Luanda.

ANGUILLA

Pop: 11,000.   *Area:* 155 sq km.
Government House, Anguilla.
Anguillan Tourist Office, 7 Westwood Road, London SW13 0LA. Tel: (020) 8876 9025.

ANTIGUA & BARBUDA

Pop: 68,000.   *Area:* 442 sq km.
High Commission of Antigua and Barbuda: 15 Thayer St, London W1M 5DL. Tel: (020) 7486 7073.

British High Commission: Price Waterhouse Centre, 11 Old Parham Road, PO Box 483, St Johns.

ARGENTINA

Pop: 37 m.   *Area:* 2.77 m sq km.
Argentine Embassy: 65 Brook Street, London W1Y 1YE. Tel: (020) 7318 1300.
British Embassy: Dr Luis Agote 2412/52, Casilla de Correntes 2050), 1452 Buenos Aires.
British Council: Marcelo T de Alvear 590, 1058 Buenos Aires.
Anglo-Argentine Chamber of Commerce, Corrientes 457, 1043 Buenos Aires.
Anglo Argentine Society, 2 Belgrave Square, London SW1X 8PJ. Tel: (020) 7235 9505.

ARMENIA

Pop: 3.7 m.   *Area:* 29,800 sq km.
Armenian Embassy: 25A Cheniston Gardens, London W8 6TE. Tel: (020) 7938 5345.
British Embassy: Charents Street 28, Yerevan 375010.

AUSTRALIA

Pop: 18.3 m.   *Area:* 7.7 m sq km.
Australian High Commission, Australia House, Strand, London WC2B 4LA Tel: (020) 7379 4334; Visa enquiries: Tel: (0900) 160 0033. Website: www.australia.org.uk or www.immi.gov.au
Also at Chatsworth House, Lever Street, Manchester M1 2DL; 2nd Floor, Hobart House, Edinburgh EH2 2DL.
Australian Tourist Commission: 10 Putney Hill, London SW15. Tel: (0870) 556 1434.
British High Commission: Commonwealth Avenue, Canberra ACT 2600, Australia.
Australian British Trade Association, Commerce House, 26 Brisbane Avenue, Canberra ACT 2603, Australia.
British Council: Edgecliff Centre, 401/203 New South Head Road, PO Box 88, Edgecliff, Sydney, NSW 2027, Australia.
The Commission on Overseas Professional Qualifications, Commerce House, Cnr Brisbane Avenue and Macquarie Street, Barton, ACT 2600.
Australian British Chamber of Commerce, 314 Regent Street, London W1R 6LN. Tel: (020) 7636 4525.
New South Wales Government Office, Australian Centre, Strand, London WC2B 4LA. Tel: (020) 7887 5871.
Queensland Government Office, 392-393 Strand, London WC2R 0LZ. Tel: (020) 7836 1333.
South Australia Government Office, Australia House, Strand, London WC2B 4LA.

Tel: (020) 7836 3455.

Victoria Government Office, Melbourne Place, Strand, London WC2B 4LJ. Tel: (020) 7836 2656.

Western Australia Government Office, Australian Centre, Strand, London WC2B 4LA. Tel: (020) 7240 2881.

Migration Agents Registration Authority. Website: www.themara.com.au. (Lists approved migration agents in Australia, UK and elsewhere.)

Concept Australia, 3 Berryfield Close, Bromley, Kent BR1 2WF. Tel: (020) 8467 8521. Also at PO Box 328, Colchester, Essex CO1 1AA. Tel/Fax: (01206) 549406. Website: www.conceptaustralia.co.uk. Migration consultants.

Challice Emigration, Rectory Farm, Top Street, Elston, Notts NG23 5NP. Tel/Fax: (01636) 525903. Migration consultants.

Four Corners Emigration, Freepost NWW1289, Manchester M22 5FR. Tel: (0345) 419453.

Workpermit.com, 11 Bolt Court, Fleet Street, London EC4A 3DQ. Tel: (020) 7495 3999. Fax: (020) 7495 3991. Website: www.workpermit.com. Migration consultants.

Ambler Collins, Eden House, 59 Fulham High Street, London SW6 3JJ. Tel: (020) 7371 0213; Fax: (020) 7736 8841. Migration Consultants. Operates Hob Net – international employment search across the Internet.

The Emigration Group, 7 Heritage Court, Lower Bridge Street, Chester CH1 1RD. Tel: (01244) 321414; Fax: (01244) 342288. Website: www.emigration.ik.com.

Ian Harrop & Associates, PO Box 12, Lechlade, Glos GL7 3YG; Tel (01376) 860850. Migration consultant.

Migrate Australia, The Flat, The Old Quarry, Arlington, Bibury, Cirencester GL7 5ND. Tel & Fax: (01285) 642869. Migration consultant.

Streamline consultants, Level 3, 79 Buckingham Palace Road, London SW1. Tel: (020) 7736 5075. Fax: (020) 7736 0282. Migration consultancy.

New Zealand & Australia Migration Bureau, 5 Manfred Road, Putney, London SW15 2RS. Tel: (020) 8874 2844. Fax: (020) 8874 1178.

The Age: www.theage.com.au. *Sydney Morning Herald:* www.smh.com.au.

AUSTRIA

Pop: 8 m.   *Area:* 84,000 sq km.

Austrian Embassy, 18 Belgrave Mews West, London SW1X 5HU. Tel: (020) 7235 3731. E-mail: embassy@austria.org.uk.

The Austrian Institute: 28 Rutland Gate, London SW7 1PQ. Tel: (020) 7584 8653.

Austrian Tourist Office: 30 George Street, London W1R 0AL. Tel: (020) 7269 0461.

British Embassy, Reisnerstr 40, A-1030 Wien (Vienna).

British Council, Schenkenstr. 4, A-1010 Wien.

Anglo-Austrian Society, 46 Queen Anne's Gate, London SW1H 9AU. Tel: (020) 7222 0366.

Arbeitsmarktverwaltung: EURO B12, Südtirolerplatz 14-16, A-6020 Innsbruck (International Jobcentre)
Die Presse: www.diepresse.at.

AZERBAIJAN

Pop: 8 m.   *Area:* 86,600 sq km.
Azerbaijani Embassy: 4 Kensington Court, London W8 5DL. Tel: (020) 7938 3412.
Ministry of Education: 1 Azadlyg Square, Baku 370016.
British Embassy: 2 Izmir Street, Baku 370065.

BAHAMAS

Pop: 300,000.   *Area:* 14,000 sq km.
Bahamas High Commission: 10 Chesterfield Street, London W1X 8AH. Tel: (020) 7408 4488. E-mail: bahamas.hicom.lond@cableinet.co.uk.
British High Commission: Ansbacher House, East Street, PO Box N7516, Nassau.

BAHRAIN

Pop: 600,000.   *Area:* 706 sq km.
Bahrain Embassy: 98 Gloucester Road, London SW7 4AU. Tel: (020) 7370 5132.
British Embassy, P O Box 114, 21 Government Avenue, North Manama 306.
British Council: AMA Centre, 146 Sheikh Salman Highway, PO Box 452, Manama 356.
Bahrain Oil Corporation: P O Box 25504, Awali. (Major employer)

BANGLADESH

Pop: 129 m.   *Area:* 148,400 sq km.
Bangladeshi High Commission: 28 Queen's Gate, London SW7 5JA. Tel: (020) 7584 0081. E-mail: bdesh-lon@dial,pipex.com.
British High Commission: United Nations Road, Baridhara Dhaka (PO Box 6079), Dhaka 12.
British Council: PO Box 161, 5 Fuller Road, Ramna, Dhaka 1000.

BARBADOS

Pop: 270,000.   *Area:* 430 sq km.
Barbados High Commission: 1 Great Russell Street, London WC1B 3NH   (020) 7631 4975.
British High Commission: Lower Collymore Rock, PO Box 676, Bridgetown.

BELARUS

Pop: 10.3 m.   *Area:* 207,600 sq km.
Belarus Embassy: 6 Kensington Court, London W8 5DL. Tel: (020) 7937 3288.
British Embassy: Ulitsa Karl Marx 37, Minsk 220030.
British Council: Minsk State Linguistic University, Ulitsa Zakharova 21, Minsk 220662.

BELGIUM

Pop: 10 m.   *Area:* 30,500 sq km.
Belgian Embassy: 103 Eaton Square, London SW1 9AB. Tel: (020) 7470 3700.
Website: www.belgian-embassy.co.uk.
Belgian Tourist Office: 31 Pepper Street, London E14 9RW. Tel: (0900) 188 7799.
British Embassy: Rue d'Arlon 85, 1040 Brussels.
British Council, rue de la Charité, 1210 Brussels.
British Chamber of Commerce: Egmont House, Rue d'Egmont 15, 1050 Brussels.
Anglo-Belgian Society: 5 Hartley Close, Bickely, Kent BR1 2TP. Tel: (020) 8467 8442.
L'Office Nationale de l'Emploi et de la Main d'Oeuvre (ONEM): Boulevard de l'Empereur 7, 1000 Brussels. (Government employment office.)
The Bulletin: www.ackroyd/be. (English language newspaper which advertises vacancies.)

BELIZE

Pop: 240,000.   *Area:* 23,000 sq km.
Belize High Commission: 19 Cavendish Square,   London W1. Tel: (020) 7499 9728.
British High Commission: PO Box 91, Belmopan.

BENIN

Pop: 6 m.   *Area:* 113,000 sq km.
Benin Embassy, 87 av Victor Hugo, 75116 Paris.
Honorary Consulate: Dolphin House, 16 The Broadway, Stanmore, Middlesex HA7 4DW. Tel: (020) 8954 8800.
British Consulate: Lot 24, Patte d'Oie, Cotonou.

BERMUDA

Pop: 60,000.   *Area:* 53 sq km.
Government Offices: Government House, Hamilton.
Bermuda Society & Secretariat, Five Trees, Wood Lane, Stanmore, Middx. Tel: (020) 8954 0652.

BOLIVIA

Pop: 8 m.   *Area:* 1.1 m sq km.
Bolivian Embassy: 106 Eaton Square, London SW1 9AD. Tel: (020) 7235 4248.
British Embassy: Avda Arce 2732-2754, Casilla 694, La Paz.

BOSNIA-HERZEGOVINA

Pop: 4.5 m.   *Area:* 51,000 sq km.
Embassy of Bosnia-Herzegovina: Morley House, 314-320 Regent Street, London
W1R 5AB. Tel: (020) 7255 3758.
British Embassy: 8 Tina Ujevica, Sarajevo 71000.
British Council: Obala Kulina Bana 4, 2nd Floor, Sarajevo.

BOTSWANA

Pop: 1.6 m.   *Area:* 582,000 sq km.
Botswana High Commission: 6 Stratford Place, London W1N 9AE. Tel: (020) 7499
0031. Visa information: 0900 160 0335.
British High Commission, Queens Road, The Mall, PO Box 439, Gaborone.
UK-Botswana Society: Whitehill, Portsmouth Road, Ripley, Woking GU23 6EW.
Tel: (01483) 225336.

BRAZIL

Pop: 170 m.   *Area:* 8.5 m sq km.
Brazilian Embassy: 32 Green Street, London W1Y 3FD. Tel: (020) 7499 0877.
Brazilian   Consulate: 6 St Albans Street, London SW1Y 4SG. Tel: (020) 7930
9055.
Brazilian Tourist Office: 47 Causton Street, London SW1X. Tel: (020) 7976 5511.
British Embassy, Avenida das Nacoes Lote 8, Caixa Postal 07-0586, Brasilia DF.
British Council: Edificio Morro Vermilho, Quadra 1, Bloco 21, SCS, 70359-900
Brasilia DF.
British Chamber of Commerce, Caixe Postal 1621, CEP 0159-970 Sao Paolo.
Anglo-Brazilian Society: c/o Brazilian Embassy. Tel: (020) 7493 8493.

BRUNEI DARUSSALEM

Pop: 325,000.   *Area:* 5,765 sq km.
Brunei High Commission: 19-20 Belgrave Square, London SW1X 8PG. Tel: (020)
7581 0521.
British High Commission: (P O Box 2197), 2nd Floor, Block D, Komplex
Bangunaa Yayasan, Jalan Pretty Bandar Seri Begawan 1921.
British Council: 45 Simpang 100, Jalan Tunku Link, Gadong, Bandar Sri Begawan
2085.

BULGARIA

Pop: 8.5 m.   *Area:* 111,000 sq km.
Bulgarian Embassy: 186 Queen's Gate, London SW7 5HL. Tel: (020) 7584 9400.
Visa information: 0900 117 1208.
Bulgarian Tourist Office: 18 Prince's Street, London W1R 7RE. Tel: (020) 7499 6988.
British Embassy: Blvd Vassil Levski 65-67, Sofia 1000.
British Council: Tulova Street 7, 1504 Sofia.
British Bulgarian Friendship Society: c/o Finsbury Library Basement, 245 St John Street, London EC1V 4NB. Tel: (020) 7837 2304.

BURKINA FASO

Pop: 12 m.   *Area:* 274,000 sq km.
Burkina Faso Embassy: 16 Place Guy d'Arezzo, 1060 Brussels. Tel: 00 32 2 345 9911.
Honorary Consulate: 5 Cinnamon Row, Plantation Wharf, London SW11 3TW. Tel: (020) 7738 1800.
British Consulate: BP 3769, c/o Tobacco Marketing Consultants. Ouagadougou.

BURMA (MYANMAR)

Pop: 49 m.   *Area:* 676,000 sq km.
Burmese Embassy: 19a Charles Street, London W1X 8ER. Tel: (020) 7499 8841.
Visa information: (020) 7499 8841.
British Embassy: 80 Strand Road, PO Box 638, Rangoon (Yangon).

BURUNDI

Pop: 7 m.   *Area:* 29,000 sq km.
Burundi Embassy: 46 Place Marie Louise, 1040 Brussels.
British Embassy: See Rwanda.

CAMBODIA

Pop: 11 m.   *Area:* 181,000 sq km.
British Embassy, 29 rue 75, Phnom Penh.

CAMEROON

Pop: 15 m.   *Area:* 475,000 sq km.
Cameroon Embassy: 84 Holland Park, London W11 3SB. Tel: (020) 7727 0771.
British Embassy: (B P 547), Le Concorde, Avenue Winston Churchill, Yaoundé.
British Council: Immeuble Christo, rue Charles de Gaulle, BP 818, Yaounde.

CANADA

Pop: 30 m.　　　*Area:* 10 m sq km.

Canadian High Commission: Macdonald House, 1 Grosvenor Square, London W1X 0AB. Tel: (020) 7258 6600. Website: www.canada.org.uk.

Immigration Department: 38 Grosvenor Street, London W1X 0AA. Tel: (020) 7409 2071 and (0906) 861 6644. Website: http://cicfnet.ingenia.com.

Canada Visa Information: PO Box 2590, Eastbourne, E Sussex BN21 3US. Send SAE with £1 stamp for self-assessment guide.

Canada House: Trafalgar Square, London SW1Y 5BJ. Tel: (020) 7258 6600.

Canadian Tourist Office: 62-65 Trafalgar Square, London WC2N 5DY. Tel: (020) 7839 2299.

British High Commission: 80 Elgin Street, Ottawa, ON K1P 5KT.

British Columbia Government Office: 1 Regent St, London SW1Y 4NS. Tel: (020) 7930 6857.

Quebec Government Office: 59 Pall Mall, London SW1 5JH. Tel: (020) 7766 5900. Website: www.immq.gouv.qc.ca.

Ontario Government: Website: www.ontario-canada.com.

New Brunswick Government: Website: www@gov.nb.ca.

Manitoba Government: Website: www.gov.mb.ca/chc/immsettl.

Saskatchewan Government: Website: www.gov.sk.ca.

Centre for Canadian Studies, University of Edinburgh, 21 George Street, Edinburgh RH8 9LD. Tel: (0131) 667 1011.

Regional Canadian Study Centre, University of Leeds LS2 9JT.

Mediacorp Canada Inc, 15 Madison Avenue, Toronto, Ontario, M5R 2S2. Tel: 00 1 416 6069. Fax: 00 1 964 3202. E-mail: mci@mediacorp2.com. Publisher and distributor of careers handbooks relating to Australia.

SIS Canada Ltd, 1 Olympic Way, Suite 424, Wembley, Middlesex HA9 0NP. Tel: (020) 8782 1142. E-mail: siscanada@yahoo.com.

Four Corners Emigration, Freepost NWW1289, Manchester M22 5FR. Tel: (0345) 419453.

Ambler Collins, Eden House, 59 Fulham High Street, London SW6 3JJ. Tel: (020) 7371 0213; Fax: (020) 7736 8841. Migration consultants. Operates Hob Net – international employment search across the Internet.

Workpermit.com, 11 Bolt Court, Fleet Street, London EC4A 3DQ. Tel: (020) 7495 3999. Fax: (020) 7495 3991. Website: www.workpermit.com. Migration consultants.

Migration Bureau, 5 Manfred Road, Putney, London SW15 2RS. Tel: (020) 8874 2844. Fax: (020) 8874 1178. Migration consultants.

Vijay Sharma Solicitors, 142 Buckingham Palace Road, London SW1W 9TR. Tel: (020) 7730 7322; Fax: (020) 7730 4150. Immigration lawyer. (Contact Mr Gohil, associate of Brownstein, Brownstein & Associates, Canada.)

The Emigration Group, 7 Heritage Court, Lower Bridge Street, Chester CH1 1RD. Tel: 01244 321414; Fax: (01244) 342288. Migration consultants.

Globe & Mail: www.globeandmail.ca.

Vancouver Sun: www.southam.com/vancouversun.

CAYMAN ISLANDS

Pop: 20,000.   *Area:* 256 sq km.
Cayman Islands Government Office: 6 Arlington Street, London SW1A 1RE.
Tel: (020) 7491 7772.
Cayman Islands Government. Government Administration Building, Georgetown,
Grand Cayman.
Northwester Co, PO Box 243, Grand Cayman. (Publishes *Cayman Islands
Handbook and Businessman's Guide.)*

CENTRAL AFRICAN REPUBLIC

Pop: 3.6 m.   *Area:* 623,000 sq km.
Central African Republic Embassy: 30 rue des Perchamps, 75016 Paris. Tel: 00 33
1 4224 4256.
British Consulate: BP 977, Bangui.

CHAD

Pop: 7 m.   *Area:* 1.3 m sq km.
Chad Embassy: Blvd Lambermont 52, 1030 Brussels. Tel: 00 32 215 1975.
British Consulate: BP 877, Avenue Charles de Gaulle, Nkjamena.

CHILE

Pop: 14.7 m.   *Area:* 757,000 sq km.
Chilean Embassy: 12 Devonshire Street, London W1N 2DS. Tel: (020) 7580 6392.
Consulate: (020) 7580 1023.
British Embassy: (Casilla 72-D), Av El Bosque, Providencia, Santiago.
British Council: (Casilla 15 T), Eliodoro Yanez 832, Tajamar, Santiago.
British Chamber of Commerce: Avenida Suecia 155C, Providencia, Santiago.

CHINA (PEOPLE'S REPUBLIC)

Pop: 1,280 m.   *Area:* 9.5 sq km.
Chinese Embassy: 49-51 Portland Place, London W1N 3AH. Tel: (020) 7636 8845.
Consular Section: 31 Portland Place, London W1N 3AG. Tel: (020) 7631 1430.
China Tourist Office: 4 Glentworth Street, London NW1. Tel: (0900) 160 0188.
British Embassy: 11 Guang Hua Lu, Jian Guo Men Wai, Beijing 100600.
British Council: Cultural & Education Section, British Embassy, 4th Floor,
Landmark Building, 8 North Songsahuan Road, Chaoyang District, Beijing 100026.
Society for Anglo-Chinese Understanding, 2 Lawnswood Avenue, Poulton le
Fylde, Lancs FY6 7ED. Tel: (01253) 894582.
Great Britain China Centre, 15 Belgrave Square, London SW1X 8PG Tel: (020)
7235 6696.

CHINA (REPUBLIC)

See **TAIWAN**

COLOMBIA

Pop: 33 m.   *Area:* 1.1 m sq km.
Colombian Embassy: 3 Hans Crescent, London SW1X 0LR. Tel: (020) 7589 9177.
Visa service: 0900 188 0890.
Colombian Consulate: 15 Great Titchfield Street, London W1.   Tel: (020) 7637 9893.
British Embassy: (Apartado Aéreo 4508), Edificio Ing Barings, Carrera 9 No 76-49 Piso 9, Bogota.
British Council: (Apartado Aéreo 089231), Calle 87 No 12-79, Bogota.
Colombo-British Chamber of Commerce, Avenida 39# 13-62, Bogota.

COMORES ISLANDS

Pop: 500,000.   *Area:* 2,171 sq km.
British Consulate: PO Box 986, Henri Fraise Fils & Co, Moroni.

CONGO

Pop: 3 m.   *Area:* 342,000 sq km.
Honorary Consulate: 131 Wandsworth Road, London SW11.   Tel: (020) 77622 0419.
Congolese Embassy: 37 bis rue Paul Valéry, 75116 Paris. Tel: 00 33 1 4500 6057.
Honorary British Consulate: Cote de l'Hotel Meridien, Rue Lyantey 26, Brazzaville. British Embassy: see Dem Gov Congo.

CONGO, DEMOCRATIC GOVERNMENT OF (formerly Zaire)

Pop: 52 m.   *Area:* 2.3 m sq km.
Embassy of Dem Rep of Congo: 26 Chesham Place, London SW1X 8HH. Tel: (020) 7235 6137.
British Embassy: (BP 8094), avenue des Trois Z, Kinshasa/Gombe.

COSTA RICA

Pop: 3.8 m.   *Area:* 51,000 sq km.
Costa Rican Embassy: 14 Lancaster Gate, London W2 3LH. Tel: (020) 7706 8844.
British Embassy: Apartado 815, Edificio Centro Colon, 1007 San José.

COTE D'IVOIRE.

See **IVORY COAST**.

CROATIA

Pop: 4.5 m.   *Area:* 56,610 sq km.
Croatian Embassy: 21 Conway Street, London W1OP. Tel: (020) 7387 1790.
British Embassy: PO Box 454, Vlaska 121/III Floor, Zagreb.
British Council: PO Box 55, 12/1 Ilica, 10000 Zagreb.

CUBA

Pop: 11 m.   *Area:* 111,000 sq km.
Cuban Embassy: 167 High Holborn, London WC1 6PA. Tel: (020) 7240 2488. Visa information: (0900) 188 0820.
Cuba Tourist Board, 154 Shaftesbury Avenue, London WC2. Tel: (020) 7240 6655.
British Embassy: Calle 34 No 702/4, Miramar, Havana.

CYPRUS

Pop: 800,000.   *Area:* 9,250 sq km.
Cyprus High Commission: 93 Park Street, London W1Y 4ET. Tel: (020) 7499 8272.
Cyprus Tourist Office: 17 Hanover Street, London W1. Tel: (020) 7569 8800.
British High Commission: P O Box 1978, Nicosia.
British Council, 3 Museum Street, (P O Box 1995), Nicosia 1097.
Turkish Rep of N Cyprus Office, 29 Bedford Square, London WC1B 3EG. Tel: (020) 7631 1920.
Cyprus Weekly: www.cyprusweekly.com.cy.

CZECH REPUBLIC

Pop: 10.3 m.   *Area:* 78,664 sq km.
Czech Embassy: 25 Kensington Palace Gardens, London W8 4QY. Tel: (020) 7243 1115. Visa information: (0900) 117 1267.
Czech Tourist Office: 95 Great Portland Street, London W1N.   Tel: (0906) 364 0641.
British Embassy, Thunovska Ulice 14, 11800 Prague 1.
British Council: Narodni 10, 125.01 Prague.
Prague Post: www.praguepost.cz.

DENMARK

Pop: 5.3 m.   *Area:* 43,000 sq km.
Royal Danish Embassy: 55 Sloane Street, London SW1X 9SR. Tel: (020) 7333

0200. Visa information: (0900) 160 0115. Website: www.denmark.co.uk.
Danish Tourist Office: 55 Sloane Street, London SW1X 9SR. Tel: (0900) 160
0109.
British Embassy, Kastelvej 36-40, 2100 Copenhagen.
British Council: Gammel Mont 12.3, 1117 Copenhagen K.
Arbejdmarkedsstryrelsen. Blegdamsvej 56, 2100 Copenhagen.
Copenhagen Post: www.cphpost.dk.

DJIBOUTI

Pop: 700,000.   *Area:* 22,000 sq km.
Djibouti Embassy: 26 rue Emile Ménier, 75116 Paris. Tel: 00 33 1 4727 4922.
British Consulate: PO Box 81, 9-11 rue de Genève, Djibouti.

DOMINICA

Pop: 75,000.   *Area:* 751 sq km.
Dominican High Commission: 1 Collingham Gardens, London SW5 0HW. Tel:
(020) 7370 5194.
British Consulate: PO Box 6, Roseau. British Embassy: see Barbados.

DOMINICAN REPUBLIC

Pop: 7.8 m.   *Area:* 48,000 sq km.
Dominican Republic Embassy, 139 Inverness Terrace, London W2 6JF. Tel: (020)
7727 6214.
Dominican Republic Tourist Board, 18 Hand Street, London WC1. (020) 7242
7778.
British Embassy: Avenida 27 de Febrero 233, Santa Domingo, DN.
British Chamber of Commerce: Apartado Posrtal 718-2. Avenida R Betancourt
1302, Santo Domingo.

ECUADOR

Pop: 12.7 m.   *Area:* 284,000 sq km.
Ecuador Embassy: 3 Hans Crescent, London SW1X 0LN Tel: (020) 7584
1367/2648.
British Embassy: Calle Gonzalez Suarez 111, Casilla 314, Quito.
British Council: Av Amazonas 1646, (Casilla 17 07 8829), Quito.
Anglo-Ecuadorean Society: Gray Ladies, 1 Whitelaw Close, Sturminster Newton,
Dorset DT10 1EJ. Tel: (01258) 472748.

EGYPT

Pop: 68m.   *Area:* 1 m sq km.
Egyptian Embassy: 2 Lowndes Street, London SW1X. Tel: (020) 7235 9777. Visa

information: (0900) 188 7777.
Egyptian Tourist Office: 170 Piccadilly, London W1. Tell: (020) 7493 5283.
British Embassy: Ahmed Ragheb Street, Garden City, Cairo.
British Council: 192 Sharia el Nil, Agouza, Cairo. (Also in Alexandria.)

EL SALVADOR

Pop: 6.3 m.   *Area:* 21,000 sq km.
El Salvador Embassy: Mayfair House, 39 Great Portland Street, London W1W. Tel:
(020) 7436 8282. Visa information: (0906) 844 4580.
British Embassy, Edificio Inter-Inversiones, Paseo General Escalaon 4828, PO Box
1591, San Salvador.

ERITREA

Pop: 3.8 m.   *Area:* 93,679 sq km.
Eritrea Consulate: 96 White Lion Street, London N1. Tel: (020) 7713 0096.
British Embassy: Zones 3/01. Emperor Yohannes Avenue, House No 4, Asmara.
British Council: Lorenzo Ta'zaz Street No 23, PO Box 997, Asmara.

ESTONIA

Pop: 1.4 m.   45,215 sq km.
Estonian Embassy: 16 Hyde Park Gate, London SW7 5DG. Tel: (020) 7589 3428.
British Embassy: Kentmanni 20, Tallinn 0100.

ETHIOPIA

Pop: 66 m.   *Area:* 1,128,000 sq km.
Ethiopian Embassy: 17 Prince's Gate, London SW7 1PZ. Tel: (020) 7589 7212.
British Embassy: (P O Box 858), Fikre Mariam Abatechan Street, Addis Ababa.
British Council: (P O Box 1043), Artistic Building, Adwa Avenue, Addis Ababa.

FALKLAND ISLANDS

Pop: 2,600.   *Area:* 12,172 sq km.
Falkland Islands Government Office: Falkland House, 14 Broadway, London
SW1H 0BH. Tel: (020) 7222 2542.
Falkland Islands Government: Government House, Stanley.
Falkland Islands Association, 16 Douglas Street, London SW1. Tel: (020) 7592
0022.

FIJI

Pop: 850,000.   *Area:* 18,300 sq km.

Fiji High Commission: 34 Hyde Park Gate, London SW7 5BN. Tel: (020) 7584 3661.
British High Commission: Victoria House, 478 Gladstone Road, Suva. (Also looks after Nauru and Tuvalu.)
British Council: Vanua House, Victoria Parade, Suva.

FINLAND

Pop: 5 m.   *Area:* 338,000 sq km.
Finnish Embassy: 38 Chesham Place, London SW1X 8HW. Tel: (020) 7838 6200. Website: www.finemb.org.uk.
Finnish Tourist Office: 30-35 Pall Mall, London SW1Y 5LP. Tel: (020) 7839 4048.
British Embassy, Itainen Puistotie 17, 00140 Helsinki.
British Council: Hakaniemenkatu 2, 00530 Helsinki.
Finno-British Trade Association, Etela Esplanaadi 2, 00130 Helsinki 10.
International Employment Service: Fabianinkatu 32, 00100 Helsinki.

FRANCE

Pop: 59 m.   *Area:* 544,000 sq km.
French Embassy: 58 Knightsbridge, London SW1X 7JT. Tel: (020) 7201 1000. Visa information: (0900) 188 7733.
French Institute: 14 Cromwell Place, London SW7 2JR. Tel: (020) 7581 2701.
French Tourist Office: 178 Piccadilly, London W1V 0AL. Tel: (020) 7491 7622.
British Embassy, 35 rue du Faubourg St Honoré, 75008 Paris.
British Council, 9 rue de Constantine, 75007 Paris.
Franco-British Chamber of Commerce: 31 rue de Boissy d'Anglas, 75008 Paris.
Association Nationale pour l'Emploi: 4 rue Galilée, 93198 Noisy-le-Grand. (State Employment Service)
Association Bernard Gregory: 53 rue de Turbigo, 75003 Paris. (Placement service to post-graduates.)
Franco-British Society: Room 623, Linen Hall, 162-168 Regent Street, London W1R 5TB. Tel/Fax: (020) 7734 0815.
International Herald Tribune: www.iht.com.

GABON

Pop: 1.2 m.   *Area:* 268,000 sq km.
Gabon Embassy: 27 Elvaston Place, London SW7 5NL. Tel: (020) 7823 9986.
British Consulate: c/o Brossette, BP 486, Libreville. Embassy in Democratic Republic of Congo.

GAMBIA

Pop: 1 m.   *Area:* 11,000 sq km.
Gambian High Commission: 57 Kensington Court, London W8 5DG. Tel: (020)
7937 6316. Gambian Tourist Office: Tel: (020) 7376 0093.
British High Commission: PO Box 507, 48 Atlantic Road, Fajara, Gambia.

GEORGIA

Pop: 5.5 m.   *Area:* 69,700 sq km.
Georgian Embassy: 3 Hornton Place, Kensington, London W8. Tel: (020) 7937
8233. Visa information: Tel: (0900) 160 0558.
British Embassy: Metechi Palace Hotel, Tblisi 380003.
British Council: 13 Chavcharaze Avenue, 2nd Floor, Tblisi 380079.

GERMANY

Pop: 82 m.   *Area:* 357,000 sq km.
German Embassy, 23 Belgrave Square, London SW1X 8PZ. Tel: (020) 7824 1300.
Website: www.german-embassy.org.uk.
German Consulates General at Norwich House, 8-12 Water Street, Liverpool L2
8TA and 16 Eglinton Crescent, Edinburgh EH12 5DG.
German Tourist Office: PO Box 2695, London W1R 0EN. Tel: (020) 7734 2600 or
(0900) 160 0100.
Goethe Institute, 50 Prince's Gate, London SW7 2PH. Tel: (020) 7411 3400.
Library and language courses.
British Embassy, Friedrich-Ebert Allee 77, 5300 Bonn.
British Council, Hahnenstrasse 6, 50667 Köln 1.
British Chamber of Commerce, Severinstrasse 50628 Küln.
Auslandsabteilung, Zentralstelle für Arbeitsvermittlung, Feuerbachstrasse 42-46,
60325 Frankfurt/Main. (Department of State Employment Service which assists
foreign job-seekers and publishes a weekly jobs bulletin *Markt + Chanc*e in
German.)
Die Welt: www.welt.de.
Frankfurter Allgemeine Zeitung: www.faz.de.
Süddeutsche Zeitung: www.sueddeutsche.de.

GHANA

Pop: 20 m.   *Area:* 239,000 sq km.
Ghana High Commission: 13 Belgrave Square, London SW1. Tel: (020) 7235 4142.
104 Highgate Hill, London N6 5HE. Tel: (020) 8342 8686.
British High Commission: (P O Box 296), Osu Link, Gamel Adbul Nasser Avenue,
Accra.
British Council: (P O Box 771), Liberia Road, Accra. (Branch in Kumasi.)

GIBRALTAR

Pop: 29,000.   *Area:* 5 sq km.
Gibraltar Government Office: Arundel Great Court, 179 Strand, London WC2R
1EH. Tel: (020) 7836 0777.
Gibraltar Government HQ: The Government Secretariat, The Convent, Gibraltar.

GREECE

Pop: 10.5 m.   *Area:* 132,000 sq km.
Greek Embassy: 1a Holland Park, London W11 3TP. Tel: (020) 7229 3850.
Greek Tourist Office: 4 Conduit Street, London W1R 8DL. Tel: (020) 7734 5997.
British Embassy: 1 Ploutarchou Street, Athens 10675.
British Council: 17 Plateia Philikis Etairias, Kolonaki Square, PO Box 34388,
Athens 10210. Branch in Thessalonika.
British-Hellenic Chamber of Commerce: 25 Vas. Sofias Avenue, Athens 10674.
OAED: Ethnikis Antistasis 8, 16610 A Kalamaki. (State employment agency)
Athens News: http://athensnews.dolnet.gr.

GRENADA

Pop: 96,000   *Area:* 344 sq km.
Grenada High Commission: 1 Collingham Gardens, London SW5 0HW. Tel: (020)
7373 7809; Grenada Tourist Office: Tel: (020) 7370 5164.
Ministry of Education: St George's.
British High Commission: 14 Church Street, St George's.

GUATEMALA

Pop: 10.7 m.   *Area:* 109,000 sq km.
Guatemalan Embassy: 13 Fawcett Street, London SW10 9HN. Tel: (020) 7351
3042.
Ministry of Education: Palaçio Naçional, Guatemala City.
British Embassy: Edificio Centro Ginanciero, 7a Avenida 5-10, Zona 4, Guatemala
City.

GUINEA

Pop: 8 m.   *Area:* 246,000 sq km.
Guinea Embassy: 51 rue de la Faisanderie, 75061 Paris. Tel: 00 33 1 4704 8148.
British Consulate: BP 834 Conakry.

GUINEA-BISSAU

Pop: 1.2 m.   *Area:* 36,125 sq km.

Guinea-Bissau Embassy: Ave Franklin D Roosevelt 70, 1050 Brussels. Tel: 00 32 2 647 0890.
Ministry of Education: Bissau.
British Consulate: Mavengro Int, CP 100, Bissau. Embassy in Senegal.

GUYANA

Pop: 975,000   *Area:* 215,000 sq km.
Guyanan High Commission: 3 Palace Court, Bayswater Road, London W2 4LP. Tel: (020) 7229 7684.
Ministry of Education: 21 Brickdam, Georgetown.
British High Commission: 44 Main Street, PO Box 10849, Georgetown.

HONDURAS

Pop: 6.5 m.   *Area:* 112 sq km.
Embassy: 115 Gloucester Place, London W1H 3PJ. Tel: (020) 7486 4880.
British Embassy: Edificio Palmira, 3er Piso, Colonia Palmira, PO Box 290, Tegucipulca.

HONG KONG

Pop: 7 m.   *Area:* 1,000 sq km.
Hong Kong Government Office: 6 Grafton Street, London W1X 3LB. Tel: (020) 7499 9821. Visa information: Tel: (0900) 160 0111.
Hong Kong Tourist Association: Tel: 020) 7533 7100.
British Consulate-General: 1 Supreme Court Road, PO Box 528, Central, Hong Kong.
British Council: Easey Commercial Building, 255 Hennessy Road, Wanchai.
British Chamber of Commerce, Harbour Road, Central District, HK.
British Council: 3 Supreme Court Road, Admiralty, Hong Kong.
South China Morning Post: www.scmp.com.

HUNGARY

Pop: 10 m.   *Area:* 93,000 sq km.
Hungarian Embassy: 35 Eaton Place, London SW1X 8BY. Tel: (020) 7235 5218.
Consular Section: Tel: (020) 7235 2664.
Hungarian Tourist Office: 46 Eaton Place, London SW1X 8BY. Tel: (020) 7823 1032.
British Embassy: Harmicad Itca 6, Budapest V.
British Council: Benczur Utca 26, 1068 Budapest.
British Chamber of Commerce: 2nd Floor, Bank Utca 6, 1954 Budapest.

ICELAND

Pop: 280,000   *Area:* 103,000
Icelandic Embassy: 2a Hans Street, London SW1X. Tel: (020) 7259 3999.
British Embassy: Laufasvegur 31, P Box 460, Reykjavik 101.

INDIA

Pop: 890 m.   *Area:* 3.3 m. sq km.
Indian High Commission: India House, Aldwych, London WC2B 4NA. Tel: (020) 7836 8484. Visa information: Tel: (0900) 188 0800.
Indian Tourist Board: 7 Cork Street, London W1X 2AB. Tel: (020) 7437 7667.
British High Commission: Chanakyapuri, New Delhi 1100021. Also Bombay, Calcutta, Madras.

INDONESIA

Pop: 213 m.   *Area:* 1.9 m. sq km.
Indonesian Embassy: 38 Grosvenor Square. London W1X 9AD. Tel: (020) 7499 7661. Visa information: (0900) 117 1210.
Indonesian Tourist Office: 3 Hanover Square, London W1X. Tel: (0900) 160 0180.
British Embassy: Jalan M. H Thamrin 75, Jakarta 10310.
British Council: S Widjojo Centre, 57 Jalan Jendral Sudirman, Jakarta.
Indonesia British Association: Lippo Life Building, 2nd Floor, Jalan HR Rasuna, Said Kav B-10, Jakarta 12910.

IRAN

Pop: 76 m.   *Area:* 1.65 m. sq km.
Iranian Embassy: 16 Prince's Gate, London SW7 1PX. Tel: (020) 225 3000.
Iranian Consulate: 50 Kensington Court, London W8 5DD. Tel: (020) 7937 5225.
British Embassy: 143 Ferdowsi Avenue, PO Box 11365-4474, Teheran 11344.
Irano-British Chamber of Commerce, Bezrouke House, 140 North Forsate Avenue, Teheran.

IRAQ

Pop: 23 m.   *Area:* 435,000 sq km.
Iraqi Interests Section: Royal Jordanian Embassy, 21 Queen's Gate, London SW7 5JG. Tel: (020) 7584 7141.
British Interests Section: Russian Embassy, House 12, Street 218, Al Khelood, Baghdad.
British Council: (P O Box 298), Waziriya 301, Street 3, Houses 22 and 24, Baghdad.

ISRAEL

Pop: 6 m.   *Area:* 21,000 sq km.
Israeli Embassy: 2 Palace Green, London W8 4QB. Tel: (020) 7957 9500. Website: www.israel-embassy.org.uk/london/.
Israeli Tourist office: 180 Oxford Street, London W1. Tel: (020) 7299 1111.
British Embassy: 192 Hayarkon Street, Tel Aviv 63405.
British Council: (P O Box 3302), 140 Hayarkon Street, Tel Aviv 61032).
Israel-British Chamber of Commerce: (P O Box 4610), 65 Alleby Street, Tel Aviv 61046.
Anglo-Israel Assocation: 9 Bentinck Street, London W1M 5RP. Tel: (020) 7486 2300).
Jerusalem Post: www.jpost.co.il.

ITALY

Pop: 57 m.   *Area:* 301,000 sq km.
Italian Embassy: 14 Three Kings Yard, London W1Y 2EH. Tel: (020) 7312 2200.
Italian Consulates: 38 Eaton Place, London W1, Tel: (020) 7235 9371;   111 Piccadilly, Manchester 2; 7-9 Greyfriars, Bedford MK40 1HJ.
Italian Cultural Institute: 39 Belgrave Square, London SW1X 8NX. Tel: (020) 7235 1461.
Italian Tourist Office: 1 Prince's Street, London W1R 8AY. Tel: (020) 7408 1254.
Anglo-Italian Society: Italian Consulate, Norfolk House, Smallbrook, Queensway, Birmingham B5 4LJ. Tel: (0121) 643 7794.
British Embassy, 80A Via Venti Settembre, 00187 Roma.
British Council, Plazzo del Drago. Via Quattra Fontane 20, 00184 Rome.
British Chamber of Commerce, Via Camperio 9, 20123 Milan.
Ufficio di Collocamento Mandopera, Via Pastrengo 16, Roma. (State employment service).
The Daily American, Via San Maria, Via 12, Roma.

IVORY COAST (COTE D'IVOIRE)

Pop: 15 m.   Area 322,000 sq km.
Embassy of Côte d'Ivoire: 2 Upper Belgrave Street, London SW1X 8BJ. Tel: (020) 7235 6991.
Anglo-Cote d'Ivoire Society: c/o Embassy.
British Embassy: (B P 2581), 5th Floor, Immeuble Les Harmonies, Angle Blvd Carde et Dr Jamot, Plateau, Abidjan.

JAMAICA

Pop: 2.5 m.   *Area:* 11,425 sq km.
Jamaican High Commission: 1-2 Prince Consort Road, London SW7 2BZ. Tel: (020) 7823 9911.

British High Commission: (P O Box 575) Trafalgar Road, Kingston 10
British Council, PCMB Building, 64 Knutsford Blvd, PO Box 575, Kingston 5.

JAPAN

Pop: 126 m.   *Area:* 378,000 sq km.
Japanese Embassy: 101-104 Piccadilly, London W1V 9FN. Tel: (020) 7465 6500.
Website: www.embjapan.org.uk.
Japanese Tourist Office: 5th Floor, 20 Savile Row, London W1X 1AE. Tel: (020) 7734 9638.
British Embassy: 1 Ichiban-cho, Chiyoda-Ku, Tokyo 102.
British Council: 2-Kagurazaka 1-Chome, Shinjuku-ku, Tokyo 162.
British Chamber of Commerce: Kowa 16 Bldg Annex, 3rd Floor, 9-20 Akaska 1-Chome, Minato-ku, Tokyo.
Centre for Japanese Studies, University of Sheffield S10 2TN. Tel: (01742) 78555.
Centre for Japanese Studies, University of Stirling, Stirling FK9 4LA.
Centre for the Study of Contemporary Japan, Essex University, Wivenhoe Park, Colchester CO4 3SQ. Tel: 01206 862286.
Japan Business Consultancy: Newton Park, Bath BA1 9BN. Tel: (01225) 874146.
Japan Society: Suite 6-9, 6th Floor, Morley House, 314-322 Regent Street, London W1R 5AH. Tel: (020) 7636 3029.
The Japan Times: www.japantimes.co.jp.   (Also publishes a directory of foreign residents and a guide for foreigners.)

JORDAN

Pop: 6.3 m.   *Area:* 98,000 sq km.
Royal Jordanian Embassy: 6 Upper Phillimore Gardens, London W8 7HB. Tel: (020) 7937 3685. Visa information: (0900) 117 1261.
Jordanian Tourist Office: 211 Regent Street, London W1. Tel: (020) 7437 9465.
British Embassy: (P O Box 87), Abdoun, Amman.
British Council: Rainbow Street, Jabal Amman, PO Box 434, Amman.
Anglo-Jordanian Society: 311 Lillie Road, London SW6 7LL. Tel: (020) 7386 0045. Website: www.manara.com.

KAZAKHSTAN

Pop: 17 m.   *Area:* 2.7m. sq km.
Kazakhstan Embassy: 33 Thurloe Square, London SW7 2SD. Tel: (020) 7581 4646. Visa information: (0900) 160 0207.
British Embassy: Ulitsa Furnanova 173, Almaty. (May move to new capital of Akmola.)
British Council: Ulitsa Panfilova 158/17, Almaty 480046.

KENYA

Pop: 30.5 m.   *Area:* 583,000 sq km.
Kenyan High Commission, 45 Portland Place, London W1N 4AS. Tel: (020) 7636 2371/5.
Kenya Tourist Office: Brooks Mews, London W1X. 1FF Tel: (020) 7355 3144.
British High Commission: (P O Box 30465), Upper Hill Road, Nairobi.
British Council: (P O Box 40751), ICEA Building, Kenyatta Avenue, Nairobi. Also in Kisumu and Mombasa.

KIRIBATI

Pop: 87,000   *Area:* 861 sq km.
Honorary Consulate: Maurice Chandler, Rutland House, 8 Brookhouse Street, Leicester LE2 0JB.
British High Commission: P O Box 61, Bariki, Tarawa.

KOREA, REPUBLIC OF (SOUTH KOREA)

Pop: 47 m.   *Area:* 99,000 sq km.
South Korean Embassy: 60 Buckingham Gate, London SW1E. Tel: (020) 7227 5500. Visa information: (0900) 844 4560.
South Korean Tourist Office: New Zealand House, Haymarket, London SW1Y 4TQ. Tel: (020) 7321 2535.
British Embassy: 4 Chung-Dong, Choong-Ku, Seoul.
British Council: Room 401, Anglican Church Annex, 3-7 Chung-Dong, Choong-ku, Seoul.

KUWAIT

Pop: 2 m.   *Area:* 18,000 sq km.
Kuwaiti Embassy: 2 Albert Gate, London SW1X. Tel: (020) 7590 3400. Visa information: (0900) 160 0160.
British Embassy: (P O Box 300), Arabian Gulf Street, Safat 13003.
British Council: (P O Box 345), 2 al Arabi Street, Mansouriyah, 13001 Safat.
Kuwait Petroleum Corporation: P O Box 26565, 13126 Safat. (Major employer)
British Council: 2 al Arabi Street, Mansouriyah, PO Box 345, 13001, Safat.

KYRGYZSTAN

Pop: 4.5 m.   *Area:* 200,000 sq km.
Kyrgyz Embassy: 119 Crawford Street, London W1H 1HF. Tel: (020) 7935 1462.
British Embassy: see Kazakhstan.

LAOS

Pop: 6.4   *Area:* 237,000 sq km.
Lao Embassy: 74 ave Raymond Poincare, 75116 Paris. Tel: 00 33 1 4553 0298.
British Embassy: PO Box 6626, Vientiane.

LATVIA

Pop: 2.5 m.   *Area:* 65,000 sq km.
Latvian Embassy: 45 Nottingham Place, London W1M 3FE. Tel: (020) 7312 0040.
Ministry of Education: Valnu Iela 2, Riga 1098.
British Embassy: 5 Alunana Iela Street, Riga 1010.
British Council: Blaumana Iela 5a, Riga 1011.

LEBANON

Pop: 3.3 m.   *Area:* 10,400 sq km.
Lebanese Embassy: 15–21 Palace Gardens Mews, London W8 4QM. Tel: (020)
7229 7265.
British Embassy: 8th Street, Rabieh, Beirut.

LESOTHO

Pop: 2.3 m.   *Area:* 30,000 sq km.
Lesotho High Commission: 7 Chesham Place, London SW1X 8HN. Tel: (020)
7235 5686.
British High Commission: P O Box 521, Maseru 100.
British Council: (P O Box 429), Hobson's Square, Maseru 100.

LIBERIA

Pop: 3.3 m.   *Area:* 111,000 sq km.
Liberian Embassy: 2 Pembridge Place, W2 4XB. Tel: (020) 7221 1036.
British Consular Agent: UNMARCO Corporation, Liberia.
British Embassy: see Ivory Coast.

LIBYA

Pop: 6.4 m.   *Area:* 1.76 m. sq km.
Libyan Embassy: 61–62 Ennismore Gardens, London SW7. Tel: (020) 7589 6120.
British Embassy, PO Box 912, Sharia Uahran 1, Tripoli.
Umm Al Jawaby Oil & Service Co Ltd, 15 Lodge Road, London NW8 8NX. Tel:
(020) 7266 4545. Major jobs recruiter for Libya.

LITHUANIA

Pop: 3.7 m.   *Area:* 65,000 sq km.
Lithuanian Embassy: 84 Gloucester Place, London W1H. Tel: (020) 7486 6401.
Visa information: (0900) 160 0385.
British Embassy: 2 Antakalnio, Vilnius 2055.
British Council: Vilnaius 39/6, Vilnius 2001.

LUXEMBOURG

Pop: 430,000.   *Area:* 2,600 sq km.
Luxembourg Embassy: 27 Wilton Crescent, London SW1X 8SD. Tel: (020) 7235 6961.
Luxembourg Tourist Office: 122 Regent Street, London W1R 5FL. Tel: (020) 7434 2800.
British Embassy: 14 Boulevard FDE Roosevelt, 2450 Luxembourg-Ville.
British Chamber of Commerce: KPMG, 121 Avenue de la Faiencerie, 1511 Luxembourg.
Administration de l'Emploi: 38a rue Philippe II, BP 23, 2010 Luxembourg.

MACEDONIA

Pop: 2 m.   *Area:* 25,700 sq m.
Macedonian Embassy: 5th Floor, 25 St James's Street, London W1V. Tel: (020) 7935 3842.
British Embassy: Veljko Vlahovic 26, 9100 Skopje.

MADAGASCAR

Pop: 17 m.   *Area:* 587,000 sq km.
Madagascar Honorary Consulate: 16 Lanark Mansions, Pennard Road, London W12 8DT. Tel: (020) 8746 0133.
Madagascar Embassy: 4 Avenue Raphael, 75016 Paris.
British Embassy: First Floor, Immeuble Ny Havana, Cité de 67 Ha, BP 167, Antananarivo. (British Council: see Mauritius)
Anglo-Madagasy Society: 11 Merritt Road, Didcot OX11 7DF. Tel: (01235) 818876.

MALAWI

Pop: 11 m.   *Area:* 118,500 sq km.
Malawi High Commission: 33 Grosvenor Street, London W1X 0DE. Tel: (020) 7491 4172.
British High Commission: (P O Box 30042), Longadzi House, Lilongwe 3.
British Council: (P O Box 30222), Plot No 13/20, City Centre, Lilongwe 3. Also in Blantyre.

MALAYSIA

Pop: 22 m.　　*Area:* 330,000 sq km.
Malaysian High Commission: 45-46 Belgrave Square, London SW1X 8QT. Tel: (020) 7235 8033. Visas information: (0900) 188 7700.
Malaysian Tourist Office: 57 Trafalgar Square, London WC2. Tel: (020) 7930 7932.
British High Commission: (P O Box 11030), 185 Jalan Ampang, 50450 Kuala Lumpur.
British Council: (P O Box 10539), Jalan Bukit Aman, 50480 Kuala Lumpur. Also in Kota Kinabalu, Kuching and Penang.
British Malaysia Industry and Trade Association: P O Box 2574, Kuala Lumpur.
British Malaysian Society: Poplar Farm, Bromley Green, Ashford, Kent TN26 2EW. Tel: (01233) 732350.

MALDIVES

Pop: 300,000.　　*Area:* 298 sq km.
Maldives High Commission: 22 Nottingham Place, London W1M 3FB. Tel: (020) 7224 2135.
British Embassy: See Sri Lanka.

MALI

Pop: 12.5 m.　　*Area:* 1.24 m. sq km.
Mali Embassy: Av Molière 487, 1060 Brussels. Tel: 00 32 2 345 7432.
British Consulate: c/o American International School of Bamakol, BP 34, Bamako.
British Embassy: see Senegal.

MALTA

Pop: 376,000.　　*Area:* 316 sq km.
Malta High Commission: 36-38 Piccadilly, London W1V. Tel: (020) 7292 4800. Visa information: (0900) 160 0395.
Malta Tourist Office: Tel: (020) 7292 4900.
British High Commission: 7 St Anne Street, Floriana.
British Council: 7 St Anne Street, Floriana, VLT 15.

MAURITANIA

Pop: 2.6 m.　　*Area:* 1 m. sq km.
Mauritanian Embassy: 5 rue de Montevideo, 75016 Paris. Tel: 00 33 1 4504 8854.
Mauritanian Honorary Consulate: 140 Bow Common Lane, London E3 4BH. Tel: (020) 8980 4382.
British Consulate: B9, 2069 Nouakchott.
British Embassy: see Morocco.

MAURITIUS

Pop: 1.1 m.   *Area:* 2,000 sq km.
Mauritius High Commission: 32 Elvaston Place, London SW7 5NW. Tel: (020) 7581 0294.
Mauritius Tourist Office: Tel: (020) 7584 3666.
British High Commission: (P O Box 1063), Les Cascades Building, Edith Cavell Street, Port Louis.
British Council: (P O Box 111), Fondoon Building, Royal Road, Rose Hill.

MEXICO

Pop: 99 m.   *Area:* 1.97 m. sq km.
Mexican Embassy: 42 Hertford Street, London W1Y 7TF. Tel: (020) 7499 8586.
Mexican Consulate: Halkin Street, London SW1X 7DW. Tel: (020) 7235 6393 and (0900)160 0230.
Mexican Tourist Office: 7 Cork Street, London W1X 1PB. Tel: (0900) 160 0230.
British Embassy: (P O Box 96 Bis), Rio Lerma 71, Col Cuauhtémoc, Mexico City 06500 DF.
British Council: (Apdo Postal 30-588), Maestro Antonio Caso 127, Col San Rafael, Mexico City 06470 DF. Also in Guadalajara.
British Chamber of Commerce: Rio de la Plata No 30, Cuauhtémoc, Mexico City 06500 DF.

MONGOLIA

Pop: 2.7 m.   *Area:* 1.6 m. sq km.
Mongolian Embassy: 7 Kensington Court, London W8 5DL. Tel: (020) 7937 5238.
British Embassy: 30 Enkh Taivny Gudamzh, PO Box 703, Ulan Bator 13.
Anglo-Mongolian Society: Department of East Asia Studies, University of Leeds LS2 9JT. Tel: (0113) 233 6740.

MOROCCO

Pop: 29 m.   *Area:* 447,000 sq km.
Moroccan Embassy: 49 Queen's Gate Gardens, London SW7 5NE. Tel: (020) 7581 5001. Visa information: (0900) 117 1260.
Moroccan Tourist Office: 205 Regent Street, London W1R 6HB. Tel: (020) 7437 0073.
British Embassy: 17 Boulevard de la Tour Hassan, (BP 45), Rabat.
British Council: (B P 427), 36 rue de Tanger, Rabat.
British Chamber of Commerce, 65 Avenue Hassan Seghir, 20000 Casablanca.

MOZAMBIQUE

Pop: 20 m.   *Area:* 801,590 sq

Mozambique Embassy: 21 Fitzroy Square, London W1P 5HJ. Tel: (020) 7383 3800.
British Embassy: (Caixa Postal 55), A. Vladimir I Lenine 310, Maputo.
Ministry of Education: Avda 24 de Julho 167, Maputo.
British Council: Rua John Issa, PO Box 4178, Maputo.

MYANMAR

(See **BURMA**)

NAMIBIA

Pop: 1.7 m.   *Area:* 824,292 sq km.
Namibian High Commission: 5 Chandos Street, London W1M 0LQ. Tel: (020) 7636 6244.
Namibian Tourist Office: Tel: (020) 7636 2924.
British High Commission: 116 Robert Mugabe Avenue, Windhoek 9000.
British Council: 74 Bulow Strasse, PO Box 24224, Windhoek 9000.

NEPAL

Pop: 24 m.   *Area:* 141,000 sq km.
Royal Nepalese Embassy: 12a Kensington Gardens, London W8 4PQ. Tel: (020) 7229 6231.
British Embassy: (P O Box 106), Lainchaur, Kathmandu.
British Council: (P O Box 640), Kantipath, Kathmandu.
Britain-Nepal Society: 3C Gunnersby Avenue, London W5 3NH. Tel: (020) 8992 0173.
Britain-Nepal Chamber of Commerce: 5 High Timber Street, London EC4V 3PA. Tel: (020) 7328 0950.

NETHERLANDS

Pop: 16 m.   *Area:* 41,000 sq km.
Royal Netherlands Embassy: 38 Hyde Park Gate, London SW7 5DP. Tel: (020) 7590 3200.
Netherlands Tourist Office: 18 Buckingham Gate, London SW1E 6LD Tel: (0906) 871 7777.
British Embassy, Lange Voorhout 10, 2514 ED The Hague.
British Council, Keizergracht 343, 1016 EH Amsterdam.
Netherlands-British Chamber of Commerce, 307-308 High Holborn, London WC1V 7LS. Tel: (020) 7405 1358.
Anglo-Netherland Society, P O Box 68, Unilever House, London EC4P 4BQ. Tel: (0207) 7353 5729.
Directoraat Generaal de Arbeidsvoorziening, Volmerlaan 1, Rijswijk ZH. (State

employment service)

Bureau Arbeidsvoorziening Academici, Visseringlaan 26, Postbus 5814, 2280 HV Rijswijk. (Specialist branch of state employment service which places highly qualified and professional people)

Intermediair: www.intermediair.nl. (Publishes jobs periodical and jobs directory for graduates.)

NEW ZEALAND

Pop: 3.7 m.   *Area:* 269,000 sq km.

New Zealand High Commission: New Zealand House, 80 Haymarket, London SW1Y 4TQ. Tel: (020) 7930 8422. Visa information: (0906) 910 0100. Website: www.immigration.govt.nz.

British High Commission, 44 Hill Street, Wellington 1. Also in Auckland and Christchurch.

British Trade Association, Commerce House, 126 Wakefield Street, Wellington.

Employment & Vocational Guidance Service of the Department of Labour: Charles Fergusson Building, Box 3705, Auckland.

New Zealand-UK Chamber of Commerce: Morley House, Regent Street, London W1. Tel: (020) 7636 4525.

Malcolm Consultants, Kingsgate House, High Holborn, London WC1. Tel: (020) 7404 0999. Migration Consultants.

Four Corners Emigration, Freepost NWW1289, Manchester M22 5FR. Tel: 0345 419453.

Workpermit.com, 11 Bolt Court, Fleet Street, London EC4A 3DQ. Tel: (020) 7495 3999. Fax: (020) 7495 3991. Website: www.workpermit.com. Migration consultants.

Ambler Collins, Eden House, 59 Fulham High Street, London SW6 3JJ. Tel: (020) 7371 0213; Fax: (020) 7736 8841. Migration consultants. Operates Hob Net – international employment search across the Internet.

Challice Emigration, Rectory Farm, Top Street, Elston, Notts NG23 5NP. Tel/Fax: (01636) 525903. Migration consultants.

Hensley & Associates, 24A Bristol Gardens, London W9 2JQ; Tel: (020) 7266 4947; Fax: (020) 7289 6562. Migration consultants.

The Emigration Group, 7 Heritage Court, Lower Bridge Street, Chester CH1 1RD. Tel: (01244) 321414; Fax: 01244 342288. (New Zealand Affiliate: Taylor & Associates)

New Zealand & Australia Migration Bureau, 70 Upper Richmond Road, London SW15 2RP. Tel: (020) 8874 2844. Fax: (020) 8874 1178.

Career Strategies New Zealand, PO Box 48-085, Auckland, New Zealand. E-mail: careerstrategies@xtra.co.nz. Job search specialists.

New Zealand Herald: www.nzherald.co.nz.

NICARAGUA

Pop: 4.7 m.   *Area:* 130,000

Nicaraguan Consulate: 58 Kensington Church Street, London W8. Tel: (020) 7938 2373.
British Embassy: Reparto Los Robles, Plaza Churchill, Aptdo 1-169, Managua.

NIGER

Pop: 11 m.   *Area:* 1.3 m. sq km.
Niger Embassy: 154 rue de Longchamp, 75116 Paris. Tel: 00 33 1 4504 8060.
British Vice-Consulate: BP 11168, Niamey.
British Embassy: see Ivory Coast.

NIGERIA

Pop: 129 m.   *Area:* 924,000 sq km.
Nigerian High Commission: Nigeria House, 9 Northumberland Avenue, London WC2 5BX. Tel: (020) 7839 8746.
Passport & Visa Office: 56 Fleet Street, London EC4. Tel: (020) 7353 3776; (0900) 160 0199.
British High Commission, Private Mail Bag 12136, Shehu Shangar Way North, Maitama, Abuja, Lagos.
Nigeria-British Chamber of Commerce, P O Box 118, Mayfield, East Sussex. Tel: (01435) 872731.
Daily Times/Sunday Times, P O Box 139, Lagos and 52-54 Grays Inn Road, London WC1X 8LT. (The leading English language newspaper of Nigeria and publisher of *Nigeria Handbook, Africa Yearbook, Trade and Industrial Directory.*)
British Council: 11 Kingsway Road, PO Box 3702, Ikoyi, Lagos. Also in Enugu, Ibadan, Kaduna, Kano, Port Harcourt.

NORWAY

Pop: 4.4 m.   *Area:* 324,000 sq km.
Norwegian Embassy: 25 Belgrave Square, London SW1X 8QD. Tel: (020) 7591 5500. Website: www.norway.org.uk.
Norwegian Tourist Office: 5 Regent Street, London SW1. Tel: (020) 6255.
British Embassy, Thomas Heftyesgate 8, 0244 Oslo.
British Council, Fridtjof Nansens Plass 5, 0160 Oslo 1.
British Business Forum, c/o British Embassy.
Anglo-Norse Society, c/o Norwegian Embassy, 25 Belgrave Square, London SW1X 8QD. Tel: (020) 7591 5500.
Norwegian-British Chamber of Commerce: Norway House, 21/24 Cockspur Street, London SW1Y 5BN.
Arbeidsdirektoratet, Holbergs Plass 7, Postboks 8127, Oslo 1. (State employment agency)
Arbeidsformidlingens Europaservice, Postboks 420 Sentrum, Ovre Slottsgate 11. 0100 Oslo 1. (State employment agency for foreign job seekers.)

OMAN

Pop: 2.7 m.   *Area:* 213,000 sq km.
Embassy of the Sultanate of Oman: 167 Queen's Gate, London SW7 5HE. Tel: (020) 7225 0001. Visa information: Tel: (0900) 160 0567.
British Embassy: P O Box 300, Ruwi, Muscat 113.
British Council: Road One, Medinat Qaboos West, PO Box 73, PC 115, Muscat. Also in Soharand and Salalah.
Anglo-Omani Society: Somers, Mounts Hill, Benenden, Kent TN17 4ET. Tel: (01580) 240819.

PAKISTAN

Pop: 156 m.   *Area:* 796,000 sq km.
Pakistan High Commission: 35 Lowndes Square, London SW1X 9JN. Tel: (020) 7664 9200. Visa information: (0900) 188 0880.
British Embassy: Diplomatic Enclave, Ramna 5, P O Box 1122, Islamabad.
British Council: Block 14, Civic Centre G6, PO Box 1135, Islamabad. Also in Karachi, Lahore and Peshawar.

PANAMA

Pop: 2.9 m.   *Area:* 77,000 sq km.
Panamanian Embassy: 40 Hertford Street, London W1Y. Tel: (020) 7493 4646.
British Embassy: Torre Swiss Bank, Urb Marbella, Calle 53, Piso 4 & 5, PO Box 889, Panama City 1.

PAPUA NEW GUINEA

Pop: 4.8 m.   *Area:* 462,000 sq km.
Papua New Guinea High Commission: 14 Waterloo Place, London SW1R 4AR. Tel: (020) 7930 0922.
British High Commission: Kiroki Street, Waigani, PO Box 212, Boroko, Port Moresby.
PNG-British Chamber of Commerce: 3rd Floor, Morley House, 314-322 Regent Street, London W1R 5AE.

PARAGUAY

Pop: 5.5 m.   *Area:* 406,000 sq km.
Paraguayan Embassy: 344 Kensington High Street, London W1H. Tel: (020) 7610 4180.
British Embassy: (Casilla de Corréo 404), Calle Presidente Franco 706, Asunciòn.
Paraguay-British Chamber of Commerce: Gral Diaz 521, 2 Piso, 2A Asunciòn.

PERU

Pop: 24 m.   *Area:* 1.3 m sq km.
Peruvian Embassy: 52 Sloane Street, London SW1X 9SP. Tel: (020) 7235 1917.
Peru Tourist Office: 10 Grosvenor Gardens, London SW1W 0BD. Tel: (020) 7730 7122.
British Embassy: (Apartado 854), Edificio El Pacifico, Plaza Washington, Piso 12, Lima 100.
British Council: (Apartado 14-0114), Calle Alberto Lynch 110, San Isidro, Lima 14.
British-Peruvian Chamber of Commerce: Republica de Panama 3563, Of 202, San Isidro, Lima.
Anglo-Peruvian Society: PO Box 13688, London SW19 5ZL. Tel/Fax: (020) 8946 8773.

PHILIPPINES

Pop: 75 m.   *Area:* 300,000 sq km.
Philippines Embassy: 9a Palace Green, London W8 4QR. Tel: (020) 7937 1600; Consulate: 1 Cumberland House, Kensington High Street, London W8. Visa information: (0900) 117 1243.
British Embassy: 15-17th Floors, Locsin Building, 6752 Ayala Avenue, Makati (P O Box 1970), Metro Manila 3116.
British Council: 7 3rd Street, New Manila, PO Box AC 168, Cubao, Quezon City, Metro Manila.

POLAND

Pop: 38.5 m.   *Area:* 313,000 sq km.
Polish Embassy: 47 Portland Place, London W1N 3AG. Tel: (020) 7580 4324. Visa Section: 73 New Cavendish Street, London W1. Tel: (0900) 160 0358.
Polish Tourist Office: 310-312 Regent Street, London W1R 7AJ. Tel: (020) 7580 8811.
Polish Cultural Institute: 34 Portland Place, London W1. Tel: (020) 7636 6032.
Anglo-Polish Society: c/o Polish Institute.
British Embassy: Aleje Róz 1, 00-556 Warsaw.
British Council: Aleje Jerozolimskie 59, 00-679 Warsaw.
British Chamber of Commerce in Poland: Ul Krolewska 27A, Suite 376, 00-060 Warsaw.

PORTUGAL

Pop: 10 m.   *Area:* 92,000 sq km.
Portuguese Embassy: 11 Belgrave Square, London SW1X 8PP. Tel: (020) 7235-5331; Consulate: 62 Brompton Road, London SW3 1BJ. Tel: (020) 7581 8722. Also in Manchester and Edinburgh.

Portuguese Tourist Office: 22 Sackville Street, London W1Y 0NP. Tel: (020) 7494 1441.

British Embassy, Rua de Sao Bernardo 33, 1000 Lisbon.

British Council: Rua de Sao Marcal 174, 1294 Lisbon Codex. Also in Cascais, Coimbra, Oporto, Parede.

British Portuguese Chamber of Commerce, Rua de Estrela 8, 1200 Lisbon.

Anglo-Portuguese Society, 2 Belgrave Square, London SW1X 8PJ. Tel: (020) 7245 9738.

Ministério do Emprego, Praça de Londres, 1091 Lisbon Codex. (State employment agency)

Robert Shaw & Associates, Rua Sampaio E Pina 70-10, 1000 Lisbon. (Private employment agency)

QATAR

Pop: 600,000   *Area:* 11,000 sq km.

Qatar Embassy: 1 South Audley Street, London W1. Tel: (020) 7493 2200. Visa information: (0906) 863 3233.

British Embassy: P O Box 3, Doha.

British Council: (P O Box 2992), Ras Al Sadd Street, Doha.

Qatar General Petroleum.Co, P O Box 3212, Doha. (Major employer)

ROMANIA

Pop: 23 m.   *Area:* 237,500 sq km.

Romanian Embassy: 4 Palace Green, London W8 4QD. Tel: (020) 7937 9666. Visa information: (0900) 188 0828. E-mail: romania@romemb.demon.co.uk.

Romanian Tourist Office: 83a Marylebone High Street, London W1. Tel: (020) 7224 3692.

British Embassy: Strada Jules Michelet 24, Bucharest 70154.

British Council: Calea Dorobalintor 14, Bucharest.

RUSSIA

Pop: 146 m.   *Area:* 17,075,000 sq km.

Russian Embassy: 5 Kensington Palace Gardens, London W8 4QX. Tel: (020) 7229 3628. Consulate: (020) 7229 8027. Visa information: (0900) 117 1271.

Russian Tourist Office: 167 Kensington High Street, London W8. Tel: (020) 7937 7217.

British Embassy: Naberezhnaya Morisa Toresa 14, Moscow 109072.

British Council: Biblioteka Inostrannoi Literaturi, Ulitsa Nikolo-Yamskaya 1, Moscow 109189.

Russo-British Chamber of Commerce, Ulitsa Ilika 6, Moscow 103684.

Moscow Times: www.moscowtimes.ru.

RWANDA

Pop: 7.7 m.   *Area:* 26,000 sq km.
Rwandan Embassy: 58 Trafalgar Square, London WC2. Tel: (020) 7930 2570.
British Embassy: (PO Box 576), Parcelle 1131, Blvd de l'Umuganda, Kacyra-Sud,
Kigali.

ST HELENA (Atlantic)

Pop: 5,700.   *Area:* 300 sq km.
Dependencies: Ascension Island (*Pop:* 1,100); Tristan da Cunha (*Pop:* 300)
Government Offices: The Castle, Jamestown.

ST KITTS & NEVIS (Caribbean)

Pop: 45,000.   *Area:* 262 sq km.
Eastern Caribbean Commission: 10 Kensington Court, London W8 5DL. Tel: (020)
7937 9522.
St Kitts & Nevis Tourist Office: (020) 7376 0881.
British High Commision: See Antigua.

ST LUCIA (Caribbean)

Pop: 160,000.   *Area:* 616 sq km.
St Lucia High Commision: 1 Collingham Gardens, London SW5. Tel: (020) 7370
7123.
St Lucia Tourist Board: 421A Finchley Road, London NW3. Tel: (020) 7431 3675.
British High Commission: NIS Waterfront Building, Castries.

ST VINCENT & THE GRENADINES (Caribbean)

Pop: 120,000.   *Area:* 388 sq km.
High Commission for St Vincent & the Grenadines: 10 Kensington Court, London
W8 5DL. Tel: (020) 7565 2874. Tourist Office: (020) 7937 6570.
British High Commission: Granby Street, Kingstown.

SAUDI ARABIA

Pop: 22 m.   *Area:* 2.15 m sq km.
Royal Saudi Arabian Embassy: 30 Charles Street, London W1X 7PM. Tel: (020)
7917 3000.
British Embassy: P O Box 94351, Riyadh 11693.
British Council: Olaya Main Road, Al Mousa Centre, Tower B, 3rd Floor, PO Box
58012, Riyadh 11594. Branches in Jeddah, Damman and Jubail.
Soudi-British Society: 21 Collingham Road, London SW5 0NU. Tel: (020) 7373
8414.

SENEGAL

Pop: 9.5 m.   *Area:* 196,000 sq km.
Senegalese Embassy: 39 Marloes Road, London W8. Tel: (020) 7938 4048.
British Embassy: BP 6025, 20 rue du Docteur Guillet, Dakar.
British Council: 34-36 Blvd de la République, BP 6232, Dakar.

SEYCHELLES

Pop: 80,000.   *Area:* 308 sq km.
Seychelles High Commission: 2nd Floor, 111 Baker Street, London W1M 1FE. Tel: (020) 7224 1660.
Seychelles Tourist Office: Tel: (020) 7224 1670.
British High Commission: Victoria House, PO Box 161, Victoria, Mahé.

SIERRA LEONE

Pop: 4.9 m.   *Area:* 72,000 sq km.
Sierra Leone High Commission: 245 Oxford Street, London W1. Tel: (020) 7287 9884.
British High Commission: Spur Road, Freetown
British Council: (P O Box 124), Tower Hill, Sierra Leone.

SINGAPORE

Pop: 4 m.   *Area:* 581 sq km.
Singapore High Commission: 9 Wilton Crescent, London SW1X 8SA. Tel: (020) 7235 8315.
Consular Section: 5 Chesham Street, London SW1. Tel: (020) 7245 0273.
Singapore Tourist Office: Carrington House, Regent Street, London W1R 7LB. Tel: (020) 7437 0033.
British High Commission: (P O Box 19), Tanglin Road, Singapore 1025.
British Council: 30 Napier Road, Singapore 1025.
British Business Association: 1st Floor, Inchcape house, 450-452 Alexandra Road, Singapore 0511.
Contact Singapore: Charles House, Lower Ground Floor, 5-11 Regent Street, London SW1Y 4LR. Tel: (020) 7321 5600. (Information on employment opportunities.)
The Straits Times: http.//straitstimes.asia1.com.

SLOVAKIA

Pop: 5.4 m.   *Area:* 49,000 sq km..
Slovak Embassy: 25 Kensington Palace Gardens, London W8 4QY. Tel: (020) 7243 0803. Visa information: (0900) 160 0360. Website: http;//slovakia.net.
Ministry of Education: Hlboka 2, 813 30 Bratislava.

British Embassy: Panska 16, 81101 Bratislava.
British Council: PO Box 68, Panska 17, 81499 Bratislava.

SLOVENIA

Pop: 2 m.   *Area:* 20,256 sq km.
Slovenian Embassy: 10 Little College, London SW1P. Tel: (020) 7222 2666. Visa information: (0900) 160 0077.
Slovenia Tourist Office, 49 Conduit Street, London W1. Tel: (020) 7287 7133.
British Embassy: 4th Floor, Trg Republike 3, 61-000 Ljubljana.
British Council: Stefanova 1/III, 61-000 Ljubljana.

SOLOMON ISLANDS

Pop: 450,000.   *Area:* 28,000 sq km.
Solomon Islands Office: 17 Springfield Road, London SW19 7AL. Tel: (020) 7946 1744.
British High Commission: Telkon House, Mendana Avenue, Honiara.

SOMALIA

Pop: 11.5 m.   *Area:* 637,000 sq km.
Somali Embassy: 60 Portland Place, London W1N 3DG. Tel: (020) 7580 7148. Closed.
British Embassy: (PO Box 1036), Waddada Zasan Geeddii Abtoow 7/8, Mogadishu. Closed.

SOUTH AFRICA

Pop: 46 m.   *Area:* 1.2 m.sq km.
South African High Commission: South Africa House, Trafalgar Square, London WC2N 5DP. Tel: (020) 7451 7299.
British High Commission: 255 Hill Street, Arcadia, Pretoria 0002; 91 Parliament Street, Cape Town.
British Council: 76 Juta Street, PO Box 30637, Braamfontein 2017. Also in Cape Town and Durban.
1820 Settlers Association: 601 Norvic, 93 De Corte Street, Braamfontein, Johannesburg 2001. (Also c/o Outbound Newspapers, 1 Commercial Road, Eastbourne BN21 3XQ.)
Beder-Harrison, 78 Marylebone Lane, London W1M 5FF. Tel: (020) 7486 3660. Fax: (020) 7486 3860. Immigration specialist.
Mallinicks, 25 Savile Row, London W1X 1AA. Tel: (020) 7333 2700. Fax: (020) 7439 0566. Immigration lawyers.

SPAIN

Pop: 40. m.   *Area:* 505,000 sq km.
Spanish Embassy: 24 Belgrave Square, London SW1. Tel: (020) 7235 5555.
Spanish Consulate-General: 23 Manchester Square, London W1. Visa information: (0900) 160 0123.
Spanish Consulates: 21 Rodney Rd, Liverpool L1 9EF; 70 Spring Gardens, Manchester M2 2BQ.
Spanish Tourist Office: 57-58 St James's Street, London SW1A 1LD. Tel: (020) 7499 0901.
Anglo-Spanish Society: 25 Woodsyre, Sydenham Hill, London SE26 6SS. Tel: (020) 8761 0955.
British Embassy: Calle de Fernando el Santo 16, 28010 Madrid.
British Council: Paseo del General Martinez, Campos 31, 28010 Madrid.
British Chamber of Commerce: Plaza de Santa Barbara 10, 28004 Madrid.
Istituto Nacional de Empleo: General Pardinas 5, Madrid. (State employment agency)
Hispanic and Luso Brazilian Council: 2 Belgrave Square, London SW1X 8PJ. Tel: (020) 7235 2303.

SRI LANKA

Pop: 19 m.   *Area:* 65,600 sq km.
Sri Lankan High Commission: 13 Hyde Park Gardens, London W2 2LU. Tel: (020) 7262 1841.
Sri Lankan Tourist Office: 22 Regent Street, London SW1. Tel: (020) 7390 2627.
British High Commission: (PO Box 1433), Galle Road, Killiputiya, Colombo 3.
British Council: 49 Alfred House Gardens, PO Box 753, Colombo 3. Also in Kandy.

SUDAN

Pop: 29 m.   *Area:* 2.5 m sq km.
Sudanese Embassy: 3 Cleveland Row, London SW1A 1DD. Tel: (020) 7839 8080.
British Embassy: (P O Box 801), Off Sharia Al Baladiya, Khartoum East.
British Council: 14 Abu Sinn Street, PO Box 1253, Khartoum East.

SURINAME

Pop: 450,000.   *Area:* 163,000 sq km.
Suriname Embassy: 2 Alexander Gogelweg, The Hague. Tel: 00 31 70 365 0844.
British Consulate: VSH United Buildings, Van't Hogerhuysstraat, PO Box 1300, Paramaribo.

SWAZILAND

Pop: 1 m   *Area:* 17,000 sq km.
Swaziland High Commission: 20 Buckingham, Gate, London SW1. Tel: (020) 7630 6611.
Swaziland Society: 4 Sybil's Way, Houghton Conquest, Bedfordshire MK45 3AQ. Tel: (01234) 742815.
British High Commission: Alister Miller Street (Private Bag), Mbabane.

SWEDEN

Pop: 8.9 m.   *Area:* 459,000 sq km.
Swedish Embassy: 11 Montagu Place, London W1H 2AL. Tel (020) 7917 6400. Visa information: (0900) 160 0110.
Swedish Tourist Office: 11 Montagu Place, London W1H 2Al. Tel: (020) 7724 5869.
British Embassy, Skarpîgatan 6-8, 115-27 Stockholm.(Also British Council)
British Swedish Chamber of Commerce, Nybrokajen 75, S-114-40 Stockholm.
International Employment Office, Arbetsmarknadsstyrelsen, Sergels Torg 12, Box 7763, 10396 Stockholm.
Anglo-Swedish Society: 43 Kinburn Street, London SE16 1DN. Tel/Fax: (020) 7231 3664.

SWITZERLAND

Pop: 7.4 m.   *Area:* 41,300 sq km.
Swiss Embassy: 16 -18 Montagu Place, London W1H 2BQ. Tel (020) 7616 6000. Visa information: (0906) 833 1313.
Swiss Tourist Office: Swiss Centre, 1 New Coventry Street, London W1V 8EE. Tel: (020) 7734 1921.
British Embassy, Thunstrasse 50, Bern 15. Consulates in Geneva, Montreux, Valais, Zürich, Lugano.
British-Swiss Chamber of Commerce, Freiestrasse 155, 8032 Zürich.

SYRIA

Pop: 16 m.   *Area:* 185,000 sq km.
Syrian Embassy: 8 Belgrave Square, London SW1 8PH. Tel (020) 7245 9012. Visa information: (0900) 160 0171.
British Embassy: Quartier Malki, 11 Mohammed Kurd Ali Street, Immeuble Kotob, Damascus.
British Council: Abu Rumaneh, Rawda, Masr Street, Hasibi/Azem Building, PO Box 33105, Damascus.

TAIWAN (REPUBLIC OF CHINA)

Pop: 20 m.   *Area:* 36,000 sq km.
Taipei Embassy: 50 Grosvenor Gardens, London SW1. Tel: (020) 7396 9152. Visa information service: (0900) 160 0315.
British Trade & Cultural Office: BTCO, 9th Floor, Fu Key Building, 99 Jen Ai Road, Section 1, Taipei.
Taipei-British Chamber of Commerce, 7th Floor, Fu Key Building, 99 Jen Ai Road, Taipei.

TANZANIA

Pop: 34m.   *Area:* 945,000 sq km.
Tanzanian High Commission: 43 Hertford Street, London W1Y 8DB. Tel: (020) 7499 8951. Website: www.tanzania-online.gov.uk.
Tanzanian Tourist office: 77 South Audley Street, London W1Y 5TA. Tel: (020) 7499 7727.
British High Commission: (P O Box 9200), Hifadhi House, Samora Avenue, Dar-es-Salaam
British Council: (PO Box 9100), Samora Avenue, Dar es Salaam.

THAILAND

Pop: 60 m.   *Area:* 514,000 sq km.
Royal Thai Embassy: 30 Queen's Gate, London SW7 5JB. Tel: (020) 7589 2944. Visa Section: (020) 7589 0173. Visa information: (0900) 160 0150.
Thai Tourist Office: 49 Albermarle Street, London W1. Tel: (020) 7499 7679.
British Embassy, Wireless Road, Bangkok 10330.
British Chamber of Commerce: Unit 1810, BB Building, 54 Asoke Road, Sukhumwit 21, Bangkok 10110.
British Council: 254 Chulalongkorn Soi 64, Siam Square, Phyathai Road, Bangkok 10330.
Thai British Business Association: Flat 4, Addiscombe, Cranborne Road, Bournemouth BH2 2BR. Tel: (01202) 314406.
Bangkok Post: www.bangkokpost.net.

TOGO

Pop: 4.7 m.   *Area:* 57,000 sq km.
British Consulate: British School of Lomé.
British Embassy: See Ghana.

TONGA

Pop: 110,000   *Area:* 700 sq km.

Tonga High Commission: 36 Molyneux Street, London W1H 6AB. Tel: (020) 7724 5828.
British High Commission: PO Box 56, Vuna Road, Nuku'alofa.

TRINIDAD & TOBAGO

Pop: 1.3 m.   *Area:* 5,000 sq km.
Trinidad & Tobago High Commission: 42 Belgrave Square, London SW1X 8NY. Tel: (020) 7245 9351. E-mail: trintogov@tthc.demon.co.uk.
British High Commission: 19 St Clair Avenue, St Clair, PO Box 778, Port of Spain.

TUNISIA

Pop: 10 m.   *Area:* 164,000 sq km.
Tunisian Embassy: 29 Prince's Gate, London SW7 1QG. Tel: (020) 7584 8117. Visa information: (0900) 188 7711.
Tunisian Tourist Office: 77a Wigmore Street, London W1. Tel: (020) 7224 5561.
British Embassy: (B P 229), 5 Place de la Victoire, Tunis. (Also British Council)
Tunisian-British Chamber of Commerce, 23 Rue de Jerusalem, 3e Etage, Tunis.

TURKEY

Pop: 66 m.   *Area:* 780,000 sq km.
Turkish Embassy: 43 Belgrave Square, London SW1X 8PA. Tel: (020) 7393 0202. E-mail:turkish.embassy@virgin.net.
Turkish Consulate-General: Rutland Lodge, Rutland Gardens, London SW7. Tel: (020) 7589 0949. Visa information: (0906) 834 7348.
Turkish Tourist Office: 1st Floor, 170/173 Piccadilly, London W1V 9DD. Tel: (020) 7629 7771.
Anglo-Turkish Society: 43 Montrose Place, London SW1X 7DT. Tel: (01420) 562506.
British Embassy, Sehit Ersan Caddesi 46A, Çankaya, Ankara.
British Consulate-General, Tepebasi, Beyoglu, Istanbul 80072.
British Chamber of Commerce, Mesrutiyet Caddesi 18, Aslittan Passaji, Kat 6, Daire 72, Tepebasi, Istanbul 80050.
British Council: Kirlangic Sokak 9, Gazi Osman Pasa, 06700 Ankara; Ors Turistik Is Merkezi, Istiklal Caddesi 251/253, Beyoglu, 80060 Istanbul.

TURKMENISTAN

Pop: 4.5 m.   *Area:* 448,000 sq km.
Turkmen Embassy: 2nd Floor, 14 Wells Street. London W1P. Tel: (020) 7255 1071.
British Embassy, 301-308 Office Building, Atin Plaza Hotel, Ashgabat.

UGANDA

Pop: 22 m.   *Area:* 236,000 sq km.
Ugandan High Commission: Uganda House, Trafalgar Square, London WC2N
5DX. Tel: (020) 7839 5783.
British High Commission: 10/12 Parliament Avenue, PO Box 7070, Kampala.
(Also British Council.)

UKRAINE

Pop: 52 m.   *Area:* 603,700 sq km.
Ukrainian Embassy: 60 Holland Park, London W11 3SJ. Tel: (020) 7727 6312.
British Embassy: 9 Desyatinna, 252025 Kiev.
British Council: 9/1 Besarabska Ploshcha, Flat 9, 252004 Kiev.

UNITED ARAB EMIRATES (UAE)
(Abu Dhabi, Dubai, Ras al Khaimah, Sharjah, Fujairah, Ajman, Umm al Qawain)

Pop: 2.4 m.   *Area:* 83,600 sq km.
UAE Embassy: 30 Prince's Gate, London SW7 1PT. Tel: (020) 7581 1281.
Consular Section: (020) 7589 3434.
British Embassy: P O Box 248, Abu Dhabi; P O Box 65, Dubai.
British Council: Villa No 7, Al Nasr Street (near All Prints), Khalidiya, PO Box
46523, Abu Dhabi. Tariq bin Zaid Street, PO Box 1636, Dubai.

UNITED STATES OF AMERICA

Pop: 275,000   *Area:* 9 m.sq km.
United States Embassy, 24 Grosvenor Square, London W1A 2JB. Tel: 020 7499
9000. Website: www.usembassy.org.uk.
Visa Branch, 5 Upper Grosvenor Street, London W1A 2JB. Tel: (020) 7499
7010. Visa information lines: (09068) 200290 (recorded) and (09061) 500590
(live).
US Information Service, 55/56 Upper Brook Street, London W1A 2LH. Tel: (020)
7499 9000 ext 2643 and 2638.
United States Consulate-General, Queen's House, Queen Street, Belfast BT1 6EQ.
Tel: (02890) 328239.
United States Consulate-General, 3 Regent Terrace, Edinburgh EH7 5BW. Tel:
(0131) 557 6023.
British Embassy: 3100 Massachussetts Ave NW, Washington, DC 20008.
www.britain.nyc.ny.us.
British Consulates/Consulates-General in Anchorage, Atlanta, Boston, Charlotte,
Chicago, Cleveland, Dallas, Denver, Houston, Kansas City, Los Angeles, Miami,
Minneapolis, Nashville, New Orleans, New York, Orlando, Philadelphia, Phoenix,
Portland, St Louis, Salt Lake City, San Francisco, Seattle.

British American Chamber of Commerce, 8 Staple Inn, Holborn, London WC1V 7QH. Tel: (020) 7404 6400. Fax: (020) 7404 6828.

Four Corners Emigration, Freepost NWW1289, Manchester M22 5FR. Tel: (0345) 419453.

Workpermit.com, 11 Bolt Court, Fleet Street, London EC4A 3DQ. (020) 7495 3999. Website: www.workpermit.com. Immigration consultants.

Frederick De Pasquale, Visa Services Inc., Devlin House, 36 St George Street, Mayfair, London W1R 9FA. Tel: (020) 7529 1423. Website: www.immigrationvisas.com. Immigration attorney.

Diane B Hinch, 24 Grosvenor Street, London W1X 9FB. Tel: (020) 7917 9680. Immigration lawyer.

LaVigne, Coton & Associates, 150 Minories, London EC3N 1LS. Tel: (020) 7264 2110. Immigration lawyer.

MACS, 49 Churncote, Telford, Salop TF3 1YL. Tel: (01952) 590722. Fax: 01952 407153. Migration consultants.

US Visa Consultants, 52 Maddox Street, London W1R 9PA. Tel: (020) 7317 6709. Fax: (020) 7317 6712.

Stan Steinger, 96 Kensington High Street, London W8 4SG. Mobile Tel: (07956) 222572. Immigration lawyer.

Richard S Goldstein, 96A Mount Street, Mayfair, London W1X. Tel: (020) 7499 8200. Immigration lawyer.

URUGUAY

Pop: 3.2 m.　　*Area:* 176,000 sq km.

Uruguayan Embassy: 140 Brompton Road, London SW3 1HY. Tel: (020) 7589 8735.

British Embassy: Calle Marco Bruto 1073, Montevideo 11300.

British Chamber of Commerce: Av Lib Brig Gral Lavelleja 1641, Montevideo.

UZBEKISTAN

Pop: 25 m.　　*Area:* 447,400 sq km.

Uzbekistan Embassy: 41 Holland Park, London W11 2PP. Tel: (020) 7229 7679.

British Embassy: Ul Gogolya 67, Tashkent 700000.

British Council: University of World Languages Building, 11 Kounoev Street, Tashkent.

VANUATU

Pop: 190,000　　*Area:* 14,800 sq km.

Ministry of Education: PO Box 028, Port Vila.

British High Commission: PO Box 567, KPMG House, Rue Pasteur, Port Vila.

British Friends of Vanuatu, 67 Beresford Road, Cheam, Surrey. (Richard Dorman)

VENEZUELA

Pop: 24 m.   *Area:* 912,000 sq km.
Venezuelan Embassy: 1 Cromwell Road, London SW7 2HW. Tel: (020) 7581 4206.
Venezuelan Consulate-General: 56 Grafton Way, London W1P. Tel: (020) 7387 6727; (0900) 117 1221.
Anglo-Venezuelan Society: c/o Schroders, 120 Cheapside, London EC2V 6DS. Tel: (020) 7622 4808.
British Embassy: (Apartado 1246), Edificio Torre Las Mercedes, Piso 3, Avenida La Estancia No 10, Ciudad Comercial, Caracas 1061.
British Council: Torre La Noria, Piso 6, Paseo Enrique Eraso, Las Mercedes/Sector San Roman, Apartado 65131, Caracas 1065.
Camero Venezolano Britanic de Comercio y Industria, (Apartado 69102), Torre Britanica, Piso 10, Letra E, Av Jose Felix Sosa, Altamira Sur, Caracas 1060A. (Venezuelan-British Chamber of Commerce).

VIETNAM

Pop: 80 m.   *Area:* 333,000 sq km.
Vietnamese Embassy: 12 Victoria Road, London W8 5RD. Tel: (020) 7937 1912. Visa Section: (020) 7937 3222; (0900) 117 1228.
British Embassy: 31 Hai Ba Trung, Hanoi; Consulate: 261 Dien Bien Phi, District 3, Ho Chi Minh City (Saigon).
British Council: 18b Cao Ba Quat, Ba Dinh District, Hanoi. Also 25 Le Duan Street, District 1, Ho Chi Minh City (Saigon).
Saigon Times Daily: www.saigon-news.com.

WEST BANK AND GAZA (Palestinian administered territories)

Pop: 1.9 m.   *Area:* 6,242 sq km.
Palestinian Delegation: 5 Galena Road, London W6. Tel: (020) 8563 0008.
British Consulate-General: 19 Nashashibi Street, Sheikh Jarrah Quarter, PO Box 19690, East Jerusalem 97200.

YEMEN

Pop: 18 m.   *Area:* 472,000 sq km..
Yemeni Embassy: 57 Cromwell Road, London SW7 2ED. Tel: (020) 7584 6607.
British Embassy: PO Box 1287, 129 Haddah Road, Sana'a.
British Council: House 7, Street 70, PO Box 2157, Sana'a.

YUGOSLAVIA

Pop: 10.5 m.   *Area:* 102,000 sq km.
Yugoslav Embassy: 5 Lexham.Gardens, W8 5JU. Tel: (020) 7370 6105. Visa

information: (0900) 160 0279.
British Embassy: Ulica General Zdanova 46, 11000 Belgrade.
British Council: Ulica General Zdanova 34 – Mezanin, 11001 Belgrade.

ZAMBIA

Pop: 10 m.   *Area:* 853,000 sq km.
High Commission: 2 Palace Gate, London W8 5NG. Tel: (020) 7589 6555.
Zambian Tourist Office: 163 Piccadilly, London W1V 9DE. Tel: (020) 7498 1188.
British High Commission: P O Box 50050, Independence Avenue, Lusaka.
British Council: (P O Box 34571), Heroes Place, Cairo Road, Lusaka.

ZIMBABWE

Pop: 12.4 m.   *Area:* 390,500 sq km.
Zimbabwe High Commission: 429 Strand, London WC2R 0SA. Tel: (020) 7836 7755.
Zimbabwe Tourist Office: Tel: (020) 7240 6169.
British High Commission: (PO Box 4490), Corner House, Somara Machel Ave and Leopold Takawira St, Harare.
Kipps Personnel Consultants, 11th Floor, Michael House, Baker Avenue, Harare.
P E Consulting Group, PO Box 8381, Causeway, Harare.
Valcol Employment Bureau, PO Box 4916, Harare.
Rio Tinto, P O Box 4490, Harare.
British Council: PO Box 664, 23 Jason Moyo Avenue, Harare.

20

Useful Addresses in the UK

Age Concern, Adastral House, 1268 London Road, London SW16 4ER. Tel: (020) 8765 7200. Website: www.ageconcern.org

Airpets Oceanic, Willowslea Farm Kennels, Spout Lane North, Stanwell Moor, Staines, Middlesex, TW19 6BW. Tel: (01753) 685571. Pet travel agent

Animal Angels, 8 Grand Parade, Station Road, Hook, Hants RG27 5DA. Tel: (01256) 764141. Website: www.animalangels.co.uk. Pet minding service.

Animal Aunts, Smugglers' Cottage, Green Lane, Rogate, Petersfield, Hants GU31 5DA. Tel: (01730) 821529. Website: www.animalaunts.co.uk. Pet minding service.

Association for Language Learning, 150 Railway Terrace, Rugby CV21 3HN. Website: www.all-languages.org.uk. Tel: (01788) 546443. Information on language training.

Association of Search & Selection Consultants, 24 St James's Square, London SW1Y 4HZ. Tel: (020) 7839 7788. Website: www.rec.uk.com.

Audio Forum, Microworld House, 2–6 Foscope Mews, London W9 2HH. Tel: (020) 7262 2178. Language books and tapes.

Avalon Overseas, Drury Way, Brent Park, London NW10 0JN. Tel: (020) 8451 6336. Fax: (020) 8451 6419. Website: www.avalon-overseas.com. International removers.

BBC World Service, PO Box 76, Bush House, Strand, London WC2B 4PH. Tel: (020) 7240 3456 and (020) 7557 2211. Website: www.bbc.co.uk/world service. Broadcasters and publishers of TV and radio programme listing journal *On Air.*

BBC Worldwide Television, Woodlands, 80 Wood Lane, London W12 0TT. Tel: (020) 8576 3040. Website: www.bbcworld.com.

Berlitz, 9–13 Grosvenor Street, London W1A 3BZ. Tel: (020) 7915 0909. Language tuition.

British Airways Travel Clinic, 156 Regent Street, London W1B 5LB. Tel: (020) 5439 9584. 101 Cheapside, London EC2V 6DT. Tel: (020) 7606 2977. Inoculation advice and treatment.

British Association of Removers, 3 Churchill Court, 58 Station Road, North Harrow, Middlesex HA2 7SA. Tel: (020) 8861 3331. Website: www.bar.co.uk.

BUPA International, Russell Mews, Brighton BN7 2NE. Tel: (01273) 208181.

Fax: (01273) 866583. www.bupa.com/int. Health insurance.

Canning, 4 Abingdon Road, London W8 6AF. Tel: (020) 7937 3233. Fax: (020) 7937 1458. Website: www.canning.co.uk. Cultural briefings.

Carbank Ltd, London Road, Ashington, West Sussex RH20 3AX. Tel: (01903) 893000. Fax: (01903) 893222. Website: www.carbank.co.uk. Car storage.

City Business Library, 1 Brewers' Hall Garden, London Wall, London EC2V 5BX. Tel: (020) 7638 8215. Has a wide range of international directories, magazines and newspapers.

Commonwealth Information Centre, Commonwealth Institute, Kensington High Street, London W8 6NQ. Tel: (020) 7603 4535. Website: www.commonwealth.org.uk

Commonwealth Publishing, 3rd Floor, New Zealand House, 80 Haymarket, London SW1Y 4TE. Tel: (020) 7930 6451. Fax: (020) 7747 9223. Website: www.nznewsuk.co.uk. Publishers of *New Zealand News UK*.

Communicaid, Queen's House, 1 Leicester Place, London WC2H 7BP. Tel: (020) 7432 3240. Fax: (020) 7432 3290. Business language programmes and cultural survival briefings.

Consyl Publishing, 3 Buckhurst Road, Town Hall Square, Bexhill on Sea, East Sussex T40 1QF. Tel: (01424) 223111. Website: www.consylpublishing. co.uk. Publishers of *Australian Outlook* and *New Zealand Outlook* and distributors of books on Australasia.

Department for Education and Skills (DfES), Qualifications and Standards Branch, Room 454, Moorfoot, Sheffield S1 4PQ. Tel: (0114) 259 4144.

Department for the Environment, Food and Rural Affairs (DEFRA), Export of Cats and Dogs Section, 1A Page Street, London SW1P 4PQ. Tel: (020) 7904 6347. PETS helpline: (0870) 241 1710. Website: www.defra.gov.uk/animalh/quarantine.

Department of Health International Branch, Room 512, Richmond House, 79 Whitehall, London SW1A 2NS. Website: www.doh.gov.uk/ traveladvice. Information on eligibility to state health facilities abroad.

Department of Health Leaflets Unit, PO Box 21, Honeypot Lane, Stanmore, Middx HA7 1AY. Tel: (0800) 555777.

Department of Trade and Industry, British Overseas Trade Board, 66–74 Victoria Street, London SW1E 6SW. Tel: (020) 7215 5000.

Department of Trade and Industry, Europe and World Trade Directorate, European Division, Ashdown House, 6th Floor, 123 Victoria Street, London SW1E 6RB. Tel: (020) 7215 4648. Certificates of Experience.

Department of Work and Pensions, Benefits Agency Overseas Branch, Tyneview Park, Whitley Road, Benton, Newcastle-upon-Tyne NE98 1BA. Tel: (0191) 228 7777.

ECA International, Anchor House, 15 Britten Street, London SW3 3TY. Tel: (020) 7351 5000. Website: www.eca-international.com. Advice on working abroad.

European Commission Representation in UK and Ireland:
Jean Monnet House, 8 Storey's Gate, London SW1P 3AT. Tel: (020) 7973 1992.

Windsor House, 9/15 Bedford Street, Belfast BT2 7EG. Tel: (028 90) 240708.

4 Cathedral Road, Cardiff CF1 9SG. Tel: (029 20) 240708.

9 Alva Street, Edinburgh. Tel: (0131) 225 2058.

Jean Monnet Centre, 18 Dawson Street, Dublin 2. Tel: Dublin 662 5113.

European Council for International Schools, 21 Lavant Street, Petersfield, Hants GU32 3EW. Tel: (01730) 268244. Fax: (01730) 267914. Website: www.ecis.org. Information on international schools worldwide.

Exeter Friendly Society, Beech Hill House, Walnut Gardens, Exeter EX4 4DG. Tel: (01392) 498063. Medical insurance.

Expat Network, Rose House, 109a South End, Croydon CR0 1BG. Tel: (020) 8760 5100. Fax: (020) 8760 0469. Website: www.expatnetwork.co.uk. Overseas jobs magazine and directory publishers; expatriate service organisation; insurance brokers.

Expat Tax Consultants Ltd, Suite 2, 2nd Floor, Shakespeare House, 18 Shakespeare Street, Newcastle upon Tyne NE1 6AQ. Tel: (0191) 230 3141. Website: www.expattax.co.uk/. Tax advisers.

Expatriate Advisory Services plc, 14 Gordon Road, West Bridgeford, Nottingham NG2 5LN. Tel: (0115) 981 6572. Expatriate financial advisers.

Expats International, PO Box 24733, London SE13 7WD. Telephone: (020) 8469 3419. Fax: (020) 8694 2484. Website: www.expats2000.com.uk. Expatriate service organisation.

Farnham Castle International Briefing and Conference Centre, Farnham, Surrey GU9 0AG. Tel: (01252) 720416. Fax: (01252) 719277. E-mail: cibfarnham@dial.pipex.com. Website: www.cibfarnham.co. uk. Country briefings.

FIDI, 69 rue Picard 85, 1080 Brussels, Belgium. Website: www.fidi.com.

Foreign & Commonwealth Office (FCO) Travel Advice Unit, Consular Dept, Clive House, Petty France, London SW1H 9HD. Tel: (020) 7270 4129. Website: www.fco.gov.uk/travel/.

Frost & Sullivan, Sullivan House, 4 Grosvenor Gardens, London SW1W 0DH. Tel: (020) 7730 3438. Business and cultural briefings.

Wilfred T. Fry Ltd, Crescent House, Crescent Road, Worthing BN11 1RN. Tel: (01903) 231545. Fax: (01903) 200868. Website: www.wtfry.com. Financial advisers.

Gabbitas Educational Consultants, Carrington House, 126–130 Regent Street, London W1R 6EE. Tel: (020) 7734 0161. Fax: (020) 7437 1764. Website: www.gabbitas.co.uk. Education advisers. See also Chapter 18.

Golden Arrow Shippers, Horsford Kennels, Lydbury North, Shropshire SY7 8DY. Tel: (01588) 680240. Fax: (01588) 680414. Pet transportation service.

The Good Book Guide, 24 Seward Street, London EC1V 3PS. Tel: (020) 7490 0900. Mail order book service.

Goodhealth International Healthcare, 5 Lloyds Avenue, London EC3N 3AE. Tel: 0870 442 7376. Website: www.goodhealth.co.uk. Medical insurance.

Grant & Cutler Language Bookshop, 55 Great Marlborough Street, London W1V 2AY. Tel: (020) 7734 2012. Fax: (020) 7734 9272. Website: www.grantandcutler.com

Hall-Godwins Overseas Consulting Co, Briarcliff House, Kingsmead, Farnborough, Hants GU14 7TE Tel: (01252) 521701. Financial and pensions advisers for expatriates.

Healthsearch Ltd, 9 Newland Street, Rugby CV22 7BJ. Tel: (01788) 541855. Impartial advice on healthcare insurance plans.

Help the Aged, St James's Walk, London EC1R 0BE. Tel: (020) 7253 0253.

Homesitters Ltd, Buckland Wharf, Aylesbury, Bucks HP22 5LQ. Tel: (01279) 777049. Website: www.homesitters.co.uk.

Howell & Associates, Hillside House, Pinewood Road, Ashley, Market Drayton, TF9 4PR. Tel: 01630 672555. Intercultural briefings for companies.

Inland Revenue Claims Branch, Foreign Division, Merton Road, Bootle L69 9BL. Tel: (0151) 922 63631.

Inland Revenue, FICO (Non-residents), St John's House, Merton Road, Bootle, Merseyside L69 9BB. Tel: (0151) 472 6208.

Inland Revenue, National Insurance Contributions Office, International Services, Longbenton, Newcastle upon Tyne NE98 1ZZ. Tel: (06451) 54811 or (0191) 225 4811. Website: www.inlandrevenue.gov.uk.

ISIS Independent Schools Information Service, 35 Grosvenor Gardens, London SW1W 0BS. Telephone: (020) 7798 1500. Website: www.isis.org.uk

Institute of Linguists, Saxon House, 48 Southwark Street, London SE1 1UN. Tel: (020) 7940 3100 Fax: (020) 7940 3101. E-mail: info@iol.org.uk. Information on language tuition.

Intercontinental Church Society, 1A Athena Drive, Tachbrook Park, Warwick CV34 6NL. Tel: (01926) 430347. Website: www.ics-uk.org.

International Private Healthcare Ltd, PO Box 488, IPH House, Borehamwood, Herts WD6 6AN. Tel: (020) 8905 2888.

Languages NTO, CILT, 20 Bedfordbury, London WC2N. Tel: (020) 7379 5131. Website: www.languagesnto.org.uk. Language course database (BLIS Professionals).

Language Studies International, 19–21 Ridgemount Street, London WC1E 7AH. Tel: (020) 7467 6500. Language tuition.

LCL Language Bookshop, 104 Judd Street, London WC1N 9BF. Tel: (020) 7837 0487. Fax: (020) 7837 0486.

Linguarama, 7th Floor, BPP House, 70 Red Lion Street, London WC1R 4NG. Tel (020) 7405 7557. Website: www.linguarama.com. Language tuition.

MASTA Medical Advisory Services for Travellers Abroad Ltd, Bureau of Hygiene and Tropical Medicine, Keppel Street, London WC1E 7HT. Tel: (020) 7631 4408 and (0891) 224100. Website: www.masta.com MASTA Travel Health Centre, 52 Margaret Street, London W1W 8SQ. Tel: (020) 7291 9333.

Mercers College, 14 Baldock Street, Ware, Herts SG12 9DZ. Tel: (01920) 465926. E-mail: mercers_college@lycos.co.uk. Correspondence courses for young people.

Manor Car Storage, PO Box 28, Clavering, Saffron Walden, Essex. Telephone (01799) 550021. Website: www.manorcarstorage.com

National Insurance Contributions Office, Inland Revenue, International Services, Longbenton, Newcastle upon Tyne NE98 1ZZ. Telephone: (0845) 915 4811 or (0191) 225 4811. Website: www.inlandrevenue.gov.uk.

National Insurance Contributions Office, Inland Revenue, International Services, 24-42 Corporation Street, Belfast BT1 3DP. (Northern Ireland residents.)

Objective Team Ltd, Bragborough Lodge Farm, Daventry NN1 7HA. Tel: (01788) 899029. Website: www.objectiveleadership.co.uk

Outbound Newspapers Ltd, 1 Commercial Road, Eastbourne BN21 3XQ. Tel: (01323) 412001. Website: www.outboundpublishing.com Publishers of *Australian News, Canada News, South Africa News, Destination New Zealand, Going USA*. Also operates mail order book service.

Overseas Resettlement Secretary, Church of England Board for Social Responsibility, Church House, Dean's Yard, London SW1P 3NX. Tel: (020) 7898 1000. Advice and introductions.

Par Air Services, Warren Lane, Stanway, Colchester, Essex. Tel: (01206) 330332. Fax: (01206) 331277. Website: www.parair.co.uk. Pet transport specialists.

Passport Agency (UK): Tel: (0870) 521 0410. Website: www.passport.gov.uk.

Globe House, 89 Eccleston Square, London SW1V 1PN.

Milburngate House, Durham DH1 5ZL.

5th Floor, India Buildings, Water St, Liverpool L2 0QZ. Serves North of England and North Wales.

Olympia House, Upper Dock St, Newport NP1 1XA. Serves South Wales, South and West of England.

Aragon Court, Northminster Road, Peterborough PE1 1QG. Serves Midlands, East Anglia, Kent.

3 Northgate, 96 Milton Street, Cowcaddens, Glasgow G4 0BT. Serves Scotland, London, Middlesex.

Hampton House, 47–53 High Street, Belfast BT1 2QS. Serves Northern Ireland.

PPP Healthcare, International Business Department, Philips House, Crescent Road, Tunbridge Wells, Kent TN1 2PL. Tel: (01892) 772002. Website: www.ppphealthcare.com.

Premier Financial Planning Group, Churchfield House, North Drive, Hebburn, Tyne & Wear NE31 1ES. Tel: (0191) 483 7805.

Recruitment and Employment Confederation, 36–38 Mortimer Street, London W1N 7RB. Tel: (020) 7323 4300. Website: www.rec.co.uk.

Robertson International, 7 Grove Park, White Waltham, Maidenhead, Berks SL6 3LW. Tel: (01628) 829090. Language training and cultural briefings.

School of Oriental & African Studies (External Services Division), Thornhaugh Street, Russell Square, London WC1H 0XG. Tel: (020) 7637 2388. Briefings and language training.

SFIA Educational Trust, 41 London Road, Twyford, Berks RG10 9EJ. Tel: (0845) 458 3690. Website: www.sfia.co.uk. Advice on children's schooling.

Spratts Animal Travel Service, 756 High Road, Goodmayes, Ilford, Essex IG3 8SY. Tel: (020) 8597 2415.

Stanfords, 12-14 Long Acre, London WC2E 9LP. Tel: (020) 7836 1321. Fax: (020) 7836 0189. Website: www.standfords.co.uk. Map shop and bookseller.

State Boarding Information Service (STABIS), DfES, Pupil Support and Independent Schools, Mowden Hall, Staindrop Road, Darlington DL3 9BG. Tel: (01325) 391272. Websites: www.stabis.org.uk and dfes.gov.uk

Dave Tester Expatriate Insurance Services, 18a Hove Park Villas, Hove BN3 6HG. Tel: (01273) 703469. Fax: (01273) 777723. Website: www.expatriate-insurance.com. Insurance broker.

Thames Consular Services, Unit 4, The Courtyard, Swab Centre, Fishers Lane, London W4 1RX. Tel: (020) 8996 2912. Website: www.thamesconsular.com. Visa service.

The Travel Bookshop, 13 Blenheim Crescent, London W11. Tel: (020) 7229 5260. Fax: (020) 7243 1552.

The Visa Service, 2 Northdown Street, London N1 9BG. Tel (020) 7833 2709. Website: www.visaservice.co.uk.

TSW International, 1st Floor, Jupiter House, Station Road, Cambridge CB1 2JZ. Tel: (01223) 363650. Tax consultants.

Colin Turner Group, City Cloisters, 188/196 Old Street, London EC1V 9BX. Tel: (020) 7490 5551. Media agency.

UK Expatriates Professional Advisory Services, 84 Grange Road, Middlesborough TS1 2LS. Tel: (01642) 221211. Financial advisers.

Universal Aunts, PO Box 304, London SW4 0NN. Telephone: (020) 7738 8937. Personal services agency.

WES Home School, 202 Bramhall Lane, Davenport, Stockport, Cheshire SK3 8TY. Tel: (0161) 456 8275. Website: www.weshome.demon.co.uk. E-mail: office@weshome.co.uk

Women's Corona Society (Corona Worldwide), Southbank House, Black Prince Road, London SE1 7SJ. Tel: (020) 7793 4020.
Website: www.coronaworldwide.freeserve.co.uk. Briefings and country reports.

World Service Enquiry, 233 Bon Marché Centre, 241–251 Ferndale Road, London SW9 8BJ. Tel: (0870) 770 3274. Fax (0870) 770 7991. Website: www.wse.org.uk. Advice on working abroad expecially in the voluntary sector. Publishes monthly *Opportunities Abroad.*

Worldwide Volunteering for Young People, 7 North Street Workshops, Stoke Sub Hamdon, Somerset TA14 6QR. Tel: (01935) 825588. Fax: (01935) 825775. Website: www.worldwidevolunteering.org.uk E-mail: worldvol@worldvol.co.uk Enquiry service which matches volunteers aged 16–25 with projects on its database. A number of careers services are linked to the database.

Year Out Group, PO Box 29925, London SW6 6FQ. Tel: (07980) 395789. Website: www.yearoutgroup.org. Website: www.yearoutgroup.org. E-mail: info@yearoutgroup.org. Information and advice for Gap Year students.

European Applications

Londres
le 18 Septembre 200X

Direction de Personnel
Société Bloggs International
Paris

Monsieur le Directeur,

Suite à l'annonce parue le 10 septembre dans The Times je me permets de poser ma candidature au poste de technicien principal.

Agé de 30 ans ju suis originaire de Portsmouth (Angleterre). Actuellement je suis employé comme technicien supérieur aux établissements Plessey à John O'Groats, et je désire trouver une situation qui soit plus en rapport avec mes capacités.

Vous trouverez ci-joint mon curriculum vitae mentionnant les études que j'ai effectuées et les postes que j'ai occupés.

Si ma proposition pouvait retenir votre attention je vous serais très reconnaissant de bien vouloir me convoquer à vos bureaux afin que je puisse vous soumettre mes certificats, diplômes et références.

Dans l'attente d'une réponse favorable, je vous prie d'agréer, Monsieur, l'expression de mes sentiments les plus distingués.

George Stephenson

Fig. 11. Application letter in French.

London
den 18 September 200X

Firma
Bloggs International A G.

Ried im Innkreis
Goethestr. 18.

Sehr geehrte Herren,

Auf Ihr Stellenangebot in der Londoner Times vom 10.09.01
bewerbe ich mich um die Stelle als Technischer Leiter und ich sende
Ihnen die erforderlichen Unterlagen – Lebenslauf,
Zeugnisabschriften usw.

Wie Sie aus den Unterlagen sehen, bin ich 30 Jahre alt, stamme aus
Portsmouth, und habe eine gute technische Ausbildung am Lands
End Technical College genossen.

Seit 1996 bin ich als Techniker bei der Firma Plessey in John
O'Groats angestellt. Jetzt aber möchte ich eine neue Stelle
aussuchen, die meinen Fähigkeiten besser entspricht.

Ich würde mich freuen, wenn Sie meine Bewerbung in die engere
Wahl ziehen könnten, und bin selbstverständlich gerne bereit, mich
persönlich vorzustellen.

Mit vorzüglicher Hochachtung,

George Stephenson

Fig. 12. Application letter in German.

Londres, 18 de Septiembre 2001

Bloggs International SA
Calle Costa del Sol, 80
Madrid

Muy Sres mios,

En respuesta a su anuncio en el Times de 10.09.01 me apresuro a ofrecerme para el puesto de director técnico en la sede de su empresa.

Tengo 30 años y soy natural de Portsmouth. Asistí al Instituto Técnico de Lands End y en 1991 aprobé el examén de Higher National Diploma. He trabajado durante los últimos tres años en la compañía Plessey en John O'Groats.

La unica razón por la que quiero dejar mi puesto es que deseo conseguir otro de más responsabilidad.

Acompaña la presente mi curriculum vitae y fotocopias de certificados de estudios uy de trabajo junto con una foto reciente.

En espera de recibir una contestación favorable, les saluda muy atentamente.

George Stephenson

Fig. 13. Application letter in Spanish.

Anita LYONS
14 Edinburgh Close,
Berwick on Tweed
Grand Bretagne
Tél: (01111) 99 99 99

Née le 30 janvier 1975, à Dundee (Écosse); 25 ans
Nationalité britannique
Célibataire

Formation

| Juillet 1993: | A Level (diplôme de fin d'études secondaires, équivalent de baccalauréat) en français, physique, économie. |
| Juin 1997: | BSc (licence en quatre ans) d'économie, Université d'Aberdeen. |

Langues:

Anglais	— langue maternelle
Français	— parlé e écrit couramment
Chinois	— notions

Expérience professionelle

1997 à 1999 Enquêtrice pour une société de marketing à Belfast
Depuis 1999 Interprète pour une société de tourisme à Penzance

Divers

| Voyages: | Séjours fréquents à l'étranger, en France, en Espagne et en Suisse. |
| Sports: | Natation, tennis, ski |

Autres Renseignements

Permis de conduire
Prête à voyager et à travailler à l'étranger

Fig. 14. A sample CV in French.

Anita LYONS
14 Edinburgh Close,
Berwick on Tweed
Grossbritannien
Tel: 01111/99 99 99

Am 30 Januar 1975 in Dundee, Schottland geboren;
25 Jahre alt
Britisch
Ledig

Beruf des vaters	Ingenieur
Konfession	r. kath
Bildungsweg	Grundschule von 1980 bis 1985
	Gymnasium von 1985 bis 1993

Leistungskurse

Juli 1993	A Level (Äquivalent des Abiturs) in Deutsch,
	Wirtschaftskunde und Mathematik
Juli 1997	BSc (vierjähriger Kurs) in Wirtschaftskunde,
	Aberdeen Universität

Sprachkenntnisse

Englisch	— Muttersprache
Deutsch	— sehr gut
Japanisch	— Grundkenntnisse

Berufstätigkeit

1997 bis 1999	Interviewerin für eine
	Marktforschungsfirma
Seit 1999	Dolmetscherin für eine Reisefirma

Ausserberufliche Interessen

Reisen:	Häufige Auslandreisen, nach Deutschland,
	Österreich und Amerika
Sport:	Schwimmen, Tennis, Skifahren

Andere relevante Informationen
Führerschein
Bereit im Ausland zu arbeiten

Fig. 15. A sample CV in German.

Anita LYONS
14 Edinburgh Close,
Berwick on Tweed
El Reino Unido
Tfo. (01111) 99 99 99

Fecha de macimiento   30 de noviembre de 1975

Nacionalidad   Británica

Estado Civil   Soltera

Educación
Julio 1993   Obtuve el certificado 'A level', en 3 asignaturas, español, francés y ciencias económicas (Este es equivalente al bachillerato y COU)

Junio 1997   Estudié 4 años para obtener el grado de BSc en las asignaturas de ciencias económicas en la universidad de Aberdeen. (El BSc es equivalente a la licenciatura)

Idiómas   El inglés como lengua materna
El español en forma adecuada
El francés que lo hablo y escribo correctamente
Tambien tengo conocimiento del alemán

Experiencia de trabajo
1997 a 1999   Tuve un trabjo con una compañía de estudios de mercado en Londres

Intereses extra-profesionales
               Natacion, tenis, esquiaje

Otros
Poseo permiso de conducir válido obtenido en 1995

Fig. 16. A sample CV in Spanish.

APPLICATION FORM / ACTE DE CANDIDATURE (*French*) / BEWERBUNGSFRAGEBOGEN (*German*) / IMPRESO DE CANDIDATURA (*Spanish*) / SOLLICITATIE FORMULIER (*Dutch*) /FORMULARIO DI CANDIDATURA (*Italian*).

Surname / Nom / Familienname / Apellidos / Naam / Cognome:

Forenames / Prénoms / Vornamen / Nombre / Voornamen / Nome:

Address / Adresse / Anschrift / Dirección / Adres / Indirizzo:

Telephone number / N° tél / Telefonnummer / N° di teléfono / Telefoonnummer / N. d telefono:

Date and place of birth / Date et lieu de naissance / Geburtsdatum und Geburtsort / Fecha y lugar de nacimiento / Plaats en datum van geboorte / Luogo e data di nascita:

Sex: male—female / Sexe: masculin—féminin / Geschlecht: männlich— weiblich / Sexo: masculino—femenino / Geslacht: mannelijk—vrouwelijk / Sesso: maschile — femminile.

Present nationality / Nationalité actuelle / Derzeitige Staatsangehörigkeit / Nacionalidad actual / Huidige nationaliteit / Cittadinanza attuale:

Fig. 17. Sample European Commission Application Form.

The terminology is taken from the different language versions of the application form used by the European Commission, whose assistance with this section is gratefully acknowledged.

Knowledge of languages / Connaissances linguistiques / Sprachkenntnisse / Conocimientos lingüísticos / Talenkennis / Conoscenze linguistiche:

Education / Études / Ausbildungsgang /Estudios / Genoten onderwijs / Studi:

Certificates and/or diplomas obtained / Certificats ou diplômes obtenus / Erlangte Zeugnisse und Diplome / Certificados o títulos obtenidos / Verworven getuigschriften of diploma's / Certificati o diplomi conseguiti:

Primary, secondary, advanced secondary or technical education / Études primaires, secondaires, moyennes ou techniques / Primarschule, Sekundarschule, Mittlere Schulbildung oder Lehrlingsausbildung / Enseñanza primaria, secundaria, media o técnica / Lager, middelbar of technisch onderwijs / Studi elementari. medi o tecnici:

Higher education / Études supérieures / Hochschulestudium / Enseñanza superior / Tertiair onderwijs / Studi superiori:

Postgraduate education / Études post-universitaires / Aufbaustudium / Estudios postuniversitarios / Postuniversitair oderwijs / Studi postuniversitari:

Published works / Ouvrages publiés / Veröffentlichungen / Publicaciones / Gepubliceerde werken / Pubblicazioni:

Office skills: typing—wordprocessing / Connaissances des techniques de bureau: dactylographie—traitement de texte / Bürotechnische Kenntnisse: Maschinenschrieben—Textverarbeitung / Conocimiento de técnicas de oficina: mecanografia—tratamiento de textos / Kennis van typen en tekstverwerking: typen—tektsverwerking / Conoscenze delle tecniche d'uffocio: dattilografia—trattamento testi:

Fig. 17. Contd.

Career to date / Expérience professionelle / Berufserfahrung / Experiencia profesional / Beroepservaring / Esperienza professionale:

Present or more recent post / Emploi actuellement occupé ou emploi le plus récent / Derzeitige oder letzte Stelle / Puesto de trabajo actual o más reciente / Huidige of laatste betrekking / Posto attuale o ultimo posto occupato:

Previous post / Emploi précédent / Vorherige Stelle /Puesto de trabajo precedente / Vorige betrekkingen / Posto precedente:

Dates—length in months—gross monthly salary / Dates—durée en mois—traitement ou revenue mensuel brut / Dauer—Dauer in Monaten—Bruttomonatsgehalt / Fechas—duración en mesessueldo o ingresos mensuales brutos / Data—duuer in maanden—bruto-maandsalaris / Date—durata in mese—stipendio mensile lordo:

Exact designation of post / Titre exact de vos fonctions / Genaue Berufsbezeichnung / Denominacion exacta de sus funciones / Nauwkeurige aanduidung van uw functie / Definizione esatta delle mansioni esplicate:

Employer / Employeur / Arbeitgeber / Empresa / Werkgever /Datore di lavoro:

Nature of Work / Nature de votre travail / Beschreibung der Tätigkeit / Descripción del trabajo / Aard van de functie / Descrizione del lavore svolto:

Reasons for leaving / Raisons pour quitter / Kündigungsgründe / Motivos del cese / Redenen voor het vertrek / Motivi dell'abbandono dell'impiego:

Fig. 17. Contd.

Period of notice required to leave your present post / Délai de préavis de votre emploi actuel / Kündigungsfrist bei Ihrer derzeitigen Stelle / Plazo de preaviso en su puesto de trabajo actual / Opzegtermijn van uw huidige betrekking / Termine de preavviso per l'impiego attualmente occupato:

Long periods spent abroad / Séjours importants à l'étranger / Längere Auslandsaufenthalte / Estancias importantes en el extranjero / Perioden van berblijf van langere duur en het buitenland / Soggiorni importanti all'estero:

Interests and skills not connected with work / Activités ou aptitudes extra-professionelles, sociales, sportives, etc. / Ausserberufliche soziale und sportliche Tätigkeiten und Fähigkeiten / Actividades o intereses extra-profesionales, sociales, deportivos, etc / Aktiviteiten of bekwaamheden buiten de beroepssfeer, bezigheden op sociaal gebied, op sportgebeit. enz. / Attività o attitudini extraprofessionali: sociali, sportive, ecc.:

Have you a physical handicap? / Avez-vous un handicap physique? / Haben Sie eine körperliche Behinderung? / Tiene usted algún impedimento físico? / Heebt u een lichamelijke handicap? / Ha una minorazione fisica?

Have you ever been convicted or found guilty of any offence by any court? If so give details. / Condamnations pénales, sanctions administratives / Vorstrafen und Disziplinarstrafen / Condenas penales, sanciones administrativas / Gerechtelijke veroordelingen en disciplinaire straffen / Eventuali condanne penali e sanzioni amministrative:

Fig. 17. Contd.

I, the undersigned, declare on my word of honour that the information provided above is true and complete.

Je soussigné(e) déclare sur l'honneur que les indications portées au présent acte de candidature sont véridiques et complètes.

Ich. der (die) Unterzeichnete, erklare ehrenwörtlich, dass die Angaben is diesem Bewerbungsfragebogen wahrheitsgetreu und vollständig sind.

El (la) abajo firmate declara por su honor que la información suministrada en el presente impreso de candidatura es verdica y completa.

Ik verklaar op erewoord dat de in dit sollicitatieformulier verstrekte gegevens waarheidsgetrouw en volledig zijn.

Io sottocritto/a dichiaro sul mio onore che le informazioni fornite nel presente formulario sono veridiche e complete.

I am willing to undergo the compulsory medical examination to ensure that I am physically fit to perform the duties involved.

J'accepte de me soumettre à la visite médicale réglementaire destinée à vérifier que je dispose bien des aptitudes physiques requises pour l'exercise des fonctions envisagées.

Ich bin bereit, mich der vorgeschriebenen ärztlichen Untersuchung zum Nachweis meiner körperlichen Eignung für die Ausübung der angestrebten Tätigkeit zu unterziehen.

Acepta someterse al reconocimiento médico reglamentario que tiene por finalidad verificar que reúne las condiciones físicas exigidas para el ejercicio de las funciones contempladas.

Ik ben bereid mij te onderwerpen aan het vvorgeschreven medische onderzoek naar de lichamelijke geschiktheid voor het vervullen van de desbetreffende functie.

Accetto di sottopormi alla visita medica regolamentare per l'accertamento della mia idoneità fisica all'esercizio delle funziono oggetto del presente bando.

Fig. 17. Contd.

22

Further Reading

COUNTRY HANDBOOKS AND GUIDES

Country Profiles for Expatriates (ECA International).

Culture Shock series (Kuperard/Times Editions): Argentina, Australia, Bolivia, Borneo, Burma, Canada, Chile, China, Cuba, Czech Republic, Denmark, Egypt, France, Germany, Greece, Hong Kong, Hungary, India, Indonesia, Iran, Israel, Italy, Japan, Korea, Laos, Malaysia, Mauritius, Mexico, Morocco, Nepal, Netherlands, Norway, Pakistan, Philippines, Singapore, South Africa, Spain, Sri Lanka, Sweden, Switzerland, Syria, Taiwan, Thailand, Turkey, Ukraine, UAE, USA, Venezuela, Vietnam.

Economist Business Travel Guides: Arabian Peninsula, China, France, Germany, Japan, SE Asia, USA.

Live and Work in... series (Vacation Work): Australia & New Zealand; Belgium, the Netherlands and Luxembourg; France; Germany; Italy; Spain and Portugal; USA and Canada.

Live and Work in... series (Grant Dawson): Canada, Central America, Japan, New Zealand, Scandinavia, USA.

Living and Working in... series (How To Books): America, Australia, France, Germany, Greece, Italy, Netherlands, New Zealand, Portugal, Saudi Arabia, Spain.

Living and Working in... series (Survival Books): America, Australia, France, Spain, Switzerland.

Living in... series (Robert Hale): France, Germany, Italy, Portugal, Spain.

Long Stays in... series (David & Charles): Belgium and Luxembourg; France; Germany; Spain.

The Traveller's Handbook, Carole Brandenberger (ed) (WEXAS). A mine of information for anyone who is likely to be visiting several countries either for business or for pleasure. Included in its extensive reference section is information on visa requirements, duty free allowances, airport departure taxes, currency restrictions, hospitals with English-speaking staff, weather information, business hours, foreign diplomatic representations in Australia, Canada, New Zealand, the USA and the UK.

Footprint Handbooks: Brazil, Caribbean Islands; East Africa, South Africa, India, Indonesia; Malaysia and Singapore; Mexico and Central America; North Africa; South America; South Asia; Thailand, Indo-China and Burma, Venezuela. (Travel & Trade Publications)

NEWSPAPERS AND PERIODICALS
(With overseas job vacancies.)

The Health Exchange: Monthly magazine for health professionals from International Health Exchange (see entry in Chapter 18) which carries overseas vacancies.

Home and Away: The monthly magazine of Expats International (see Useful Addresses in the UK), which deals with all matters of concern to expatriates, including finance, family matters, overseas jobs markets. Subscribers, many of whom are on overseas contracts, also receive an extensive list of vacancies in the UK and abroad, and can have their details circulated to employers registered with the organisation.

Nexus: A monthly magazine from Expat Network (see Useful Addresses in the UK), which has articles on working abroad and an extensive section devoted to job advertisements with a bias to construction, oil and gas, engineering and utilities.

Opportunities Abroad: A monthly vacancy bulletin from Christians Abroad (see Useful Addresses in the UK) concentrating on voluntary and non-governmental organisations. Subscribers receive a copy of a guide to these organisations which is updated annually.

Overseas Jobs Express: A fortnightly paper which contains features on working abroad and overseas vacancies. Subscriptions: 20 New Street, Brighton BN1 1UF. Website: www.overseasjobsexpress.com. Tel: (01273) 440220. Fax: (01273) 440229.

NEWSPAPERS & PERIODICALS
(General)

The Economist: The Economist Subscription Centre, PO Box 471, Haywards Heath RH16 3GY. Tel: (01444) 475647. Fax (01444) 445572. E-mail: economist.subs@qss-uk.com. Weekly international news magazine which also carries a selection of international job advertisements.

The Guardian Weekly: Weekly digest of news from the *Guardian*. Subscriptions: 164 Deansgate, Manchester M60 2RR. Tel: (0161) 832 7200.

The Independent International: 1 Canada Square, London E14 5DL. Tel: (020) 7293 2488. Website: www.independent.co.uk.

On Air: BBC World Service. (See Useful Addresses in the UK). Monthly magazine which lists details of BBC World Service radio and TV programmes.

Resident Abroad and *The International,* Financial Times Magazines, Maple House, 149 Tottenham Court Road, London W1P 9LL. Tel: (020) 7896 2525. Fax: (020) 7896 2172.

The Week: Bradley Pavilions, Pear Tree Road, Bradley Stoke North, Bristol BS32 0BQ. Tel: (01454) 620070. Fax: (01454) 620080. Weekly digest of British and foreign press.

The Weekly Telegraph: Weekly newspaper featuring articles and news items from *Daily Telegraph*. Subscriptions: PO Box 14, Harold Hill, Romford RM3 8EQ. Tel: (01708) 38100.

GENERAL BOOKS

Culture and Interpersonal Communication, William D. Gudykunst and Stella Ting-Toomey (Sage).
Culturegrams: The Nations Around Us. (Ferguson Publishing Co, USA.)
Culture's Consequences, Geert Hofstede (Sage).
Europa World Book (Europa). Contains background information and directory of addresses for every country in the world.
Handbook for Development Workers Overseas (Returned Volunteer Action).
Handbook for Women Travellers, M. and G. Moss (Piatkus).
International Relocation, W. Coyle and S. Shortland (Butterworth).
Living and Working Abroad: A Practical Guide; *A Wife's Guide*; *A Parent's Guide* (Kuperard).
Mind your Manners, John Mole (Nicholas Brealey).
Planning to Work Abroad (ECA International).

Portable Careers, Linda Greenbury (Kogan Page).
Riding the Waves of Culture, Fons Trompenaars (Nicholas Brealey).
Travelling Alone – A Guide for Working Women, R. Bailey (Macdonald Optima).
Women Overseas: a Practical Guide, N. Piet Pelon and B. Hornby (Chartered Institute of Personnel and Development).
Working Abroad: The Daily Telegraph Guide to Working Overseas, Geoffrey Golzen (Kogan Page).
Worldwide Personal Tax Guide (Ernst & Young).

WORK GUIDES AND DIRECTORIES

Au Pair & Nanny's Guide to Working Abroad, S. Griffiths and S. Legg (Vacation Work).
Casual Work on the Mediterranean and the Canary Islands (Island Publishing).
Contact Directory series (Expat Network): Far East, Middle East, SE Asia.
Directory of Jobs & Careers Abroad (Vacation Work).
Directory of Summer Jobs Abroad (Vacation Work).
Directory of Work & Study in Developing Countries (Vacation Work).
Finding a Job in Australia (Island Publishing).
Getting a Job in... (How To Books): America, Australia, Canada, Europe, France, Germany.
International Directory of Executive Recruitment Consultants, Executive Grapevine, 2nd Floor, Cottonmill Lane, St Albans AL1 2HA. Fax: (01727) 844779.
International Directory of Voluntary Work, D. Woodworth (Vacation Work).
International Fax Directory (Jaeger & Waldman).
Teach English as a Foreign Language, S. Tyson-Ward (How To Books).
Working Holidays (Central Bureau – annual).
Working Holidays in Australia (Island Publishing).
Working in Ski Resorts – Europe, V. Pybus and C. James (Vacation Work).
Work Your Way Around the World, Susan Griffiths (Vacation Work).
Worldwide Volunteering for Young People. (How To Books).

Index

Abu Dhabi, see United Arab Emirates
accommodation, 59, 65, 98-100
accountancy careers, 187-188
adaptability, 22
adjustment, 16, 68-70, 98
Afghanistan, 155-156, 268
age, 23
agricultural posts, 111, 188
Albania, 146, 269
Algeria, 150, 151, 269
allowances, 59-60
Andorra, 141-145, 269
Angola, 164-167, 269
Anguilla, 177, 269
Antigua, 269
applications, 40-52, 315-322
application forms, 48-52, 323-327
Arabs, 149-154
Argentina, 175, 270
Armenia, 155-156, 270
Asia, 155-161
au pair jobs, 188-189
Australia, 137, 180-183, 185, 270-271
Austria, 141-145, 271
aviation careers, 189
Azerbaijan, 155-156, 271

Bahamas, 271
Bahrain, 271
balance, 22
Baltic States, 145
Bangladesh, 156-157, 271
banking, 80-81, 105
banking careers, 189
Barbados, 272
BBC, 104
Belarus, 146, 273
Belgium, 141-145, 273
Belize,177, 273
Benin, 273
Bermuda, 177, 273
bibliography, 328-331
Bolivia, 274
Bosnia-Herzegovina, 146, 274

Botswana, 164, 274
Brazil, 175, 176, 274
briefings, 25, 72-75
British Council, 29, 75, 125, 195-196,
    268-310
British Embassies/Consulates, 29, 105, 107,
    108, 268-310
British Virgin Islands, 177
broadcasting careers, 209-210
Brunei, 158, 274
Buddhism, 159
Bulgaria, 146, 275
Burkina Faso, 275
Burma (Myanmar), 157, 275
Burundi, 163, 275

Cambodia, 157, 275
Cameroon, 275
Canada, 137, 168-170, 174, 276
car, 81, 88, 96, 105
careers guidance, 23, 33
Caribbean, 177, 178-179
catering careers, 120, 200-201
Cayman Islands, 177, 277
Central Africa, 163-164
Central African Republic, 277
Central America, 175-177, 178-179
Central Asia, 155
Central Bureau, 110, 117-118
certificates of experience, 143
Chad, 275
chambers of commerce, 29, 139, 268-310
charities, 126-127
Chartered Institute of Personnel and
    Development (IPD), 134, 135-136
children, 65-68, 82, 105
Chile, 277
China, 158, 277
Christians Abroad, 23, 26, 75, 102, 128-129
church, 102
climate, 17, 69
clothing, 82
clubs, 104
Colombia, 278

Comores Islands, 278
Congo, 278
Congo (Dem Rep), 163, 278
Commonwealth Secretariat, 122-123, 125, 228
communications careers, 190
companionship, 101-102
competence, 18
computer jobs, 191-192
Confucianism, 159
consular assistance, 107-108
construction, 120, 191
consultancy, 122, 192-193
contacts, 28-29, 110, 140
contracts, 58, 59-60, 76-77, 123-124, 129-130
Corona Worldwide, 67, 75, 93
Costa Rica, 175, 278
cost of living, 60
Cote d'Ivoire, 287
Croatia, 146, 279
Crown Agents, 124
Cuba, 177, 279
cultural associations, 75, 89, 268-310
cultural differences, 20-21, 69-71, 159-160
culture shock, 97-98, 105
currency, 60
curriculum vitae (CV), 44-48, 320-322
Cyprus, 141, 145, 279
Czech Republic, 141, 145, 279

Dean Associates, 67
Denmark, 141-145, 279-280
Department for Education & Skills (DFES), 32-33, 67
Department for International Development (DFID), 28, 124, 133
Department of Health, 85
diplomacy, 22
diplomatic careers, 194-195
directories, 30
dismissal, 106-107
dissatisfaction with job, 105-106
Djibouti, 280
Dominica, 280
Dominican Republic, 177, 280
driving licence, 81
dual income families, 61
Dubai, see United Arab Emirates

East Africa, 163-164
Eastern Europe, 145-146, 147-148
ECA International, 23, 73-74, 75, 100-101
Ecuador, 280
Edmonds K, 107
Egypt, 149, 151, 280-281

elderly relatives, 68
electronics careers, 197
El Salvador, 281
embassies, 29, 105, 139, 268-310
emigration, 136-138
empathy, 22
employers' credentials, 58-59
employment agencies, 30-32, 144, 217-268
engineering careers, 197
entertainment careers, 210-211
Eritrea, 163, 281
Estonia, 145, 281
Ethiopia, 163, 281
EURES network, 32
European Economic Area (EEA), 141
European Union, 137-138, 141-145
European Union careers, 125, 138, 144, 197-199
European Council for International Schools (ECIS), 66, 234
exchange schemes, 117-119
Executive Grapevine, 32
Expat Network, 34, 75, 107
expatriate community, 102
Expats International, 34, 107
experience, 19-20

Falkland Islands, 177-178, 281
family, 62-68, 135
Farnham Castle International Briefing and Conference Centre, 73
financial matters, 83-85
financial careers, 199-120
Fiji, 281-282
Finland, 282
Foreign & Commonwealth Office, 28, 75, 94
foreign employers, 39-40, 58-59
foreign environment, 16-18, 68-71, 97-98
France, 147, 282
future career, 129-131

Gabbitas Educational Services, 67
Gabon, 282
Gambia, 283
Gap Year, 109, 114-117, 156-157
Georgia, 155-156, 283
Germany, 141-145, 147, 283
Ghana, 163, 283
Gibraltar, 141-145, 284
government organisations, 124-125
Greece, 141-145, 284
Grenada, 284
Guatemala, 284
Guinea, 284
Guinea-Bissau, 284-285

Guyana, 177, 285

Haiti, 177
health, 85-86, 87
healthcare careers, 120, 202-203
Herin R, 176
Hinduism, 159
Hints to Exporters, 76
Hofstede G, 70-71
Hogg C, 21
holiday jobs, 110-113
home in UK, 87-88
Honduras, 285
Hong Kong, 158, 285
hotel industry careers, 121, 200-201
Howell & Associates, 74
Hungary, 141, 145, 285

Iceland, 141, 286
immigration formalities, 137, 138, 169-170,
    171-172
Independent Schools Information Service
    (ISIS), 67
India, 156-157, 286
Indian Subcontinent, 156-157
individualism, 70
Indonesia, 157-158, 286
information sources, 72-76
information technology careers, 191-192
insurance, 87-88
International Organisation for Migration
    (IOM), 176, 216
international organisations, 125-126, 138,
    214-216
Internet, 27, 110, 172
investment, 84-85, 138, 139
Iran, 150, 155-156, 286
Iraq, 150, 286
Islam, 150-151, 159
Israel, 152-153, 287
Italy, 141-145, 147, 287
Ivory Coast (Côte d'Ivoire), 287

Jamaica, 287-288
Japan, 159, 288
job advertisements, 26-27, 41
job applications, 40-52
Job Centres, 32-33, 145
job expectations, 61-62, 100-101
job interviews, 52-64
job search, 25-36
Jordan, 288
journalism, 209

Kazakhstan, 155-156, 288
Kenya, 163, 289

Kiribati, 289
Know How Fund, 145
Korea (North), 158
Korea (South), 158-159, 289
Kuwait, 149, 289
Kyrgyzstan, 155-156, 289

language difficulties, 40, 107, 146-147
language learning, 88-90, 103, 105
Laos, 157, 290
Latin America, 175-177, 178-179
Latvia, 145, 290
law careers, 201
Lebanon, 149, 290
leave, 59, 65, 77
lecturing posts, 195-196
leisure careers, 210-211
leisure interests, 103-104
Lesotho, 290
Liberia, 163, 290
Libya, 149, 150, 290
Lithuania, 145, 291
luggage, 90
Luxembourg, 141-145, 291

Macedonia, 146, 291
Madagascar, 291
Malawi, 291
Malaysia, 157-158, 292
Maldives, 292
Mali, 292
Malta, 145, 292
manufacturing jobs, 202
marketing and sales careers, 202
Mauritania, 292
Mauritius, 293
media agencies, 33
media jobs, 208-210
Medical Advisory Service for Travellers
    Abroad (MASTA), 86
medical careers, 202-203
Mercers College, 66
Mexico, 191, 293
Middle East, 149-154
military careers, 203-204
mining careers, 204-205
minority status, 17
missionary work, 205-207
misunderstanding, 17
Mongolia, 293
Morocco, 149, 293
motives, 13
Mozambique, 164, 293-294
Myanmar (Burma), 157, 275

Namibia, 164, 294

nannies, careers for, 188-189
national insurance, 90-91
Nepal, 294
Netherlands, 141-145, 294-295
New Zealand, 137, 183-185, 186, 295
next of kin, 95
Nicaragua, 295-296
Niger, 296
Nigeria, 163, 296
non-governmental agencies (NGOs),
    126-127
North Africa, 149-154
Norway, 141, 296
nursing careers, 202-203

oil and gas industry careers, 120, 207-208
Oman, 149, 297
open-mindedness, 22
Overseas Placing Unit, 32-33

Pacific islands, 185, 186
Pakistan, 156-157, 297
Panama, 297
Papua New Guinea, 297
Paraguay, 175, 297
passport, 91
patience, 22
pension, 92-93
permanent posts, 132-138
personal qualities, 20
Peru, 298
pets, 96
Philippines, 157, 298
photographs,
Poland, 141, 145, 298
police careers, 208
Portugal, 141-145, 298-299
power distance, 71
preparation, 80-96
private sector recruitment, 123-124,
    217-268
professional associations, 29
publishing careers, 208-209

Qatar, 149, 299
qualifications, 19, 40, 142-143

readjustment, 135-136
recruitment, 25, 37-57, 217-268
recruitment consultants, 30-32, 144,
    217-268
re-entry, 135-136
relief organisations, 121-122
removals, 90
resignation, 105-106
resourcefulness, 22

returnees, 131, 135-136
Romania, 146, 299
Russia, 146, 299
Rwanda, 163, 300

St Helena, 300
St Kitts & Nevis, 300
St Lucia, 300
St Vincent & the Grenadines, 300
salary, 59-60, 77, 78-79
Saudi Arabia, 149, 300
School of Oriental and African Studies
    (SOAS), 74
seasonal employment, 114
secondment, 133-134
secretarial work, 210
Senegal, 163, 301
selection tests, 53
self-assessment, 21-23
self employment, 131, 138-140, 144-145
separation, 64, 67-68
Seychelles, 64, 67-68, 301
settling in, 97-108
shopping, 92-93
short professional assignments, 122-123
short-term work, 109-123
show business careers, 210-211
Sierra Leone, 163, 301
Singapore, 157-158, 301
Slovakia, 301-302
Slovenia, 302
social customs, 20
social security, 91, 92
Solomon Islands, 302
Somalia, 163, 302
South Africa, 164-165, 302
South America, 175-177, 178-179
South East Asia, 157-158
Southern Africa, 164
Spain, 141-145, 147, 303
speculative applications, 28-34
speculative letters, 41-44
speculative visits, 34-35
specialist journals, 26
sports activities, 104
sports coaching, 210-211
spouses, 23, 62-65
Sri Lanka, 156-157, 303
State Boarding Information Service, 67
state employment agencies, 32, 144
staying on, 130-131, 139-140
Sudan, 163, 303
suitability, 18-23
Suriname, 303
Swaziland, 304
Sweden, 141-145, 304

Switzerland, 145, 304
Syria, 304

Taiwan, 158, 305
Tajikistan, 155-156
Tanzania, 163, 303, 305
taxation, 83, 138
teaching careers, 117-118, 120, 144, 195-196
technical cooperation, 120, 211-212
technical writing, 144, 210
termination bonus, 59
Thailand, 157-158, 305
Thorndike T, 177
Togo, 305
tolerance, 22
Tonga, 305-306
tourism careers, 212-213
trade unions, 29
training careers, 195-196
translating, 144, 197-199, 210
travel, 94, 103
Traveller's Bookshop, 76
Traveller's Handbook, 95
Trinidad & Tobago, 306
Trompenaars F, 21, 71
Tunisia, 151, 306
Turkey, 145, 148, 306
Turkmenistan 155-156, 306
Turks and Caicos, 177

Uganda, 163-164, 307
Ukraine, 146, 307
United Arab Emirates, 149, 307
United Nations, 125-126, 138, 214-216
United States of America (USA), 137, 170-174, 307-308
uncertainty avoidance, 71

Uruguay, 308
useful addresses, 311-316
utilities, 121, 215
Uzbekistan, 155-156, 308

vacancy bulletins, 26
vaccinations, 86
value for money, 18
values, 18, 70-71
Vanuatu, 308
Venezuela, 309
Vietnam, 157-158, 309
visits on spec, 34-35
visas, 25, 95, 105
voluntary service, 119, 127-129
voting rights, 96, 105, 108

WES Home School, 66
West Africa, 163
West Bank and Gaza, 150, 152, 309
Wheatley D, 57
wives, 23, 62-65
women abroad, 71, 102-103
Women's Corona Society, 67, 75
work patterns, 13
work permits, 95
working holidays, 110-113
working practices, 18
Worldwide Volunteering for Young People, 110-111, 116

Yemen, 309
Year Out Group, 115
Yugoslavia, 146, 309-310

Zambia, 164, 310
Zimbabwe, 164, 310